FOR VALOR

Defending the Faith for Those of Worth

Corby Shuey

DEFENDER

CRANE

For Valor: Defending the Faith for Those of Worth
By Corby Shuey

Defender Publishing
PO Box 5 Crane, Mo 65633
Copyright ©Thomas Horn

All rights reserved. Published 2023
Printed in United States of America.

ISBN: 9781948014717

A CIP catalog record of this book is available from the Library of Congress

Cover design by Darrin Giesinger

Unless otherwise noted, all Scripture quotations are from the New American Standard Bible Translation 1995.

∞

To Jesse and Jaime for possessing the boldness of faith to ask the question. May we all be steadfast and immovable, abounding in joy as we walk faithfully in accord with the will of our Lord! In this no one labors in vain (1Corinthians 15:58). To God be the glory forever and ever and ever, Amen!

Appreciation and Acknowledgments

I would like to express my gratitude to a number of individuals who have contributed to the formulation of this book. Dr. Michael Lake has been instrumental in contributing insight into my work. He has been a consistent source of encouragement and wisdom. Thank you, Dr. Lake, for helping me in the opportunity to study the Holy Word of God. I also thank Dr. Justin Elwell. Dr. Elwell is a man of integrity and compassion. I thank him for his generosity, encouragement, and thoughtfulness in those times when I most needed a brother to offer words of hope. I thank Pastor Chris Smith, a fellow brother and warrior in Christ, for his instruction, correction, and words of truth. Pastor Chris has been a mentor and valuable influence. Lastly, I thank David Laughery for his efforts in helping to edit this writing. I thank you for your wisdom, kindness, and time as you read through the initial drafts of this work.

CONTENTS

Preface. 1

PART ONE

The Serpent Speaks
The Voice of Chaos

1. Pensamiento Serpentino 9
2. Lullabies from the Father of Lies. 25
3. Critical Theory. 73
4. Interlude
Today Is Still Called "Today"! 83

PART TWO

The Spirit Speaks
The Word, the Sword of Our God and King

5. Luke 23:27–32
Behold the Days Are Coming 91
6. Ephesians 4:17–19
Those Who Walk in Futility 107
7. Jeremiah 16:16–18
I Will Send Out Hunters 115
8. Zechariah 10
Weak Shepherds and a Wandering Flock 129
9. Psalm 2
The King of Zion! 137

PART THREE

The People Must Speak
For Valor, for Those of Worth

10. The Glass Divide 149
11. Priesthood of Believers 167
12. A Call to Arms for the Priesthood of Flint 175
13. "No Greater Valor" 201
14. Restoring the Mirror of God Almighty! 213

Coda 229
About the Author 230
Bibliography 233
Notes 243

And Jesus answered and said to them, "See to it that no one misleads you. For many will come in My name, saying, 'I am the Christ,' and will mislead many. You will be hearing of wars and rumors of wars. See that you are not frightened, for those things must take place, but that is not yet the end. For nation will rise against nation, and kingdom against kingdom, and in various places there will be famines and earthquakes. But all these things are merely the beginning of birth pangs.

"Then they will deliver you to tribulation, and will kill you, and you will be hated by all nations because of My name. At that time many will fall away and will betray one another and hate one another. Many false prophets will arise and will mislead many. Because lawlessness is increased, most people's love will grow cold. But the one who endures to the end, he will be saved. This gospel of the kingdom shall be preached in the whole world as a testimony to all the nations, and then the end will come."

MATTHEW 24:4–14

PREFACE

So often in our daily lives we are barraged with the negative. We encounter negativity in the media, advertisements, politics, and even other people. Voices monotonously repeat the sounds of the negative as if acting as farmers working to grow a crop of despair. These voices seek to cultivate pessimism in the field of society. They expect to harvest a crop of the melancholy grown on the hearts of humankind. The fruit of the crop tastes of bitterness. The bitterness is yet another ingredient which elevates the distrust we feel as we look across the scope of the current climate of our world.

Whether the voices speak from a place of intentionality or if the voices unintentionally echo divisive sound bites, the result remains the same. The field has been fertilized. The fruit has been grown. The taste of bitterness lingers on the tongue. The heart of humanity has been reminded of the negative. The voices repeat. The drone of the negative perpetually reverberates in our ears. Inevitably we tend to reciprocate the melody in our speech and attitudes. The negative is repeated. It is an unfortunate affliction that we so often choose to dwell on the pessimistic. Our fallen human nature seems to be drawn to negativity. Maybe the draw is a result of the curse of sin. The fallen nature seeks what is familiar.

It is not surprising that those who do not know Jesus as their Lord and Savior dwell on the negative. What hope can they turn to other than the familiarity found with despair? As I stated, the negative is familiar. The commonality that we can find with the negative in the fallen state of mankind serves as a strange comfort for those who do not know the true and only source of eternal hope. To be honest, I do not know how those who are lost can continue. How do those who do not have the hope and joy of knowing Jesus possess the strength to endure the negativity we are bombarded by routinely, day in and day out? Our prayer, in the contemporary climate of our culture, must be that the Church is able to continue to represent the mercy of our Savior to a world laden with desperation. We have an incredible opportunity, as the Church, to offer something different than what the world promotes. We have a consistent and eternal hope in Jesus!

While it is not surprising for those without faith to dwell on negativity, what I do find surprising is the fact that so many people of faith choose to fill themselves with the negative. We often hear voices from those of faith that should resound with the hope of Jesus regurgitating the same negative drone found in the culture from which we to be set apart. We hear teaching and preaching that is burdened with the negative. This is especially true of teaching that deals with current events or with eschatology. The airwaves are filled with both men and women who present a pessimistic view of reality. They degrade the state of the Church to becoming irrelevant and shackled in weakness. Darkness, in the view of many, is threatening to destroy the hope of God. There are books which have been written outlining the demise of mankind. Bookstores, which are unfortunately becoming a rarity, are filled with publications that dwell on the work of the enemy rather than the hope of the Overcomer. Countless videos, podcasts, and sound bites can be found on the Internet propagating gloom. These videos focus far too much attention on the darkness and far too little on the hope of our light. Too often we investigate the negative while focusing too little effort on the hope of salvation.

Now, I must say, it is wise to be aware of the workings of the enemy. It would be folly to completely ignore the strategies of those who hate God. Our Savior gives us this instruction found in the book of Luke:

"Behold, I send you out as sheep in the midst of wolves; so be shrewd as serpents and innocent as doves" (Luke 10:16). We dwell as sheep in the den of wolves. This is true. We must be aware of the predator. Our ignorance of the predator will lead to death for the sheep and a full belly for the wolves. Our Savior instructs us to be as shrewd as serpents as we keep watch of the wolves. Jesus tells us to be informed of the strategy of our enemy. We are to be watchful of where the wolves walk, exposing the traps they intend to spring upon the sheep. In our efforts to keep watch, we must also remain as innocent as doves. Jesus reminds us to be wary of our surroundings, knowing that we walk in enemy territory, but at the same time, we are to keep our eyes fixed upon Him as our hope and peace. Innocent as doves, we are to be as Christians, knowing that Jesus has overcome is the promise spoken by the voice of our Savior (John 16:33). Therefore even the sheep who find themselves surrounded by wolves shall have no fear. This promise of our God, the Almighty, is found in the book of Isaiah:

> But now, thus says the LORD, your Creator, O Jacob,
> And He who formed you, O Israel,
> "Do not fear, for I have redeemed you;
> "I have called you by name; you are Mine!
> "When you pass through the waters, I will be with you;
> "And through the rivers, they will not overflow you.
> "When you walk through the fire, you will not be scorched,
> "Nor will the flame burn you.
> "For I am the LORD your God,
> "The Holy One of Israel, your Savior;
> "I have given Egypt as your ransom." (Isaiah 43:1–3)[1]

He has redeemed us by His sacrifice! His blood was poured out for the salvation of all who call upon His name! His resurrection from the grave serves as a reminder of the eternal covenant that He upholds for His people. He calls us by name, stating that we are His! The waters of despair will not flow over us. The fire of destruction will never scorch our flesh. He is the Lord our God, our Savior!

As I stated, so often we hear the rumblings of the negative both in secular society and in the Church. We hear the negative that thirsts after our attention, and far too often we give in. Thus the negative is remembered and the promises forgotten. I have written this book in the attempt to remind the reader of the eternal hope of the Church. We do not live in overwhelming darkness as a weak Church without hope. The Church will prevail because it is His. God will have a people who will bear His name with integrity (1 Peter 2:4–5). This book is divided into three parts. While I do not want to dwell on the negative, in the first part of the book, I will deal with some of the hardships that we face as the people of faith. I do this in an effort to reveal the antagonist of our souls. I will address a few tactics of the enemy that have been shaping our society. These tactics are deployed with the intention of erasing the identity of God's creation from memory. The second part of the book is an expository exploration of the Holy Word of our Lord. In this section, I will look at the instructions given by God to His people. We are not without recourse. God has given us clear directives as we fight the good fight of faith. Lastly, part three addresses our response. As we look at the workings of the devil, knowing the instruction of our heavenly Father, we must respond. The Church must stand in its authority given by God Almighty. We must focus our attention on the overcomer as He equips us to overcome. Therefore, I write to encourage. I write to offer hope in a day when hope is most needed. To God be the glory!

Challenge and Blessing

As you read this work, I pray that you are encouraged. I pray that you come to realize your purpose as His royal priest serving your Heavenly Father. I pray that you are emboldened in faith. I pray that the reassurance of the promises of Jesus strengthens you to meet the challenges of our day. We are not without hope. Know this, beloved: We are His, and He goes before us placing the dread of His good name in the hearts of all those who stand against the hope of mercy (Isaiah 59:19–20). May you be blessed by our Savior in your walk of faith. May He guide and lead your every step, and may you be willing to follow.

Preamble

Chaos is a complex, unwanted visitor. It is birthed of subtility and originates as an unnoticed breeze slithering through the boughs of the tree, silently gaining strength, growing into a storm collecting debris along its meandering path of deception, chaos. The storm of chaos eventually vomits forth a heap of ruin. The storm of chaos regurgitates all that it was allowed to consume as it lurches forth along its path toward deception. The landscape utterly changed as a result of the subtle violence of the storm. Chaos, a storm that moves in silence, often unnoticed, carries the penalty of hell in its wake. Chaos returns, like a dog to its vomit, repeating folly in a cycle that is allowed to be left unbroken (Psalm 26:11). "That which has been is that which will be, and that which has been done is that which will be done. So there is nothing new under the sun" (Ecclesiastes 1:19). So goes the plight of mankind, lazily sunbathing under the tree. We enjoy the shade. Reprieve from the Son is a welcomed favor offered by the storm of deception. It is better to be ignorant than to be responsible. Ignorance foolishly gives the false hope that responsibility can be avoided. In our ignorance, we can claim that we did not know, therefore we cannot be held responsible. It is often the choice that the sunbathers make as they bask in the shade of the tree.

Chaos is a juggernaut that moves in silence, only being noticed when its stomach becomes distended, full of the vittles of human weakness. Chaos gorges itself upon our willful blindness. We wade through its excrement on this fallen dirt. When its belly stretches to the point of pain from gluttony, the silence is broken. By a guttural retch, we notice. Chaos then takes form in our blindness. Suddenly all the putridity that was ignorantly allowed to decompose within the juggernaut's belly is felt.

The confusion of chaos is unleashed into our consciousness, demanding our full attention. Chaos is a complex, unwanted visitor. It is birthed in subtility. Grows in purposeful, willful ignorance, and then becomes realized in a heap of ruin. The consequences of allowing the wretch to thrive throws discord into all facets of reality.

To push against chaos feels futile, daunting, and desperate. By the time the storm of chaos is realized, the vast extension of the difficulties wound within seem impossible to overcome. We deem it a futile task to even try, so we, at times, reluctantly submit to the course set by societal progression. It is just the way that it is; rejection of the "just the way that it is" grates against the general level of complacent comfort in chaos that we have grown accustomed to living in. If we find within ourselves the determination to try to climb to the top of the mountain of chaos to lop off its head, determination quickly fades and is replaced by dismay as we look upon the staggering height of the mountain we must climb. Desperate, we feel the frost-dense air on our feet and legs as it slides down the mountain of chaos. Shuddering, we stand aghast in the cold emptiness of the human condition that fell victim to the slithering in the tree.

It is startling to realize that chaos lurks in subtility. This reality is diametrically opposed to what we perceive chaos to be. But it is true. Chaos is unseen until it is unleashed. Chaos is a silent destroyer until destruction comes. Where is chaos when it is silent? Where is chaos when walking along the merry path of life and all seems well? Where is chaos when the storm slithers high up in the tree beyond the sight of the sunbathers? Where is chaos when we close our eyes?

Chaos is birthed in subtility. "Now the serpent was more crafty than any beast of the field which the Lord God had made" (Genesis 3:1). It speaks, wooing us to listen, to question, to doubt, to die. Chaos from silence to subjugation; so go the lullabies from the father of lies.

PART ONE

The Serpent Speaks

The Voice of Chaos

1

PENSAMIENTO SERPENTINO

The serpent speaks. It has been speaking into our thoughts since the Fall. Its voice, a whisper of lies, quietly plants seeds that grow into vines of cancerous thorns in our flesh. *Pensamiento serpentino* ("serpentine thought") is the corrupt part of our being that has, unfortunately, been tuned in to the frequency broadcast from chaos in the tree. As when the serpent slithered through the boughs of the tree in the garden, its influence can be felt slithering through the boughs of our minds. If left unchecked, the result is bitterness, anger, and exile.

Pensamiento Serpentino, a poem written by Luis Miguel Valdez, delves into the thought of the serpent. Luis Valdez is a Mexican-American playwright and founder of *El Teatro Campesino* ("The Farm Workers' Theater").[2] The Theater was founded in 1965 amid the United Farm Workers Movement. The theater utilized art to bring to light the difficulties of migrant farming in California. Valdez has won numerous awards for his work in theater. He is also an educator who held professorships at the University of California (UC) Berkeley; UC Santa Cruz; Fresno State University; and California State University Monterey Bay.[3] Valdez was also a member of the Chicano movement, which can be described as a radicalized Mexican-American mechanism protesting for social and political change.[4]

I write of Valdez only to give a very brief introduction to what influences his writing. I am not making any judgments on the validity of the movements he was part of, nor do I intend to delve into the intricacies of the climate of American culture during the social revolution of the 1960s. I only bring up this abbreviated history of Valdez to facilitate an examination of the poem, *Pensamiento Serpentino*. His influence can still be found within our system of education. His writing is concerning because he exalts a false religion. He embraces the serpentine thought. In this work, Valdez writes of the influence of the false god Quetzalcoatl, an ancient Aztec god that takes the form of a feathered serpent. The name is derived from the Nahuatl language meaning "feathered serpent." Additionally, the name can be translated as "precious serpent." Nahuatl is an ancient language spoken throughout central Mexico. In the poem *Pensamiento Serpentino*, Valdez romanticizes the ancient Mayan and Aztec culture. He longs for a revolt against the oppression from what he calls the *gabacho*, a derogatory term applied to foreigners of a different origin. "In Mexico, *gabacho* refers to sugar cane chews that are white in color and are usually spit out."[5] Although Valdez writes of the plight of migrant workers as they fought for equal opportunities, his work contains an underpinning of division based on racial disharmony. I am not discounting the strides we have made in America during the social reform of the 1960s. Nor do I suggest that the reform bringing to light equality for all people was meaningless or unnecessary. Obviously, we are all created in the image of our Heavenly Father, whether our skin is darker or lighter. We are all one race called "human." All people should be afforded the God-given freedom to live in peace. But we live in a corrupt world that has been tainted by the saliva of the serpent as it whispers its lies in our ears. I remind my readers that I am only concerned with the work of Valdez as it relates to the poem, *Pensamiento Serpentino*. I am concerned with the negative spiritual poison that can be found throughout this work. This poison speaks of the curse issuing forth from the father of lies. The serpent seeks to divide so that we fall. My only concern in examining this work by Valdez is to shed light on the subtility of the serpent's speech.

In the poem, *Pensamiento Serpentino*, Valdez refers to a false god of ancient mythology. Quetzalcoatl is the central figure wound throughout this work. The god Quetzalcoatl, who pervades this writing, is considered to be the patron god of the Aztec priesthood. Quetzalcoatl was worshipped in both Aztec and Mayan cultures. This god also takes on the names Kukulkan and Gucumatz, depending on the region. The god was worshipped for various reasons throughout history. It was known as a god of vegetation and earth. Quetzalcoatl was known as the god of war and human sacrifice. It also came to be known as the god of death and rebirth. Within the mythos surrounding this god is the notion of life from destruction. The myth suggests that Quetzalcoatl was one of four sons of the god Tonacateuctil. In this mythos, the brothers constantly fight, resulting in the destruction of the world. This destruction occurs four times across numerous ages.[6] Quetzalcoatl is credited for attacking his brothers with a stone club and stopping the destruction of the earth. Quetzalcoatl, in this legend, has brought forth a fifth age, the one in which we are currently living. This fifth age was thought to usher in a golden age of mercy, justice, and learning. But this perfect order was destroyed when a demonic god, Tezcatlipoca (meaning "smoking mirror") deceived Quetzalcoatl.[7] Tezcatlipoca usurped Quetzalcoatl's authority, leading to the degeneration of the golden age. Tezcatlipoca tricked Quetzalcoatl into embracing the practice of human sacrifice. It is thought, in the myth, that one day Quetzalcoatl will restore the golden age.

In this very brief summary of the myth surrounding this god, the voice of deception can be discerned. The influence of the father of lies lulls us to complacency by spinning yarns of falsehood. I gave you this summary in order to provide an understanding of the thought processes of Valdez as he writes. The whisper of the great serpent can be felt in the reading of his work. Valdez embraces the myth and, as we will see, confuses this god, Quetzalcoatl, with Jesus our Savior. This blasphemous assertion is the effect of early exploration of the conquistadors of Spain in this region.[8] The myth of Quetzalcoatl was intermingled with truth found in the Word of God. Over the course of time, and due to a lack of correction by the Church, the myth grew in deceiving influence. But this is how chaos is birthed. It is a quiet, unnoticed visitor, born of subtlety and ignorance.

We will now examine this aforementioned poem by Valdez. I am not going to look at each stanza of the work in full. I intend to choose only a few sections to examine. I aim not to fully criticize the poem, but to expose the entwined lies from chaos on the tree that lead to destruction. The majority of the poem is written in the Spanish language, intermingled with English. I have provided the original content as it appears in the writing. I have also provided an English translation in parentheses. I will comment briefly on selected stanzas. The full poem is found in a collection of Valdez' early works.[9] The selected stanzas of the poem that appear in this writing are taken from that book. (Please refer to the "works cited" section for full bibliographic information regarding this work.)

The poem opens as follows:

Pensamiento Serpentino ("Serpentine Thought")
Teatro ("Theatre")
eres el mundo ("you are the world")
y las paredes de los ("and the walls of the")
buildings mas grandes ("largest buildings")
son ("are")
nothing but scenery.

Valdez opens this work by declaring that we are all in a grand play being carried out in the theater of the world. Even the largest monuments are naught but a scene in this theater of humanity. The world that we perceive is but a stage set to entertain the onlooking, self-serving gods. We are pawns; the world around us, a backdrop. This is a nihilistic opening stanza alluding to the futility of existence.

Valdez goes on in subsequent stanzas to elaborate on this grand play. He writes that it is the greatest pantomime on earth written in the tongues of men. We are in a great improvisation role, playing master and slave, rich and poor. The purpose of this poem is to point to, in Valdez' words, a spiritual truth. He goes on to write:

pero underneath it all
is the truth
the Spiritual Truth
that determines all material ("that determines all subjects")
la energia that creates the ("the energy that creates the")
universe
la fueza con purpose ("the force with purpose")
la primera cause de todo ("the first of all")
even before the *huelga* ("even before the strike")
la First Cause de Creation
Dios ("God").

Valdez suggests that a god is responsible for being the author of life—*la fueza con purpose*, "the force with purpose," as the author puts it. He states that this god is the first of all, meaning the primary god. The phrase, "the first cause of creation brought forth reality before the strike," is hard to nail down. Interpreting it in context of the protest Valdez participated in may allude to the strikes that occurred during the migrant farming protests of the 1960s. But within the context of the poem, the phrase occurs as Valdez expounds on the god who created. If the phrase is read in this context, could Valdez be thinking about the strike of the serpent as it inflicted humanity with its venom in the garden? The "force with purpose," as suggested in this poem, would have been created prior to this strike. In any case, it is hard to discern what Valdez means. He does not circle back to this thought during the remainder of the writing. It is clear, however, that the god Valdez attributes with the power of creating is not the God of the Bible, as we will discover. The poem continues:

Los indios knew of this ("The Indians knew of this")
long ago

hace mucho anos que cantaban ("they have been singing many years")

en su flor y canto ("in its flower and song")

de las verdades ("of the truths")

CIENTIFICAS Y RELIGIOSAS ("science and religion")

del mundo ("of the world").

Valdez attributes the indigenous people with the knowledge of truth found in both science and religion. This theme carries throughout the poem. Valdez writes as if he is longing for the ancient understanding of the indigenous peoples to arise again. He calls for this ancient knowledge to regain authority in modern thought. Also carried throughout the poem is the notion of harmony between humanity and nature. The writing suggests that we have lost the understanding, in our contemporary form, to be in harmony with the world around us. In order to restore harmony, according to Valdez, we must revert to the old ways. Another concept is brought forth in this work. The Aztec and Mayan civilizations held to a moral code of behavior toward others, called in the ancient Nahuatl language *in lak' ech* ("you are my other me"). This phrase was considered a greeting of humility and an acknowledgment of the collective universality of all human beings. In other words, you are me and I am you as we are one, shimmering resonance harmonizing to the song in the vast cosmos. The intent of the phrase is also "affiliated with the Mayan definition of the human being, which they called '*huinik'lil*' or 'vibrant being.' In this regard, we are all part of the same universal vibration."[10] Our perception of the human other is but a vulgar conception of the grandness of life hidden behind the material. There is no good or bad. There is only the eternal vibration of the universe. In the words of Valdez, *eres el mundo* ("you are the world"). This thought is, firstly, presumptuous in its self-absorbed, grandiose exaltation of who we are in regard to a Holy God. The thought is, secondly, deadly, as it slithers its way into the mentality of society, prompting sinners to prop themselves up on a foundation that is faulty. The poem continues:

But reality *es una Gran Serpiente*
a great serpent
that moves and changes
and keeps crawling
out of its
dead skin
despojando su pellejo vielo ("stripping its old skin")
to emerge
clean and fresh
la nueva realidad nace ("the new reality is born")
de la realidad vieja ("from the old reality")

Reality is a grand serpent. In many ways this is true. For those who refuse to recognize the liberation in Christ, an elaborate diorama unfolds before them, deceiving them, lulling them into complacent cooperation with the serpent's ancient scheme: "You can be like God, your eyes will be opened (Genesis 3)." This is the lie that opened the rift leading to broken fellowship with our God. To the unrepentant, our reality is a result of the curse introduced into this world by the vile serpent. It crawls through time, shedding its skin, moving and changing along with progress. It reinvents itself, perfecting its venom in order to sufficiently possess the potency to corrupt. The serpent emerges into its new skin, into a new reality of chaos reigning over the unconcerned. The lazy sunbathers bask in the glow of gleaming white light reflected by the fangs of the cursed creature as it speaks false promises. A new reality is born with each passing age; a reimagined serpent arises, bringing the workings of the old. Solomon tells us:

That which has been is that which will be,
And that which has been done is that which will be done.
So there is nothing new under the sun.
Is there anything of which one might say,
"See this, it is new?"

15

Already it has existed for ages
Which were before us.
There is no remembrance of earlier things;
And also of the later things which will occur,
There will be for them no remembrance
Among those who will come later still. (Ecclesiastes 1:9–11)

There is no remembrance, none to recall the earlier things. Therefore, the latter things will be allowed to occur. For Valdez and others who share his mindset, this is truth. Life is but a cycle of reimagined deception regurgitated repeatedly. They call forth the old truths, ancient wisdom of the serpent, because they choose not to remember. Thus, the cycle continues because there is nothing new under the sun.

Valdez goes on in this poem to name prominent figures in history who have shaped our world. He declares that none of these individuals will be able to liberate the oppressed from the oppressors. Valdez cites a text called the *Popul Vuh*. This is an ancient text used by Mayan priests. The text recounts how ancient false deities created the world.[11] He also cites an ancient text referred to as the *Chilam Balam*.[12] The title means "jaguar priest or spokesman of the jaguar."[13] This text contains "detailed understanding of astronomy and calendrics, including a method for predicting both solar and lunar eclipses."[14] The book also documents the "history, rituals, prophecies, astronomy, architecture, mythology, calendar, songs, and incantations of the local Maya peoples."[15] A prominent theme in this work is the return of the god Quetzalcoatl.[16] It was believed that the return of this god would revive the golden age of the Aztec/Mayan cultures. It is alarming that Valdez refers to an obviously pagan document. He references this document as he leads into the praise of the only one, in his view, who is able to bring liberation to this world. Valdez names Quetzalcoatl as the source of liberation, calling upon this god to return to deliver the people from their plight.

While the praise of a false deity is surprising, the red flag, from a Christian perspective, is the title of the text cited by Valdez, that being *Chilam*

Balam. "Balam," also spelled "Balaam," should sound familiar to our Christian ears. Balaam was a prophet who was commissioned by Balak, king of Moab, to curse the Israelites (Numbers chapters 22 through 24). The curse was ineffective and actually became a blessing, to the bewilderment of both Balaam and Balak. This connection alone brings uneasy thoughts to the intent, making an association with a book and a prophet attempting to curse God's people. But what is more striking is discovered in a deeper investigation of the demon sharing the name "Balam." In the book, *The Lesser Key of Solomon Goetia: The Book of Evil Spirits,*[17] "Balam" is defined according to its true nature. The Goetia is obviously a perversion of truth filtered through the mouth of lies. This work is part of a larger collection of occult magic texts and demonology written in the seventeenth century known as the *Lemegeton.* In this text, Balam is defined as the "king of hell." This entity is said to have three heads—that of a bull, a man, and a ram—as well as the tail of a serpent, and he rides upon a bear.[18] It is said that he is able to speak true answers out of his wit, giving insight into the past, present, and future, and he commands forty legions of spirits. This demon takes its name from the false prophet Balaam, or vice versa. Both the demon and the prophet share the desire to rise against the people of God. They also share the inability to do so.

Valdez dances to the lullabies of the snake in the tree. He is influenced by the deception that has poisoned the well of those who reject the source of Living Water (John 7:37–38). The association Valdez draws between liberation from forbidden knowledge and the lies of the serpent have caused men to fall since the garden. The lies inspiring this poem do not end with Balam. Valdez continues, in the writing, to call for a new day, a rebirth of the days of the past. He calls for the movement of the fifth sun. This event, as a reminder, is marked by the return of the snake god to usher in an age of liberty. He advocates that mankind become sons of this movement, calling humanity to be made alive, one with the cosmos. He cries for justice between God and man. Justice, according to the blasphemous twisted thought, will only be achieved when humanity recognizes that *Jesucristo* is Quetzalcoatl. Valdez holds that this false god is the true image of Jesus our Lord. Valdez suggests that all humanity must come to recognize this truth. Again, this man is deceived. The Bible is quite clear on who our Savior is. Jesus tells us in the book of John: "I am the way and the truth and the life" (John 14:6). No one can know salvation unless they know the one and only source. God claims sole authority as the one divine being who has the power to save. Through the prophet Isaiah, God declares, "I am the Lord, and there is no other; Besides Me there is no God" (Isaiah 45:5). Quetzalcoatl is a demonic imposter masquerading through the imaginings of prideful mankind. Its limited authority has been crushed under the feet of our Savior because Jesus is the one and only King, eternally (Genesis 3:15)!

Valdez goes on in this poem calling to rise against the *gabacho* (foreigners of different origins) influence over the indigenous people. He gives insight into a rejection of capitalism, decrying the practice. He suggests the capitalistic model should be removed like waste matter. This is language that sounds all too familiar to our ears. Valdez rallies social unrest because it will bring forth the *Nahui-Ollin*, the fourth movement of the fifth sun. The Quetzalcoatl myth holds that the fifth sun is the rebirth of humanity though the shed blood of the feathered serpent itself. Quetzalcoatl pours forth its own blood to revive mankind. But because the plumed serpent's blood was shed, it now requires human sacrifice, the blood of mankind, to be shed in order to keep the world intact.[19] Valdez closes this poem with the words:

That Great Spiritual ReBirth
Men will go to the stars
Only *con Dios en su Corazon* ("only with god in your heart")
Asi lo dispone la Evolucion ("this is how evolution has it")
Asi lo dispone THE GREAT ("so has the great feathered serpent of the universe")
FEATHERED SERPENT OF THE UNIVERSE.
Asi los dispone Dios ("god arranges them that way")
Asi sea ("so be it").

Pensamiento serpentino, the thoughts of the serpent. The influence of the father of lies slithers through the dark recesses of our thoughts, revealing itself in ways that are hidden, subtle. Its words quietly chant the drone of deceit. The drone resonates with our fallen nature. If we harden our hearts to the voice of truth, we give ourselves over to the deception. Paul tells us in the book written to believers in Rome:

> For those who are according to the flesh set their minds on the things of the flesh, but those who are according to the Spirit, the things of the Spirit. For the mind set on the flesh is death, but the mind set on the Spirit is life and peace, because the mind set on the flesh is hostile toward God; for it does not subject itself to the law of God, for it is not even able *to do so,* and those who are in the flesh cannot please God.
>
> However, you are not in the flesh but in the Spirit, if indeed the Spirit of God dwells in you. But if anyone does not have the Spirit of Christ, he does not belong to Him. [10] If Christ is in you, though the body is dead because of sin, yet the spirit is alive because of righteousness. (Romans 8:5–10)

We live in difficult times. Our enemy masquerades as an angel of light (2 Corinthians 11:14) and will use things that sound innocent to our ears to draw us down the spiral of deceit. Though ideas presented by Valdez may be laced with truth, we can see that an examination of the foundation on which his thought is built upon is dark. The same is true for our society. As we will see in this next section, noble intentions can be founded on the vilest of lies. It is essential for those of faith in Jesus to use the utmost discernment as we stand firm in faith. If we set our minds on things of the flesh, we will only find death. Our hearts will become calloused to God's counsel (Ephesians 4:19). A callus does not develop overnight. It is acquired over time through the repetition of an action. In the same way, our hearts do not become calloused toward God instantly. Our hearts become hardened over time because of our lack of attention or disinterest in the repetition of deceit spoken by the fallen one. Therefore, set your hearts to the things of God. Live according to the Spirit who is the breath of life in a dying world. With this in your heart, you will find life in Christ Jesus, our Savior.

I bring to light this poem by Luis Valdez not to slander the man, but to shed light on his beliefs. In this work, we can see the beginnings of the unrest in our society. Some of the unrest is warranted, I admit. The fight to end racism, the struggle to view each person as having value, and treating others with dignity are noble. But this concept is not born of humanity. The value that should be found in all human life is not a concept imagined by mankind. It is a truth from God Most High. He tells us in His Word that we are to "'love the Lord your God with all your heart, and with all your soul, and with all your mind, and with all your strength.' The second is this, 'You shall love your neighbor as yourself.' There is no other commandment greater than these" (Mark 12:30–31). We are to love God above all. We are to love His Word above all. We are to praise Him not because He demands it out of His anger, but because He first loved us (1 John 4:19). He created us to be in fellowship with Him (Romans 8:16). He descended to earth, walked among us, and died on the cross only to resurrect three days later to redeem us of sin, because of love (1 Corinthians 15:3–4). We are to be reflections of the love that God has for us to others. Now, love does not mean blind tolerance to sin. This seems to be a popular interpretation of what it means to love. I cannot address this in full now, as this subject would take quite some time to develop. But suffice it to say that love comes with responsibility. Love comes with obedience to our Savior. To others does not mean ignoring the sin in their life so that they fall off the cliff of lies that will end up in a heap of death. Love means to walk alongside our brothers and sisters reflecting the light and truth of our God. Love means teaching others the Word and how to apply the Word to their lives so that they, too, can find freedom from sin (Galatians 5:1).

What I am addressing in this poem by Valdez is the perversion at the base of his thought. We can feel this same perversion of purpose socially in our day. We should fight for justice among people. We should strive for the abolition of tyrannical governments, but this struggle to fight against what is deemed an oppressor seems to be sailing quickly to its logical end: the destruction of all that is founded on truth being replaced by rampant individualistic relativism. The one truth in God is sought to be exchanged for the truth of the individual. The difficulty in this mindset is that all truths cannot be equally true at the same time. The drive to reach individual, secular liberty from all that are deemed born of the patriarchy leads directly into the servitude of chaos left unchecked in the unfettered human mind. What we feel in our society now, what we can see at the core of Valdez' writing, is birthed from critical theory. I will address the philosophical tenets of critical theory later. We are now seeing the climax of this theory coming to its logical end in our society.

The purpose for examining the poem, *Pensamiento Serpentino* was to bring to light the concept of *in lak'ech* mindfulness. As I briefly explained earlier, this concept finds origination from a principal Mayan teaching on appropriate social conduct. The term can be loosely interpreted to mean "you are my other me." In other words, you are an aspect of me as we are one in the grand scope of the cosmos. We are in relationship to one another because humanity is an eternal, vibrant spirit attempting to find the right ways to harmonize with the universe. Not only does this thought extend to other people, it also extends to what are considered non-human persons. A brief definition of non-human person is as follows:

According to legal terminology, legal personhood is not exactly synonymous with human being. The law divides the world between two entities: things and persons. According to the Nonhuman Rights Project executive director, attorney Kevin Schneider, personhood is best understood as a container for rights. Things have no rights, but once an entity is defined as a person it can obtain some rights. So, a "non-human person" refers to an entity that is guaranteed some rights for limited legal purposes.[20]

Non-human rights claim validity in the sentience of the non-human entity. Lak' ech mindfulness suggests that not only should we view our human other as an extension of ourself, but we should also seek harmony with our non-human other. This argument to extend basic human rights to other sentient beings logically flows into the realm of artificial intelligence (AI). This very subject is under consideration, as writer Eun Suk Yang suggests. In an article titled "Predicting the Legal Personhood of AI through the Fate of Two Chimpanzees in the Matter of Nonhuman Rights Project, Inc. v. Lavery," the author writes:

Often, a "best friend" inherits a fortune. Thus, some may imagine a future in which people will wish to bequeath their fortune to a humanoid robot whom they consider their "best friend." Thinking that "[w]ell you seem like a person, but you're just a voice in a computer," one may think that interacting with an artificial being sounds absurd. However, forming such connections with an artificial being is not as implausible as it may seem, as one man in Japan married a video-game hologram in an $18,000 marriage ceremony. Recently, the advancements in Artificial Intelligence ("AI") are enabling these realities once thought to be fiction. Technological developments in AI have been applied to tasks once thought to be impossible, such as piloting drones. In 2018, Google displayed its AI that displays the realism and the natural fluctuations in human vocal conversation. These technological advancements are overcoming limitations in specific areas, if not in its entirety, of the Turing test. As humanity comes closer to developing more complete humanoid AI, as seen by sophisticated AIs such as Google Duplex, more humans may inevitably form emotional bonds and relationships with them.

These developments impose the question of whether AIs could ever be granted the legal status of people.[21]

This subject is a pressing issue, especially as we continue to plow into the future of advanced technology. I cannot delve too deeply into this topic now. I simply want to make an observation as to how slippery the slope becomes when we begin a debate on the status of non-human entities. I also highlight this topic because it connects to the concept of *in lak'ech* mindfulness. Human and non-human entities are, in this worldview, different forms of cosmic energy seeking harmony. Unfortunately, the concepts of *in lak'ech* have been trickling down into the framework of the educational field. These absurd, if I can use a term to suggest what they truly are, ideas are influencing the way we teach basic concepts to our children. This is the disturbing aspect for me as a Christian and a father. Not only are these absurd concepts being taught in the realm of self-awareness, but as we will see in this next section, they influence the objectivity that should be standard in mathematics education.

LULLABIES FROM THE FATHER OF LIES

The father of lies speaks lullabies into the ears of culture. The lullabies, designed to quiet the voice of truth that is found within the spirit of all people (Romans 1:20), desensitizes us to sin. We are without excuse if we listen to the lies and reject the voice of truth found in the Word of God. Unfortunately, the influence of the father of lies manifests in the thoughts of humanity due to the hardness of our hearts (Ephesians 4:18). We cling to pride, elevating the ignorance as understanding. In this section, I will present a cursory overview of the lullaby's affliction on our current society with its melody of deceit. We will look at how our common enemy perverts reason, truth, and logic, twisting them to serve his own agenda. I will address four distinct attacks against purity. These attacks can be clearly discerned to be manifested in the chaos we feel currently taking form. The attacks are designed to pervert God's design for humanity. I have provided distinction between these four attacks that are to be brought to light by giving them titles. All four revolve around the deconstruction of God's design. I have named the four attacks that I will discuss the deconstruction of: knowledge, identity, biology, and truth. I will close this section by shedding light onto the philosophical source that has contributed to the manifestation of deception running rampant in the thoughts of mankind. The enemy seeks to cause confusion so that we lose the definition of what it means to be children of God. This is very much the focus of the deception: our children, the next generation. Those who will carry the light of life as a beacon of hope are those who are targeted. The enemy strives to entice us to neglect the call of passing on the knowledge of God to those who follow us (Romans 1:18–26). We suffer on multiple fronts under the attack of the fallen one. It is not a pleasant venture to write of such things, but a herald offering a warning without the weight of evidence finds no listeners. I write to warn. I encourage caution to those who have ears to hear. While the subjects addressed in the following pages are not pleasant, do not fret. We have a King who has overcome! We serve a risen Savior who has conquered sin and has put an end to death (Isaiah 25:8). We find peace as children of the Living God. We are His: "Be strong and courageous, do not be afraid or tremble at them, for the Lord your God is the one who goes with you. He will not fail you or forsake you" (Deuteronomy 31:6). Our Lord goes with us; find peace in this promise.

The Deconstruction of Knowledge

We start with mathematics and the deconstruction of knowledge. It is not a favorite subject of mine, but at least there was a time when math was considered a constant or objective truth. Two plus two was equivalent to four. There does not seem to be any room in mathematics for interpretation or diversion from objectivity. Obviously, theoretical mathematics delves into the realm of hypothesis, but it is still based on predictable mathematical constants.[22] Postmodernism has levied a heavy blow to objectivity, reason, and absolute truth. Postmodernism posits a relativistic outlook, finding truth only in the individual and/or the moment in time. What was formerly considered objective truth that presumably remains constant outside of and independent of an individual is now replaced with logic—or should I say "preferences" that are given over to personal narrative.[23] Sciences that traditionally have been celebrated as being founded on objective truth have now fallen victim to the rejection of tradition. This trend is seen in all of its stark, confused state in an article titled, "Living Mathematix: Towards a Vision for the Future." The article was written by Dr. Rochelle Gutierrez, who holds a professorship at the University of Illinois at Urbana-Champaign. She is a professor in the department of education who has won numerous awards for her research. The focus of her work is on changing the way mathematics is taught in order to make it more accessible.

In this article, Dr. Gutierrez seeks to push education in mathematics to what she calls "mathematix." This spelling of the term removes the gender/traditional approach to math education, which opens, in her view, the concept of math to "different knowledges, different ways of knowing, and different knowers."[24] She suggests that we incorporate the concepts of *in lak'ech*, reciprocity, and *Nepantla* mindfulness into our educational practices so that we have opportunity as humanity to "learn from other-than-human persons, which, in turn may change our relationship with them."[25] We know the definition of *in lak'ech* already. She also applies the term "reciprocity." This term is defined as "a process of exchanging things with other people in order to gain a mutual benefit."[26] Dr. Gutierrez suggests that we need to apply a reciprocal approach to knowledge acquisition, understanding that we gain knowledge from other-than-human persons. We, reciprocally, should return the favor of the imparted knowledge to the other-than-human person. Dr. Gutierrez defines other-than-human persons as animal, plant, and even inanimate objects. She suggests that a reciprocal approach to mathematics education can be found by returning to indigenous knowledge. She writes:

> Indigenous knowledges recognize that we are part of a system of intelligent and sentient beings, also referred to as persons, with interconnected spirits, including rocks and bodies of water. Plants, for example, have lived on this planet for millions of years before humans. In that sense, plants are our brothers/sisters and have developed ways of efficiently using space, relating with other living beings, and sustaining life not just for themselves but for others, often with few resources at any given moment.[27]

What I would have done for a math teacher that was a rock, a pond, or maybe an apple tree when I was in middle school! At least, if the teacher was an apple tree, maybe we could have snacked during class! I am obviously being silly, but the ideas presented by Dr. Gutierrez are not. They are strikingly bizarre. Remember, she holds the responsibility for developing educational theories that are taught to college students who in turn become teachers who in turn pass this knowledge down to our children—who in turn are afflicted with yet another layer of chaos to contend with in this already confusing world. Be warned!

Dr. Gutierrez also puts forth the notion of *Nepantla*. This is a "Nahuatl word for the space between two bodies of water, the space between two worlds. It is a limited space, a space where you are not this or that but where you are changing. You haven't got into the new identity yet and you haven't left the old identity behind either."[28] Nahuatl is an ancient language spoken by the Aztecs. This term is applied in the modern context to describe a place of transition found when we live in the mental space between the past and the future. Dr. Gutierrez describes the term in this way:

> Nahua metaphysics recognizes the shared collective consciousness of the cosmos. As such, a person is both *in* Nepantla and *is* Nepantla. That is, I am situated within a space of tensions and multiple realities that is called Nepantla. And, by virtue of being in that space, I am also the thing called Nepantla; I contribute to its essence. Therefore, Nepantla dictates how we move though the world."[29]

In this view, absolutes are nonessential, as we, being human, are only an organism, amid billions of other organisms looking back at the past to interpret the future. All is fluid. We all contribute to a collective understanding of the universe.

Dr. Gutierrez acknowledges *Nepantla*, a place of transition, by suggesting that "there is no absolute universalism or absolute relativism.

That is, there is no umbrella term which all forms of mathematics can collapse and explain everything in reality."[30] No absolutes, no truth. There is, in this view, nothing we can look to or count on in this life as a constant. All is one, all is changing, all is dependent on personal experiences and interpretations of the self. How dismal, confusing, and lonely it would be to hold this worldview. Yet if we scan the narrative of the popular trends of our day, the voices of many call out from such a lonely place. Truth is an interpretation. All knowledge is legitimate, regardless of any basis on facts. Dr. Gutierrez picks up this thought by stating, "All knowledge is legitimate, partial, interdependent. In fact, with respect to ignorance, learners do not just lack knowledge, they have 'misknowledges' (i.e., stereotypes, incorrect knowledge) about others."[31] A definition of "misknowledges," according to this article, is an interpretation of the world that is perceived, by others, as being based on a preconceived stereotype. In other words, someone who holds "misknowledge" is someone who does not fit into the narrative pushed forth by those who seek to deconstruct norms.

On a side note, reading what has been written about concepts such as "misknowledge" or the denial of absolute truth may sound foreign or distant from what is necessary for the everyday. However, this is the very argument used by those who seek to delegitimize faith. They argue that there is no absolute truth; there is nothing in this life that we can recognize as being a constant source of truth. Thus, faith in God is invalid, in their view. As Christians, we know this to be a lie. God defines Himself in His Holy Word as being self-existent and without origin (Colossians 1:17). God is immutable (Malachi 3:6). God is full of perfect, unchanging wisdom (Romans 11:33). To argue against an absolute understanding of our world is to argue against God. That is why recognizing the fallacy of the rejection of absolutes is vital. Denial of an absolute, objectifiable truth is the antithesis of foundational knowledge in what is real. Standards of knowing, apart from objectifiable truth, become relegated to one's individual preferences. Reality is then an interpretation based on the emotional state of the interpreter. In this writing, I am most concerned with faith. I am most concerned with the preservation and bolstering of faith. It is clear that the enemy of faith seeks to denigrate those who profess love for our Savior, Jesus. **We must recognize the lies of the enemy, no matter how insignificant they are perceived to be. We must call out these lies, offering recourse to blind acceptance.**

Dr. Gutierrez goes on to say that she chooses to see "the interconnections between Indigenous and Whitestream knowledge of mathematics."[32] In this article, a great emphasis is placed on Indigenous knowledge. She suggests that it is vital to revert back to the ancient knowledge of our ancestors. She cautions against viewing the world in the context of the present, because the present is laden with "Whitestream" knowledge. Dr. Gutierrez defines the term "Whitestream" in this way: "I choose the term Whitestream instead of European American to highlight the role of global White supremacy in the enterprise of mathematics education."[33] Mathematics education, in her view, is plagued with white supremist dominance. I am not sure where this thought originates. Looking at the development of math, we can trace its origins to Mesopotamia. We have examples of both geometric and algebraic calculations in Babylon and Egypt that date to as early as 1750 BC.[34] The suggestion that math is plagued with white supremacist dominance may just be an echo of the current climate the world seems to be suffering through. We can feel a sense of unease as we contemplate the state of the world we live in. We live in the *Nepantla*, to use the words of Dr. Gutierrez. *Nepantla*, a place of tension, a place between two worlds. We live in a time of transition.

The central theme throughout the article by Dr. Gutierrez is deconstruction. She calls for the deconstruction of the traditions at the core of knowledge acquisition, stating that "knowledge is a political process, not a neutral product."[35] To a degree she is correct. We are influenced culturally. Those born into a particular region in our world will hold to a certain standard of normative behavior for that particular region. Politicians, media personalities, and social-change activists do utilize propaganda to manipulate society. It is therefore wise to use discernment to filter truth from the chaff. However, knowledge based on what is true transcends the garbage fallen humanity attempts to add to the mix. To reject foundations of knowledge acquisition outright is dangerous, because it opens the door to repeating the mistakes of the past. Standards are good because they protect from mistakes and serve as markers toward excellence. When we travel, we often use a map. In doing so, we can foresee the path to get from point A to point B. Many alternate routes can be taken with varying degrees of effectiveness, but the map remains essential. It provides the information necessary to prevent us from getting lost because of our own wanderlust. The map ties us to reality. In the same way, the practice of knowledge acquisition has been forged through experience. Some paths toward knowledge are efficient, others not so. The mistakes and the successes that have been discovered in the past serve to inform the present and the future. Though, there may be aspects found within the standards that have been developed to best direct learning that are tainted with human error, the map is still necessary. The map is necessary because it keeps us grounded in reality. The map provides facts that are constant. To divorce ourselves from a source that provides knowledge that is constant is folly. If having a map to direct us in mundanity is important, how much more vital are the instructions leading to eternal life?

In the Word of God, we find the instructions to live a set-apart life that is founded on fellowship with our Savior. This Word leads to eternality with our King! Argumentation that suggests we dissociate ourselves from a standard of moral thought can only lead to unfettered debauchery. To step aside from a centralized standard of ethical behavior curses the heart of mankind to chase after every evil imagining. It happened before. Noah was instructed to build an ark because "the wickedness of mankind was great on the earth, and that every intent of the thoughts of their hearts was only evil continually" (Genesis 6:5). Judgment fell upon the earth because humanity sought after the lust of the flesh. God's Word is our one and only roadmap to stay on the path leading toward righteousness. To stray from this path leads to death.

A summation of the influences that inform the attitude of deconstruction felt in our culture today is found in a statement offered by Dr. Gutierrez. She suggests:

> In social justice mathematics tradition, students are taught to use classical mathematics as a tool to read and write the world. But, in general, the tool itself is not questioned. Recognizing the limitations of using the master's tools to dismantle the master's house leads me to argue that we must also be willing to question and reconceptualize what counts as mathematics in the first place, thereby taking up issues of epistemology and ontology.[36]

She puts forth a call for "dismantling the master's house." She comments that utilizing standards that have been set forth regarding math instruction is futile in the efforts of some to terraform the face of math procedure. It is therefore, in her view, necessary to devise alternative avenues to bring tradition to its knees for the sake of progress. "Progress into what?" is the question. She suggests that it is necessary to take issue with epistemology itself. Epistemology deals with the nature of knowledge in contrast to opinion. It investigates knowledge to determine if it is a valid, substantive truth or simply opinion. Additionally, Dr. Gutierrez calls for the deconstruction of ontology. This term refers to the nature of being. She calls into question the validity of the framework that is commonly accepted through which we define mathematics. In her view, the framework is invalid given the state of our world.

I know Dr. Gutierrez is speaking about mathematics. Why then have I spent so much time looking at her system of thought? Firstly, the scope of her writing reaches out to teaching and learning in general. She pushes for epistemic changes in how we transfer knowledge. As I stated earlier, there is validity in tradition. Removing all traces of tradition leads to chaos. Secondly, as I also stated earlier, I am most concerned with issues of faith. How then does this examination of mathematics education connect with faith? Dr. Gutierrez and others who share her worldview target faith, especially the Christian faith, because it is deemed intolerant. Those who hold to the teachings of the Bible are categorized as zealots of a tradition. They are religious zealots who have utilized fear to control the masses as the world was colonized. It is a religion of political control, in the view of those who oppose faith. Therefore, it follows, as the argument for the dismantling of the master's house in the field of mathematics goes, so goes the deconstruction of traditional values established in Scripture. The master's house will be torn down and thrown in the fire of progressivism.

We are in a time of deconstruction. The traditions that have been in place are being dismantled in an attempt to build a better tomorrow, a tomorrow that is unleashed from the bounds of what is deemed part of the white-supremacist mentality of colonialization. We live in a time marked by the deconstruction of knowledge. Truth is relative. What is known is relegated to the individual. Knowledge is only valid if it pertains to the individual and as long as it does not infringe on the expression of others. Gutierrez shares this idea of dismantling the norm along with others in the educational field. In an article written for the Tudschrift Voor Genderstudies forum of Amsterdam University, titled "In Lak' ech: You Are My Other Me," authors Aurora Perego and Christine Quinan celebrate the deconstruction of norms. We move into the deconstruction of identity.

The Deconstruction of Identity

Identity involves whom we perceive ourselves to be as we relate to the world around us. A general, basic definition of this term is: "who a person is, or the qualities of a person or group that make them different from others."[37] Identity is another victim of the deconstruction. Identity has become a political weapon to dismantle norms of expression. The concept of identity has been taken to the nth degree. No longer is identity an indicator of what makes an individual distinct from another; it has now devolved to becoming a thought that is so specific to a given individual that a particular proclivity expressed as identity within an individual is almost non-relatable to others. What I mean by this is that we have come to a point in our society where individual expression has been loosed from all bounds. To hold a general collective understanding of human identity is disregarded in our day as restrictive. This general human identity has been replaced with a concept known as "expressive individualism." This concept can be described, in a brief manner, as the expression externally of what an individual perceives the self to be internally. In this view, the inner feelings are predominant, and they must be expressed externally, with the inner self being the true self regardless of societal normativity. Culturally there has been a shift in our view of the self. This shift can be witnessed in examining the placement of the self within the context of the larger world. In our contemporary context, what makes up our being is not the self relative to a larger context in which we as a human race collectively agree upon. The concept of the self—who we are within, our feelings, desires, lusts, perceptions of individual being—has become primary. The inner self is the starting point through which the external self is determined, refined, and expressed. How we interpret, interact, and dwell in reality is determined from within. It is for this reason that human identity is suffering from deconstruction.

Identity is being reconfigured by the voice of chaos. Many people in our world struggle with identity. They struggle with knowing who they are as the self in conformity or conflict toward inner feelings played out in the matrix of external expression. It is the elevation of the inner self that causes many people to struggle with sin as a mechanism of self-definition. We live in a culture wherein sin is celebrated as a viable aspect of personal identity. I make this statement not out of judgment. I do not write these words to pass judgment on anyone in any struggle they face. Nor do I write from a position of dismissal. Clearly, we can see that many people are conflicted with issues of identity. To dismiss the conflict and disregard the person is apathetic. Holding such attitudes only increases the difficulty of allowing lines of communication to remain available. I make this statement out of concern for those who struggle. I write these statements out of love in an effort to speak hope and truth. To love is to be willing to warn. To love is to be willing to remind others of truth. To love is to be willing to communicate. We must be willing to openly communicate, speaking hope into all situations we struggle with as humanity. To do this is to allow the Holy Spirit the opportunity to work. It is ultimately by the power of our Savior Jesus Christ that we awaken from the slumber of sin. I recognize that conversing about the topic of identity is difficult. I tread lightly as I address the issue of identity—not out of fear of persecution, but out of love for those who are confused as to who they truly are in the eyes of a loving God and Father. As the Church, it is imperative that we confront the difficulties we can see in our world with compassion (2 Timothy 2:24–26). Too often we are quick to disregard the struggle of our human other. It is time for His Church to stand as bastions of truth driven by compassion for the revelation of salvation for those are lost.

May the words I write be glorifying only to God. May these words serve as expressions of His hope toward a world stricken with darkness. May He reveal His light to those who need Him most. May His name be made great upon this earth. Praise be to our God and Father, our Savior, Amen.

As alluded to earlier, we live in a time when we can identify as something so uniquely distinct from any other person that we become self-defined. General categories of personal identity can no longer contain the array of more contemporary forms of self-identity. Collectively, this trend toward self-definition can be corralled within a development in human behavior that has come to be known as the transgender movement. The transgender movement has demanded the attention of the world. It has become a juggernaut that is trampling opposition, marching behind the banner of intolerance and racism. To question the motives of the movement means being branded a fool. The movement has taken ground in all aspects of life, from the media to education. Vaughan Roberts, who is an author, conference speaker, and rector of St. Ebbe's Church in Oxford, suggests the cause magnifying the force by which the LGBTQ+ movement has gripped the attention of the world is the fact that "our culture has now largely rejected the concept of objective truth, at least when it comes to the big issues, such as meaning and morality."[38] This statement is not an opinion held by Reverend Roberts; it is an unfortunate fact. Objective truth founded on healthy social norms has been rejected and replaced by individual subjectivity to personal preferences informed by one's own interpretation of society. It is therefore necessary for a commonly accepted understanding of social normativity to fall prey to the individual. Any commonly held system of belief that comes into conflict with individual expression is deemed an act of the most heinous violence. Reverend Roberts goes on to say:

> Within ourselves as individuals. If we think that truth is subjective, then we certainly won't let any external authority tell us what to think or how to behave-whether it's the government, a religion or our family. It's up to us to draw our own conclusions and live our own lives.[39]

The individual is an authority unto itself defined by the self. As a culture, we have been slowly conditioned to move away from standards of truth, especially if the truth comes from the Bible. We have grown accustomed to ideologies that strive to dismantle traditional concepts of ethical behavior. Chaos in the tree, how we have listened to thee. The transgender movement has been such a dominant voice directing the course of contemporary thought because we have sat under the influence of the tree, soaking in the sun as if everything is just fine. The Church is lazily "sinbathing" in complacent affluence. I use the fabricated word "sinbathing" intentionally. This word describes the state of what we refer to as the Church in context of our cultural milieu. We have been too busy sinbathing, dipping our toes in the pool of sin and ignoring the plight of those who do not have faith. The serpent has been left to ravage the landscape in plain sight of those who should be standing guard for the truth.

Our Messiah warns of the time leading up to His return. He tells us of the time before the judgment of sin. He warns:

For as in those days before the flood they were eating and drinking, marrying and giving in marriage, until the day that Noah entered the ark, and they did not understand until the flood came and took them all away; so will the coming of the Son of Man be. (Matthew 4:38–39)

Wickedness will be unchecked in the human heart. Each person will be given over to fall victim to the lusts of one's own heart because the proclamation of truth from the people of God is mumbled incoherently in dread. The prophet Jeremiah writes through the inspiration of the Holy Spirit, telling us that the human heart "is more deceitful than all else and is desperately sick; who can understand it? I, the Lord, search the heart, I test the mind, even to give each man according to his ways, according to the results of his deeds" (Jeremiah 17:9–10). The Lord warns us of the condition of the sinful heart; it finds wickedness in its nature. God declares that He is the sole authority to search the hearts of mankind. He gives us over to the desires of our heart. If we desire to seek after the lusts of the flesh, it is ours. If we choose to seek the things of God, He makes Himself known to us. It is for this reason that sin has gained such influence over humanity in this age. The Church has done a poor job of defending the faith, which in turn has caused the hearts of the people to fade to apathy. Culturally, individualism is celebrated. The individual has been allowed to disengage from commonly held standards of ethical conduct in exchange for preferences enflamed by sin.

Reverend Roberts picks up this theme in a comment regarding the contemporary disposition of the culture: "There's a deeply rooted conviction that everyone is free to define themselves as they wish, and no one has the right to question that self-definition."[40] The thirst for deconstruction flows through all aspects of reality driven by the incessant lust of the culture. The intersectionality of the culture's desire to dismantle tradition permeates even to the individual. No longer is the identity inherent in an individual commonly defined by the culture. Identity has been dismantled. The individual has become a god unto oneself. Identity can no longer be defined in a concise entry in the dictionary. Identity, as realized in the contemporary frame of reference, cannot be defined. We have come to a place where all individuals can create an identity based on whatever they wish. Not only that, but one's identity can be changed, modified, morphed, or discarded at will. Yet even with all of this inconsistency, others must and are demanded to observe specific pronouns that are chosen, modified, morphed, or discarded. Disregarding a chosen pronoun is seen as violence. Chaos and confusion, discord and division are the harbingers giving a sign marking the end of what we have come to know as human. The devolution of the social construct arising from a collective moral consideration founded upon the biblical standard is clearly recognized as everyone does what is right in their own eyes (Judges 17:6).

In a paper written by Dr. James Fearon, professor of political science at Stanford University, a definition that encompasses identity in the contemporary context is provided. He offers this quote regarding identity originally given by Stuart Hall:

> Identity emerges as a kind of unsettled space, or an unresolved question in that space, between a number of intersecting discourses…. [Until recently, we have incorrectly thought that identity is] a kind of fixed point of thought and being, a ground of action…the logic of something like a "true self." …[But] identity is a process, identity is split. Identity is not a fixed point but an ambivalent point. Identity is also the relationship of the Other to oneself.[41]

Dr. Fearon suggests that identity is a process. Our self-identity is no longer defined by characteristics that are deemed noble by the larger context in which we live. Identity is now a point of contradiction; it is ambivalent, in this view. An individual can choose to exist in a place that is in opposition to culturally accepted norms. Additionally, an individual can choose to adopt expressions of identity that are in opposition to oneself. There are those who choose, then, to live in a world of tension. *Nepantla*, a place between two worlds, is the chosen dwelling of many in modern culture. This is a place of noncommittal, a place of amorphous abstraction where definitions can be altered based on feeling. We have come to a point in our culture where "any attempt to try to 'correct' a person's gender identity so that it conforms to their biological sex is now increasingly seen as unacceptable. It is now the body rather than the mind that is often treated, with hormones or surgery being used to change the body so that it conforms to a person's sense of identity."[42]

Reverend Roberts comments on the difficulty we face when counseling those who struggle with gender/identity dysphoria. He is correct in stating that no longer is the dysphoria treated through the mind; it is addressed in the body. The enemy of our souls has manipulated humanity through the enticements of the flesh to focus on the carnal. The physical, the material, the here and now are deemed the only form of acceptable, tangible truth.

The dominant secular culture attempts to center our humanity on sexuality. We are identified by our sexual lusts or aversions. Identity has become carnal. The expression of our gender or our identity, according to contemporary standards, is not a function of a divine design by a creator, but a condition of self-expression. Sexual identity has even moved away from actual physical, biological characteristics that scientifically have defined sexual identity. Sexuality is now a sliding scale of malleable sexual preferences determined, seemingly, by the mood of the day. We have stepped away from identifying ourselves as humans, first, who secondarily possess characteristics of either male or female, to sexually driven expressions of identity based on the perversion of sexual lust. The culture perverts the purity of our humanity, causing it to take a back seat to immoral sexual desire posing as personal liberation. Our identity as children of God should be the priority. Sexuality is an expression of a marriage covenant for the purpose of procreation and unity of a couple. It is disheartening to witness so many people who are driven by sexual appetites who choose to give up their true identity for fleeting bursts of physical or emotional pleasure. Yet this is common, accepted, and even endorsed socially. I do not address any particular group in this statement. Sexual immorality is a plague that affects both the secular culture and the Church alike. Too often, the Church ignores the sexual immorality within for the sake of directing attention to the sins found without. This is a mistake, as all sexual sin must be addressed—especially for those who claim faith in Jesus. It is our responsibility to be witnesses of His authority in our lives.

Not only is sexual desire masquerading as individual identity, the liberation of the biological definition of gender identity is often encouraged. It has become almost a rite of passage for an individual to openly discard the biological self in exchange for the constructed self. To conform to biology is seen as submission to the authority of the patriarchal system of oppression. It is thus vital to liberate oneself from the bonds of a worldview that is antiquated, outdated, and irrelevant to human emancipation.

It is essential that we remember who we are as the people of God. We are not a construct of a system of collective belief. We are created in the image of a loving, merciful God. The Church must prepare to counsel people who struggle with identity issues in a compassionate manner, helping them to see that they are unique and beautiful children of a loving Father. We can no longer sit, as the Church, in ignorance, turning a blind eye to what the devil is trying to do to our fellow brothers and sisters. The Church must address issues of difficulty in honesty, from a biblical perspective.

In a book titled, *Coequal and Counterbalanced: God's Blueprint for Women and Men,* Dr. John Garr examines human development from conception. His purpose is to bring to light the false teaching that human sexuality and or gender expression is based on personal choice rather than biological standards. Dr. Garr starts this discussion at the point of conception. He explains that when an egg is fertilized, the embryo contains all of the genetic information necessary to create a human child. Both male and female characteristics are fully present in this early stage of development. He writes, "It is not that the embryo in this indistinguishable form has no gender: it just contains all of the building blocks for *both* genders."[43] Like Adam before the separation of Eve, the embryo contains all of the genetic information to construct a life. This genetic information for biological development of gender distinction remains present in the growing infant up until the eighth week of gestation. This fact is cited by Dr. Garr through a source called "Pediatric Endocrinology: Psychology, Pathophysiology, and Clinical Aspects."[44] I specifically make note of where Dr. Garr is gathering his information, because he is not simply making conjecture. He is not writing based on a presuppositional bias informed by the Christian worldview. Dr. Garr is reading academic source material to develop his arguments. His position is based on empirical, scientific evidence based on observed datum.

Dr. Garr continues: "Until the sixth week of gestation, then, 'the fledgling embryo has two sets of ducts—Wolffian for male, Mullerian for female—an either/or infrastructure held in readiness."[45] At this point in the development of the embryo, a process begins within the brain of the baby to release chemical information that will determine biological sex. If the *Y* chromosome is present in the DNA of this baby, the brain releases testosterone that directs the body to develop as a male. If no *Y* chromosome is present, the body develops as female. The characteristics of the opposite sex in the embryo are resorbed as a result of the natural ontogenesis of the new life growing in the mother's womb. The important fact is that early on in the maturation of the baby, biological gender is established and made distinguishable. Dr. Garr states: "This biological fact obviates many arguments by unisex sociologists who have declared that gender differences are entirely the result of environmental factors."[46] Environment, therefore, is not a factor contributing to the biological indicators of gender. The gender of an individual is settled within the first few weeks after conception.

There are many people who suffer from gender dysphoria. Unfortunately, rather than helping people who are dealing with this condition work through their dysphoria from a biblical perspective, counseling them with true insight, many psychologists are prescribing hormone-therapy treatments that are administered according to the feelings of the individual experiencing dysphoria. Hormone therapy is described in an article published by Translational Andrology and Urology. In the article, titled "Hormone Therapy for Transgender Patients," they explain:

> The number of transgender individuals seeking cross-sex hormone therapy has risen over the years. The administration of exogenous virilizing hormones is considered medically necessary for many transgender individuals. Many transgender men seek therapy for virilization and the mainstay treatment is exogeneous testosterone. Transgender women desire suppression of androgenic effects and often use anti-androgen therapy with feminizing exogenous estrogens.[47]

Virilization can be a condition that springs from the administration of progestin during pregnancy. Progestin is a drug that prevents miscarriage, and it was commonly induced to pregnant women in the 1950s and '60s.[48] An article published by the Intersex Society of North America explains:

> Virilizing hormones can be born into a continuum of sex phenotype which ranges from "female with larger [female anatomy]" to "male with no [male anatomy]." It is noteworthy that the use of progestin is not effective in the prevention of miscarriage. Virilization is related to chemically induced man-made drug intended to serve the good but ultimately this drug inhibited normal infant development. This unfortunate procedure may have been the catalyst that flung open the door for the debate of gender identity that our culture struggles with today. In another article titled Virilization published by Merck Manual, it is stated "Virilization is caused by excess production of androgens usually because of a tumor in or enlargement of

an adrenal gland or a tumor in an ovary or abnormal hormone production by the ovaries."[49]

The article continues:

Enlargement of the ovaries due to certain types of cysts may cause virilization, but such cases are almost always mild. Sometimes, a congenital abnormality in an enzyme (a protein) in the adrenal glands can also cause virilization. Such an abnormality is often diagnosed in childhood or adolescence and is termed congenital adrenal hyperplasia.[50]

The typical treatment for such cases comes in the form of exogenous hormones. The hormones can be used to treat individuals who suffer from virilization. Testosterone treatments for men and estrogen treatments for women were developed to be administered to individuals suffering from this condition. It appears that these treatments were meant to be administered to biologically male or female individuals who experience an increase in the opposite sex characteristics that are exaggerated through various medical conditions. The hormones were developed to stabilize male testosterone in men and estrogen levels in women.[51]

Thus, the inception of gender dysphoria appears to be medical, not psychosocial. Yet, there is an increasing drive to make gender dysphoria an internal, individual struggle with self-expression as the individual struggles to relate to a society who, in their own perception, rejects their personal expression of sexuality. I am not trying to downplay the plight of those who suffer from this type of dysphoria; for those living with this disorder, their perceptions are very real. What I am getting at is the fact that, traditionally, this was seen as a medical condition and was treated as such. Gender dysphoria has morphed into a psychological condition, but rather than treating individuals with therapy that assists them with this disorder, we seem to be encouraging them to embrace the disorder. The individual then becomes the disorder, and their self-identity is the disorder.

An article published by the NHS titled "Treatment of Gender Dysphoria" gives a chilling synopsis of contemporary procedures to treat gender dysphoria, beginning with children. The article states:

> If your child has gender dysphoria and they've reached puberty, they could be treated with gonadotrophin-releasing hormone (GnRH) analogues. These are synthetic (man-made) hormones that suppress the hormones naturally produced by the body.
>
> Some of the changes that take place during puberty are driven by hormones. For example, the hormone testosterone, which is produced by the testes in boys, helps stimulate [male anatomy] growth.
>
> GnRH analogues suppress the hormones produced by your child's body. They also suppress puberty and can help delay potentially distressing physical changes caused by their body becoming even more like that of their biological sex, until they're old enough for the treatment options discussed below.
>
> GnRH analogues will only be considered for your child if assessments have found they're experiencing clear distress and have a strong desire to live as their gender identity.[52]

So many disturbing things appear in this brief statement. It is apparent that modern medicine is approaching this disorder from the standpoint of acceptance and exaltation rather than from correction. The treatment for children suffering from this disfunction, in view of this article, is one of counsel to embrace the gender that one *feels* is the most appropriate. When this baseline of feeling is established, the children are administered a series of *man-made hormones* that will suppress the natural development of the body. In this view, the feelings an individual is experiencing in the moment far surpass the factual evidence of biology. It is startling that professional counselors and doctors are enabling children to make lifelong decisions at such a young, naive age. Gonadotrophin-releasing hormone (GnRH) affects the pituitary gland of the brain.[53]

The development of this hormone appears to have been implemented to assist individuals psychologically who are struggling with a deficiency of naturally occurring hormones produced by the brain for a given gender. Males were given a hormone treatment that aided the body in producing testosterone and conversely, for women, they were administered treatments to aid in the production of estrogen. The levels of estrogen in women, especially during pregnancy, can vary. This hormone was developed to assist with this naturally occurring variance. As stated in an article titled "Gonadotrophin-Releasing Hormone:"

> The variations in levels of GnRH receptors during pituitary development, the menstrual cycle, pregnancy, lactation, and oophorectomy in the presence or absence of estrogen replacement suggest that such changes are physiologically important.[54]

The introduction of this type of hormone treatment was initially meant to help individuals experience a stabilization of hormonal secretions in the body. The initial usages of this treatment are further explained on the National Cancer Institute website. They define GnRH in this way:

> A hormone made by a part of the brain called the hypothalamus. Gonadotropin-releasing hormone causes the pituitary gland in the brain to make and secrete the hormones luteinizing hormone (LH) and follicle-stimulating hormone (FSH). In men, these hormones cause the [male anatomy] to make testosterone. In women, they cause the ovaries to make estrogen and progesterone. Also called GnRH, LH-RH, LHRH, and luteinizing hormone-releasing hormone.[55]

This therapy is now being used for those suffering from gender dysphoria. The hormones are administered to individuals to help suppress naturally occurring hormones. In addition to the suppression of naturally occurring hormones, the brain is introduced to hormones associated with the opposite sex. We have taken this treatment initially designed to help, and altered its functionality to further confusion within the society.

Another alarming admission toward the practice of hormone therapy is that the induced hormones are man-made. We are introducing the body to chemicals that are not naturally occurring in an effort to suppress the designed development. The treatment is not medical, but psychosocial, as stated in the article by the NHS. They write:

> GnRH analogues suppress the hormones produced by your child's body. They also suppress puberty and can help delay potentially distressing physical changes caused by their body becoming even more like that of their biological sex, until they're old enough for the treatment options discussed [in a later section of the article].
>
> GnRH analogues will only be considered for your child if assessments have found they're experiencing clear distress and have a strong desire to live as their gender identity.[56]

The purpose of hormone therapy in adolescents is to suppress the natural development of characteristics determined by biological sex. This determination is based on the emotional distress of an individual at a given, brief moment in early development. I am not trying to downplay the emotional crisis an individual is experiencing. We all know that when we are in the midst of turmoil, our emotional state is exceedingly real. Often choices made during periods of crisis are based on emotional reactions to external and internal stimuli. Long-term consequences are often neglected as the fight or flight response kicks in to assist us through the period of turmoil. Especially during adolescence, emotional stability can fluctuate dramatically. It is disheartening to know that, again, professional therapists, counselors, and doctors are encouraging children to fully engage in temporal emotional responses. Rather than offering man-made chemicals to counter natural development, we should be offering solid, truth-centered counseling and truly taking the time to walk alongside people who suffer from this dysphoria. Our Messiah will give us rest from our burdens (Matthew 11:28–30). Rest will not come from *man-ufactured* substances. We are fearfully and wonderfully made by a loving Father (Psalm 139:14). We are imparted with the image of our Creator (Genesis 1:27; 1 Corinthians 15:49). He promises to never leave us or forsake us (Deuteronomy 31:6).

The dysphoria experienced by some in our culture, categorized as transgenderism, is a prominent warning pointing to the deception spoken forth by the serpent. Historically, slavery has been defined as "submission to a dominating influence."[57] It appears as if slavery has evolved. The horror of slavery has mutated. Slavery, once the oppression via a dominating influence, has moved through slavery to systems, policies, and politics. From slavery to politics/policies, we have gone to enslavement under the guise of social activism or reform. The dominating influence that has power over the masses is social angst that leads to the dismantling of norms for the sake of the dismantling. It now appears that we have fallen into the possible final state of slavery: slavery to individualism. The devil has found a way to make us slaves unto ourselves. We are slaves to the pride of the self. We elevate ourselves to the level of gods, claiming sovereignty in our sin. No one, nothing, can dissuade us from the pursuit of the elevation of the self. It is for this reason we see the dismantling of what is considered traditional social order in the world today. Those who are slaves to the self must dispose of standards of conduct that have been established through the traditions of biblical morality and the lessons of history in order to shape a future wherein the fetters of God are broken. The psalmist cries out in disbelief as he contemplates the arrogance of a people who are so filled with hate that they attempt to make war with God.

> Why are the nations in an uproar
> And the peoples devising a vain thing?
> The kings of the earth take their stand
> And the rulers take counsel together

Against the Lord and against His Anointed, saying,
"Let us tear their fetters apart
And cast away their cords from us!" (Psalm 2:1–3)

The people bound to slavery of the self want the fetters to be dashed upon the rocks of progress. In this light, progress is the rejection of God. The God of our Bible is deemed to be a suppressor of individualism. The serpent in the tree speaks the same lies throughout time. "You will be like God," it repeats, "eat therefore of the fruit of death." And so those who love their own sin to destruction eat. Sin reserves its dominance over them (Romans 6:14).

The transgender movement is a stark exemplifier of the drive to destroy ethical norms for the sake of enslavement to individualism. This movement has given voice to the underlying pattern of deceit the serpent has been employing to manipulate humanity. The transgender movement relates to the destruction of identity. The enemy desires for humanity to forget who they are and in whose image they have been created (Genesis 1:27). The devil seeks to mold humankind into its own image, one corrupted by pride. The enemy knows that the prideful suffer the most from the lack of hearing. The prideful are the most closed to counsel because they are a counsel unto themselves.

It is for this reason that I have devoted so much time elaborating on the transgender movement in this writing. I do not write with the intent to degrade anyone. Nor do I incite others to mistreat anyone. I am writing to expose the crippling lies of the enemy as he attempts to influence our children. The serpent's desire is to steal the future and bring decay to the fruit of the Church. If the fruit is corrupt, the tree springing forth from the fruit will also be born out of corruption. I again do not promote the mistreatment of anyone. Instead, I bow my knee in prayer to a Holy God and ask for His help. The Church is called to be His witness even in this age, and it is only by the impartation of wisdom flavored with mercy of our Holy God that we can begin to minister to those who struggle in this falling world. It is only by His strength that we will be able to walk in compassion to win the hearts of those who have given themselves over to the slavery of the self and bring them back to God. My heart breaks for those struggling with gender dysphoria. I am not in any way passing judgment on anyone, nor do I elevate myself. For I am one of the vilest of sinners Christ, our Messiah, has saved (1 Timothy 1:14–16). My heart breaks for those who suffer in willful sin. Those who embrace the bondage of sin have decided to close themselves off to the mercy of God, choosing, rather, to harden their own heart. **Be a witness; live your faith in the everyday.** Show those who are slaves to sin the love of God so that His Holy Spirit can work to soften their hearts unto repentance. Salvation comes to those who repent, with the authority to turn them away from their sin (Luke 15:7).

The effects of the transgender movement give evidence of the enemy's desire to destroy human identity. When we step away from who we are, as identifiable children given life by the Living God, the theater of war is set to bring destruction to biology. Human biology finds itself in the guillotine constructed by the violent thirst, in modern culture, to dismantle anything that is perceived as being a facet of normalized understanding passed on through the traditional school of thought. The regressive nature of deception initially begins with the deconstruction of knowledge. The enemy deceives those who choose to be unaware, to regard knowledge as relative and pertinent to an individual's experience. If knowledge is a concept that is determined to be relative to an individual's perception, then knowledge moves from a foundation based on external, empirical truth to a foundation carved into the sands of human malleability. The enemy attempts to shape human cognition with the hammer of chaos. When empirical knowledge defining humanity described biblically is lost, our innate human identity as children of the Living God can be reduced to preferences associated with feelings, opinions, or rebellion. Human identity is now founded on subjective preferences, which can be altered at any given moment due to any given set of circumstances. Identity grounded in objective truth has become obsolete. No longer does an individual need to conform to norms of the self. The self can be whatever the self wants to be, liberated from normative behavior, while also free to experience hell—the *hell* of arrogance. If the bookends that give structure to the definition of the self are discarded, the biological science of human identity can be deemed irrelevant, insufficient, and inhibiting to personal expression. "Pride goes before destruction, and a haughty spirit before stumbling" (Proverbs 16:18). Pride of life in one's own arrogance will bring stumbling before the feet of the beast of destruction. We enter the realm of the self-imposed god. We return to the time in antiquity when a pharaoh became god—a man-made god, the god of personhood. The difference we can see with the deification of humankind in the modern world is found in the recognition that there is more than one pharoah. All people have the sinful capacity to be gods unto themselves. Self-worship born of the self-made god of arrogant humanity falls from the lips of so many. What a pitiful thing to worship the created over the Creator.

Therefore God gave them over in the lusts of their hearts to impurity, so that their bodies would be dishonored among them. For they exchanged the truth of God for a lie, and worshiped and served the creature rather than the Creator, who is blessed forever. (Romans 1:24–26)

The Apostle Paul clearly defines the cause that has effectually brought about the demise of humankind—the exchange of truth for lies, the elevation of the created above the authority of the Creator. Those who choose to remain condemned to their sinful lives are given over to the lusts of the flesh. We enter the age of the almighty "ME," where the "I" is the only concern. We enter the realm of science fiction made reality.

The Deconstruction of Biology

We have come to the end of ourselves. The end of the human. We now tread at the boundary of what denotes human distinction. The devil has been working for millennia to breed disdain for the human condition into the consciousness of the masses. We have been conditioned through the influence of the liar, subtly over time, to despise our created identity as unique individuals knit together by a loving God (Psalm 139:13). The very thought that we have been born into a body and given a spirit that has been designed by our Heavenly Father has become revolting. It has become an untruth that must be rejected and redefined. The human, therefore, has become a plaything of chaos. The human now suffers from a plethora of disorders, afflictions, dysphoria, and limitations that may or may not be grounded on factual reality. The human suffers tragically in both reality and fiction, the actual and the imagined. We seem to invent disorders along with endless pharmaceutical remedies contrived to address the disorders *ad nauseum*. All of these afflictions, real or contrived, are designed by the enemy of God to cause His children to be drawn back unto themselves. Slavery to the self through incessant reminders of affliction, disorder, and dysphoria are poisoning the human condition. Our enemy wants us to grow to hate biology so that we devise avenues to reduce, even eliminate from the human vocabulary what are perceived as biological constraints. The enemy has bred discontent within the human heart, leading to the continual, perpetual drive for change, for more, for the new. What was is not good enough. What *will be, will be* coveted only in the chase to attain the *will be*. When the *will be* is grasped, it no longer is sufficient to satiate the cravings of human desire to discover the next *will be*. In this context, biology is a suggestion, an antiquated blueprint for a foundation that has been redesigned by those who proclaim to possess enlightenment. The human "I," defined as an individual given life by the Sovereign God, has become the "they," the "ze," the "ver," the "xem," or the "xyrs."[58] As I stated earlier, we have come to the end of humanity as we become transhuman. The widespread drive leading to the apotheosis of man has been reborn. As in the days of old, when man thought himself to be a god, we come to an awakening in the liberated self. Where all who seek godhood of the self are afflicted with the ability to taste pride, the gods of the old have awakened.

The transhumanist movement is a massive, multifaceted philosophy.

Proponents of the movement appear to perceive organic humanity as a thing of the past, a limitation that evolution through technological advances will alleviate. The movement seeks to fortify widespread disdain for biological humanity by deeming it a mundane restriction in the process of true human enlightenment. What is perceived to be organic, biological characteristics of life have become limitations of human physiology because of the advancements in technology. Transhumanism, simply stated, is driven by the desire to remedy the biological limitations of the human. This is an attack against the organic; it is the deconstruction of biology. Nick Bostrom, professor at Oxford University and director of the Future of Humanity Institute, defines "transhumanism" in this way:

> Transhumanism is a loosely defined movement that has developed gradually over the past two decades. It promotes an interdisciplinary approach to understanding and evaluating the opportunities for enhancing the human condition and the human organism opened up by the advancement of technology. Attention is given to both present technologies, like genetic engineering and information technology, and anticipated future ones, such as molecular nanotechnology and artificial intelligence.[59]

The God-given human condition is determined to be outdated. Biological humanity is dead. There are some who seek, in the transhumanist movement, to give rise to a new, improved human. This human is autonomous, freed from the bonds of being a child of God. We have now come to a place in technological advancement that pride in the knowledge of human ingenuity surpasses submission to the higher authority in God. We can be our own gods. We can worship the god of modern-day personhood. I write in a very general way when making these statements. There have been significant advancements in medical technologies that have aided in the plight of individuals suffering with any number of afflictions. The issue of technological integration with the biological human is delicate and complex. It is a matter of ethical consideration that is beyond the scope of this writing. I make reference to the transhuman movement to shed light on the subject for the people of God. Transhumanism is an ethical issue that must be considered in the context of our Christian worldview. We must develop dialogue using discernment given by God to navigate this point of concern. It is vital that the Church addresses difficult matters influencing our culture in order that we have a biblical answer to give (1 Peter 3:14–16). Additionally, we must know how to counsel our children as they are confronted with contemporary matters of contention toward faith. We cannot ignorantly give our children over to the whims of a godless society. As the Church, we must address difficult ethical decisions from a biblical perspective for the sake of those who have worth: our children.

As I stated, the transhuman movement is massive and multifaceted. It spans concepts from biomedical technology to artificial intelligence to neurotechnology. I do not intend to write on each aspect of this globular movement at this time, with the exception of one. I will comment briefly on the tentacle of the transhumanist movement that I find the most frightening: the arm that touches the very language by which we are made, our DNA.

Friedrich Miescher is credited with the first discovery of DNA, as he conducted experimentation with human white blood cells in the 1860s.[60] The continued study of DNA has led scientists to develop knowledge in the areas of paternal, genealogical, and forensic testing. It has also contributed to advancements in fetal diagnosis, preimplantation, and pharmacogenomics. Experimentation in this field of study has opened the door to discoveries in genetic engineering and the manipulation of the biological genetic code. The engineering of DNA was theoretical until the 1970s, when Peter Berg created the first recombinant DNA.[61] The process of developing lab-generated, recombinant DNA is "created through the combination of elements of DNA from different organisms. By introducing genetic material from one organism to another, this discovery established the principles of modern genetics, and was the basis of many future experiments."[62] Recombinant DNA is a method of combining genetic material from one or more organisms and creating genetic sequencing that normally would have been present. Recombinant DNA becomes part of the original DNA molecule. It is a new strain of DNA manufactured in the lab through the persistence of fallen man. This is a frightening thought, as we truly have no long-term scientific data to analyze effects of recombinant DNA (rDNA) in organisms. An article written by the National Center for Biotechnology Information sheds an alarming light upon the rDNA introduction in human specimens that are found in current vaccines. The article suggests:

> When a single recombinant DNA molecule, composed of a vector plus an inserted DNA fragment, is introduced into a host cell, the inserted DNA is reproduced along with the vector, producing large numbers of recombinant DNA molecules that include the fragment of DNA originally linked to the vector. Two types of vectors are most commonly used: E. coli plasmid vectors and bacteriophage λ vectors. Plasmid vectors replicate along with their host cells, while λ vectors replicate as lytic viruses, killing the host cell and packaging the DNA into virions.[63]

A plasmid, as mentioned in the quote above, is "a small, circular, double-stranded DNA molecule that is distinct from a cell's chromosomal DNA."[64] Plasmids occur naturally in the cells of bacteria. Bacteria often benefits from the existence of plasmids because they act as a conduit through which bacteria can gain antibiotic resistance. Bacteria cells divide rapidly. The genetic information contained within the bacteria cell is cloned, including the plasmids that might be present. This process is described in an excerpt from a book titled *An Introduction to Genetic Analysis*. The authors describe the process of creating lab-generated rDNA in bacterial cells:

> The basic procedure is to extract and cut up DNA from a donor genome into fragments from several genes and allow these fragments to insert themselves individually into opened-up small

autonomously replicating DNA molecules such as bacterial plasmids.[65]

The DNA of a donor genome is fragmented and comingled with bacterial, or, as the authors suggest later, viral plasmids. Plasmids act as carriers, referred to as vectors, transmitting information and replicating information from the donor genome to the introduced genetic strand. Plasmids therefore enhance the bacteria cells' survival by transferring information to the cloned cells generated from the original. Plasmids have been used experimentally in order to "clone, transfer, and manipulate genes."[66] Plasmid vectors can be inserted into DNA for the purposes of cloning genetic information on a large scale, essentially creating "factories to copy DNA fragments in large quantities."[67] The altered genetic code is then able to replicate much more efficiently and completely through the presence of vector transformation. As the genetic information is cloned between the donor DNA and the plasmid vectors, the original information is considered to be transformed. As noted in the article, "Making Recombinant DNA":

> An individual transformed cell with a single recombinant vector will divide into a colony with millions of cells, all carrying the same recombinant vector. Therefore, an individual contains a very large population of identical DNA inserts, and this population is called a clone.[68]

The manufactured genetic information is able then to be cloned throughout the donor's genetic code.

Recombinant DNA experimentation revealed to the scientific community the ability to introduce genetic information across species of organisms. Dr. Leslie Pray describes this development in genetic engineering as follows:

> Researchers learned that recombinant DNA could be introduced into the SV40 virus, a pathogen that infects both monkeys and

humans. Indeed, in 1972, Stanford University researcher Paul Berg and his colleagues integrated segments of phage DNA, as well as a segment of *E. coli* DNA containing the galactose operon, into the SV40 genome. (The *E. coli* galactose operon is a cluster of genes that plays a role in galactose sugar metabolism.) The significance of their achievement was its demonstration that recombinant DNA technologies could be applied to essentially any DNA sequences, no matter how distantly related their species of origin. In their words, these researchers "developed biochemical techniques that are generally applicable for joining covalently any two DNA molecules" (Jackson *et al.*, 1972). While the scientists didn't actually introduce foreign DNA into a mammalian cell in this experiment, they provided (proved) the means to do so.[69]

The understanding of combining genetic information through recombinant DNA has revealed the shocking reality that scientists now have the ability to merge the genetic makeup of various organisms. A startling admission is discovered in the article titled "Making Recombinant DNA." The authors suggest that rDNA is an unnatural union of DNAs from nonhomologous sources, usually from different organisms. Some geneticists prefer the alternative name "chimeric DNA, named in recognition of the mythological Greek monster Chimera."[70] The term "nonhomologous," as you probably can determine, means "being of unlike genetic constitution."[71] Thus, the applied word for this manufactured genetic creation, Chimera, is fitting. The process of combining genetic information from diverse organisms is done on the covalent level. In other words, the genetic alteration of an organism's DNA code occurs within the atom. A covalent bond is an "interatomic linkage that results from the sharing of an electron pair between two atoms. The binding arises from the electrostatic attraction of their nuclei for the same electrons."[72] Recombinant DNA bonds are therefore not fleetingly superficial; they occur within the atomic, foundational construction of an organism. Dr. Pray makes note that when this initial discovery in rDNA was made, a voluntary moratorium was enacted in the scientific community. She suggests:

> Clearly, scientists have always been aware that the ability to manipulate the genome and mix and match genes from different organisms, even different species, raises immediate and serious questions about the potential hazards and risks of doing so— implications still being debated today.[73]

Science itself is nervous about the implications this knowledge has brought forth. There is no telling what results will come about by knowing such genetic manipulation is possible. The World Health Organization (WHO), in response to the advancements in genetic research in the field of rDNA vaccines, suggests the following in a statement released to define the standards of vaccine research:

> The field of DNA vaccination is developing rapidly. Vaccines currently being developed use not only DNA, but also include adjuncts that assist DNA to enter cells, target it towards specific cells, or that may act as adjuvants in stimulating or directing the immune response. Ultimately, the distinction between a sophisticated DNA vaccine and a simple viral vector may not be clear. Many aspects of the immune response generated by DNA vaccines are not understood. However, this has not impeded significant progress towards the use of this type of vaccine in humans, and clinical trials have begun.[74]

Two things in the above statement are alarming to me, and they should alarm the reader as well. First, WHO, an organization comprised of world-class scientists charged with managing the health of the world, state they are "unclear" regarding the differences between sophisticated DNA vaccines and simple viral vectors. This admission of uncertainty does not bolster confidence in an organization that proposes the potential need for mandated vaccinations.[75] The second comment that I find alarming is as follows, taken directly from the WHO address as they consider the implications of advances in rDNA: "Many aspects of the immune response generated by DNA vaccines are not understood."[76] The immune response of humans when introduced to a lab-generated DNA vaccine is "not understood." Again, these admissions of uncertainty come from the organization that watches over the health and safety of the global population. It is frightening to think that scientific advancements have allowed us to learn how to edit, manipulate, erase, and combine the DNA of various organisms, yet the implications of doing so are not understood. The long-term effects of experimentation in this field are shrouded with uncertainty. We have yet to fully realize the effects genetic experimentation will bring forth.

Before I move on, let me say this: In making the statements regarding vaccinations, I do not desire to push the reader toward an opinion that would prevent one from taking a vaccine. That decision rests within you as you consider your individual circumstances. I write on these things only to provide information. I encourage the reader to use discernment in making decisions by collecting a comprehensive knowledge base so that the decisions are coming from an informed position. It is never a good idea to act in desperation or ignorance when making decisions, especially if they could affect long-term health. I encourage you to pray that God directs your steps. I encourage you to submit yourself to His authority as He leads according to His will. Lastly, I encourage you to think for yourself with the God-given intellect imparted to you by our loving Father. Our Messiah encourages us with these words found in the book of John:

My sheep hear My voice, and I know them, and they follow Me; and I give eternal life to them, and they will never perish; and no one will snatch them out of My hand. My Father, who has given them to Me, is greater than all; and no one is able to snatch them out of the Father's hand. I and the Father are one. (John 10:27–30)

We are His. Those who trust in Jesus as their Savior are His. We are firmly held within His hands. Nothing can snatch us from the steady, loving grip of our Father. Find hope in this truth. The world is filled with confusion. Do not worry about the decisions you are tasked to make. Be informed, but do not worry. We are His.

Because we have chosen, as the human race, to walk the path that has led us to the capacity to alter God-given genetic information, we are now faced with ethical problems that are yet to unfold. We do not even know the questions to ask to fully address the depth of ethical difficulties surrounding the advanced genetic developments of recent history. We, through scientific inquisitiveness, have found the guidebook that adds man-created definition to the foundation of organic life. We hold within our hands, whether benevolent or violent, the ability to redefine what is known as human. The alarming aspect of these advancements is the ability to erase, change, or add information to the genetic makeup we are given at birth.

The implications of genetic experimentation are extensive. There have been noble advancements in DNA research that have been beneficial to ease human suffering. The debate of ethics regarding continued advancements in genetic research is therefore diverse, divisive, and demanding. I write from the perspective of a Christian trying to navigate this ever-changing world. I write from the perspective of a father and husband who is concerned for the well-being of his family. I write from the perspective of a shepherd guiding the flock to use discernment when wandering in the pastures of this world. To address issues of genetic research is difficult, to say the very least. Additionally, I possess much less than could even be considered adequate knowledge of this field. But what I do know is this: We are in a war. The devil is at war for our bloodline. The enemy's strategy is to separate us from the Word and the love of our Heavenly Father. The devil wants us to forget our identity as children of God and exchange it for an identity born of corruption. Since the Fall of man, humanity has been cursed with the introduction of rebellion into our nature (Genesis 3). In the garden, the serpent injected into the bloodline of humanity the knowledge of pride.

The enemies of God know that within our DNA we carry the complex messaging system of life. The devil, by enticing humanity through advancements in genetic engineering, deceives us into altering our own God-given genetic structure. There is life in the blood, and lucifer[77] knows this. The book of Leviticus reveals this truth: "For the life of the flesh is in the blood, and I have given it to you on the altar to make atonement for your souls; for it is the blood by reason of the life that makes atonement" (Leviticus 17:11). In context, the Lord is giving the people of Israel instructions on the sacrificial system, which allowed for a temporary atonement for sin through the shed blood of an animal. This sacrificial system was designed to point us to the coming Messiah, who would shed His own blood for the remission of sin once and for all. There is power in the blood. The blood of our Savior has the power to save souls if we are repentant and turn to Him for salvation. The blood of Messiah has the power to restore us from our fallen condition. His blood also has the power to condemn those who reject the provision of God. Our blood cries out to God for either restoration or judgment. There is no neutrality.

The beginning of Leviticus 17:11 states "the life of the flesh is in the blood." It was only when God breathed into Adam that Adam became a living being. Prior to the breath of God entering Adam, there was only dust. Adam was formed in the image of God out of the dust of the earth (Genesis 2). Though Adam was formed into the physical representation of man, he did not inherit the spiritual "image" of God until the breath of God enlivened his spirit. God imparted upon Adam the essence of life. God's eternal life force entered Adam's body. The blood is the conduit that carries this life force throughout our bodies.

The war rages regarding the deconstruction of biology on the battlefront of xenotransplantation. For many years, the scientific community has been attempting to grow human body parts and organs within other species of animals for the purpose of human transplantation.[78] The drive for growing lab-developed human organs is due to a shortage of donor organs. An article on pbs.org reports that around "150,000 people around the world join the waiting lists for new heart, kidney or liver. Half die before they can get one."[79] This shortage has led to extensive research in the development of xenotransplantation, a word meaning to transplant organs, tissue, and cells from one species of animal to an animal of a different species. The transplants work best in species that have the most genes in common, meaning that it is genetically less difficult to transplant an organ from a mouse to another mouse, because the animals share similar genetic coding. It is a significantly more difficult task to transplant an organ from one species to another that has a different genetic makeup. Transplants are harder to achieve in species that have fewer genes in common. There is always some form of rejection to transplanted organs, but scientists have been working to overcome the rejection. The same article describes a breakthrough in xenotransplantation research:

> In 1992, British scientists succeeded in breeding a pig, called Astrid, with human "flags" on her cells. They put genes (DNA) for the human flags into the pig embryos and put them into the wombs of surrogate sows.[80]

The flags placed within the pigs help suppress rejection of transplanted organs. The flags block the body's natural tendency to reject foreign matter. Essentially, the flags tell the rest of the body, "there's nothing to see here." The flags disguise the true origin of the transplanted organ so the body accepts the transplant more readily.

The article goes on the explain:

> Since 1992, herds of transgenic pigs have been bred both in Europe and the United States which have human flags on their cells.... US scientists are very close to cloning piglets which have human flags on their cells. So they should be a reliable source of transgenic pig organs.[81]

The scientific community has been working to breed pigs and other animals that possess genetic markers found in human DNA.

These markers, bred into various species, allow for the genetic makeup of that animal to accept genetic material that is foreign to its species. In this experimentation, we enter turbulent waters. God gives clear direction in the Creation account that every living thing will reproduce after its own kind (Genesis 1:24). Species of the living creation are to remain separate. Animals and humans are distinct creations God never intended to intermingle. God created man in His image, imparting us with attributes of His character (Genesis 1:24–31). It was not and is not in God's design to allow different species to intermingle. As God spoke Creation into our reality, He declared that both animal life and human life will reproduce after their own, distinct kinds. This means a genus of one animal species cannot breed with that of a different species. We know this to be scientifically accurate. Dogs cannot breed with cats, as they are genetically in different biological families, or genus. We can see that God does not allow for the mixing of genes outside of what He refers to as "kinds." The Hebrew word used for the word "kind" is (H4327-מִין *min*). This word refers specifically to differentiations within species. The scientific community applies the term "kinds" to the genus level of taxonomic classification. Humans and animals are to remain segregated according to their own species, kind, or genus.

The scientific community has been developing technologies that allow for the interspecies comingling of genetic information that, under normal circumstances, would be impossible. We are beginning to discover how to mix the DNA of one species with another. The scientific community has adopted the phrase "chimera" as a term to define this type of research. The term "chimera" is defined as "an organism or tissue that contains at least two different sets of DNA, most often originating from the fusion of as many different zygotes (fertilized eggs). The term is derived from the Chimera of Greek mythology, a fire-breathing monster that was part lion, part goat, and part dragon."[82] The mythologic Greek Chimera was a monstrous, fire-breathing horror composed of various animals who ravaged the countryside of Lycia. It is fitting, scientifically, to apply the term as a descriptor to the practice of infusing human genetic information in cross-species xenotransplantation.

An article published by the *Chicago Tribune*, titled "Scientists Take the First Steps to Growing Human Organs in Pigs," reports on current breakthroughs in this research that have led to "working on making humanized pancreases, hearts and livers in pigs. The animals would grow those organs in place of their own, and they'd be euthanized before the organ is removed."[83] Within the pigs would grow human organs that would be harvested when needed. The pigs possess the genetic markers allowing for human organs to grow within them. This increases the ability of the human specimen who will then receive the pig-grown organ to accept the transplant. This process intermingles human and swine DNA. From what has been discovered thus far regarding plasmid vectors and rDNA advances, the DNA-implanted cross species may have the ability to be replicated, cloned indefinitely.

Additionally, to make the transplant of these human/pig organs easier for the body to accept, researchers are now experimenting on taking DNA samples from an individual in need of an organ transplant. They would then inject pig embryos with the person's DNA and grow organs with the specific person's individual DNA. Within the swine and the human would exist a covalent bond of the genetic information. Again, the ramifications of dabbling in this experimentation are bewildering to consider. There is no telling what xenotransplantation of genetic material will do to the health of both human and animal. There already exists considerable concern for the "cross-species transmission of infectious pathogens."[84] Research is being conducted to determine if porcine endogenous retroviruses can be produced from recombinant events between interspecies genetic manipulation in vitro. "Endogenous retroviruses are the result of an infection of germ cells with a retrovirus leading to the integration of the viral genome as DNA copy (provirus) in all cells of the organism."[85] In cell replication, human endogenous retroviruses (HERVs) occur naturally. They are typically defective and non-infectious. HERVs are needed for the basic physiological functions of human development. It is also interesting to note that HERVs proteins serve in the development of immunity of an embryo in vivo, as an article published by the National Center for Biotechnology Information suggests:

> Although HERVs are replication inactive, it is important to note that proteins encoded by HERVs and endogenous retroviruses of other mammalians are utilized for physiological functions of the host. The Env proteins are required for the generation of a functional placenta using the fusion competence of this protein. Interestingly, in different species different proviruses were utilized for this function. In addition, Env proteins may be involved in immunosuppression required for the survival of the embryo and recent data suggest that endogenous retroviruses are involved in the regulation of the innate immunity.[86]

HERVs aid in the generation of the placenta. The presence of human endogenous retroviruses supports the survival of the young life in the womb. They also assist in the natural development of innate immunity.

It is logical to conclude, then, that the introduction of genetic information into the designed genetic makeup of a human would alter or diminish natural development. Research is being conducted to determine how experimentation in chimeric DNA affects both the human as well as the animal. There is much to be understood, if it can be understood. But just the fact that we have come to a place in medical technology where these things are conceivably possible is frightening. We are consumed with extending and making our material lives more comfortable. We are in a continual search for the fountain of youth leading to an extended existence in the physical. We miss, in our human lust to cling to this fallen life, the only answer to new life and a new existence. God offers us a whole and perfect life through the redemption of His Son. Apart from this truth, we grasp only at straws leading to further depravity.

The purpose of what has been written above is to bring us to a point where we are baffled by the drive to alter our DNA. Again, I admit that there have been beneficial advances that have aided in alleviating suffering. But, at the same time, unchecked knowledge, freed from the limits of a moral lawgiver, finds limit only in the extent of human depravity. John Adams is quoted as saying:

> We have no government armed with power capable of contending with human passions unbridled by morality and religion. Avarice, ambition, revenge, or gallantry would break the strongest cords of our constitution as a whale goes through a net. Our Constitution was made only for a moral and religious people. It is wholly inadequate to the government of any other.[87]

I know he was speaking in the context of the Constitution during the establishment of our country, but the principle of the statement applies. Morality is only a consideration if the people choose restraint. When we choose to become unhinged from "morality and religion," the limits of human passions are unknowable. Humanity, as Mr. Adams suggests, is like a whale breaking through the net of logical, moral constraint. Humanity has been loosed to fall victim to depravity. Chaos, born in silence, elevated by ignorance, and manifested in tribulation causes the mayhem we experience. Chaos is a result of listening to the voice of the snake in tree.

Chaos in the tree has confused knowledge. It has caused truth to be exchanged for a lie (Romans 1:25). It has caused good to be called evil and evil to be called good (Isaiah 5:20). The deconstruction of knowledge has led to the deconstruction of identity. From the deconstruction of the identity as unique children created of God, we moved into the deconstruction of biology. When scientifically observed facts of biology are deconstructed, truth itself finds little place to find rest under the tree of chaos. Herein lies the rise of the emerging Church, the deconstruction of truth. It is this Church that we find coalescing in the wake of deconstruction. It is this Church that has listened to the whispers of chaos, falling victim to its seductions. It is this Church that has embraced disharmony with the Word of God in exchange for conformity with this world. It is this Church that is in the balances and has been found wanting.

The Deconstruction of Truth

The "emerging church" can loosely be defined as a movement within modern thought that devalues objective truth in exchange for an emotional or feelings-centered connection. This contemporary movement seeks "to reach the lost by focusing on relationships and developing a 'story,' 'journey of life' that is expressed through the 'narrative' of learning."[88] The emerging church tends to focus on relationships rather than biblical truth: "There is sometimes an ambiguous, feelings-oriented desire to experience God and also share in the lives of people as they seek to find God in their way."[89] In this theology, all truth is relative to the believer, and the walk to God is one of individual choice. A person's faith is a collection of life experiences developed on a journey of awareness of his or her own personal God. The emerging church finds its theology in a system referred to as "apophatic theology." This theology can be defined as follows:

> The key to apophatic theology is tied up in the word "mystery." Much of who and what God is, is a mystery to us. We are finite and we cannot define an infinite God without misrepresenting Him by our limitations in thought and language. Therefore, the best thing we can do is refrain from our temptation to define Him—we just worship Him. This is apophatic theology. According to the emerging church, we don't go to church to learn about God; we go to worship God. We don't go so that we can better understand, articulate, and defend our faith; we go to commune with fellow believers. Our goal is not to confirm our beliefs, but to deconstruct our "unfounded" beliefs so that we can truly worship God in mystery.[90]

While we are limited in our finite minds to fully understand the infinite, I believe God offers insight into attributes that define who He is as well as who we are in relation to Him. He is not a mystery that is unknowable. He wants to reveal Himself to us so that we can commune with Him (1 John 4:11–13). We are to be in fellowship with God through the redemption of our Savior (John 14:20–21). The apophatic approach to theology can lead to error through reductivism. If God, because of human limitation, cannot fully be grasped, we must then deconstruct the definition of God to an amorphous, distant concept beyond the grasp of cognition. God cannot be defined. Therefore, we can worship God by defining Him in a way that is comfortable to our flesh. Faith found in modernity functions according to the desires of the flesh rather than submission to the will of God. God defined by the human "I." This is the theology of emergent religion.

Secular culture has actively tried to remove religion through atheism. Secular science seeks to provide answers to the origin of life apart from a divine Creator. Society has worked tirelessly to make us so enamored in the self that we could care less about existential truth. Though the efforts to remove God from the vocal cords of the modern individual have been intense, the desire for humanity to lose faith in a Creator has not been successful. Humanity continues to seek answers to the big questions in life through religion. Secular humanism has been proved to be insufficient to deal with foundational issues of existence. People continue to seek comfort in faith. There is an innate understanding of a Creator that is found in all of us (Romans 1:18–21). We can now begin to see the emergence of universalism in Christian thought. Deception of the masses has incorporated a new guise, because the manipulators of social thought cannot get rid of that innate characteristic people harbor within themselves to believe in a higher power.

Disciples of Deception

At this point, I want to talk about two individuals who, in my opinion, are charged with promoting this cultural ideology: psychotherapist Carl Jung and religious studies and philosophy scholar Huston Smith. By the term "disciples of deception," I mean to describe the function of their beliefs. A disciple is a follower of a teacher. In the two cases I will highlight, both individuals follow deceiving spirits.

The first disciple, Carl Jung (1875–1961), was a psychologist and psychotherapist. He worked to establish what is known as analytical psychology and promoted the power of the unconscious. He briefly worked alongside Sigmund Freud. He was also the author of numerous books.

Jung believed in the evolution of thought. By this, he means that we are a reflection of our unconscious past experiences. What we think and do is driven by the parts of the brain that lie behind our conscious perception. We determine throughout our life to comply or deny the unconscious influences behind our motivation. He believed that human behavior is comprised of psychic archetypes.

Archetypes constitute the structure of the collective unconscious— they are psychic innate dispositions to experience and represent basic human behavior and situations. Thus mother-child relationships are governed by the mother archetype. Father-child—by the father archetype. Birth, death, power and failure are controlled by archetypes. The religious and mystique experiences are also governed by archetypes.

The most important of all is the Self, which is the archetype at the center of the psychic person, his/her totality or wholeness. The center is made up of the utility of conscious and unconscious reached through the individuation process.[91]

In this view, the human condition was built upon archetypal constructs found within the unconscious and passed on by our ancestors. These constructs are generated by a "universal consciousness"[92] that exists beyond perception and time. The "universal consciousness" offers definition to corporeal reality. The reality we perceive is founded upon collective experiences of human collective consciousness. This consciousness informs the present. Our behaviors are determined by an interplay of the conscious reality we live in physically and the unconscious heritage all humans share. Our unconscious self influences our conscious self. Our behaviors are either in compliance with the acceptable archetype or contrary to the archetype. Humanity, in this view, is a projection. We, as people, can choose to fit the presupposed category or deny the category.

The ultimate goal of Jungian psychology is something he terms "individuation."[93] This is defined as "the achievement of self-actualization through a process of integrating the conscious and the unconscious."[94] To be a complete individual, according to Jung, we must move beyond the interplay of the conscious and unconscious and harness the power of both. This enables the individual to be fully realized, utilizing the collective consciousness to direct our present reality. We can move beyond the limitations of societal expectation. We can create our own definition. We are not bound to anything, because reality is what we perceive. To quote the comedian Bill Hicks: "We are all one consciousness experiencing itself subjectively, there is no such thing as death, life is only a dream, and we are the imagination of ourselves."

There is much more that I could write about Jung's philosophy. I do not intend to expound any further in this limited examination. I simply want to provide a general perspective of the origins that direct the deception that we are faced within our day. Obviously, there are many dangerous things when one holds a belief system similar to Jung. Accepting these beliefs opens the door for deception and confusion. By Jung's own admission, he was influenced by demons. In his own words, Jung wrote:

> There was a demonic strength in me, and from the beginning there was no doubt in my mind that I must find the meaning of what I was experiencing in these fantasies. When I endured these assaults of the unconscious, I had an unswerving conviction that I was obeying a higher will, and that feeling continued to uphold

me until I had mastered the task. I have had much trouble getting along with my ideas. There was a demon in me, and in the end its presence proved decisive. It overpowered me, and if I was at times ruthless it was because I was at the grip of the demon.[95]

Such sad, tragic words. Our pride often gets in the way of a simple understanding of life. We confuse the truths of God with grandiose imaginings. We can easily become so inflated by our own intellect that when deception lurks in the shadows of our thoughts, we do not recognize it, nor can we do anything to stop it. We can never forget to cling to the knowledge found in the Word of God. There is one source of life and truth. God breathed life into Adam. We see this pattern repeated when Jesus breathed the Spirit into the apostles during the birth of the Church. Our bodies and spirit are functions of being made alive by God, nothing else.

I now move to examine another disciple of deception, professor of religion and philosophy, Huston Smith. Smith was a professor at MIT, Syracuse University, and UC Berkeley. He authored fifteen books about religion and philosophy. He proclaimed to be a Christian, but also a practitioner of multiple faiths. He believes that "God has to speak to each person in their own language, in their own idioms."[96] What he means by this is not that God can speak different languages, but that God presents Himself to each individual uniquely. Religious differences are necessary so that God can be revealed to a particular culture based on cultural preferences. He claimed essentially that all religions are the same:

> I do not think it matters almost infinitely that we practice one of the authentic religions, but if you mean does it make any difference. The answer is not as long as each is followed with equal intensity, sincerity and dedication.[97]

The authentic religions in Smith's understanding are Christianity, Judaism, Islam, Buddhism, Confucianism, and Hinduism. He believes each of the religions possesses truth; the difficulty lies in the degree to which a follower of a given religion is devoted. In Smith's view, a person can choose to follow whatever religion or multiple religions they want, as long as they do it with integrity.

Smith states he attended a Methodist church that served as a grounding, but his "spiritual center was in the Vedanta Society, whose discussion groups and lectures fed" his soul.[98] The Vedanta Society is an orthodox understanding of Indian philosophy found in Hinduism. When Smith discovered Buddhism, he described it as a "tidal wave" breaking over him. With each new religion, new insights were made available; one religion builds upon another. He states:

> In none of these moves did I have any sense that I was saying goodbye to anything. I was just moving into a new idiom for expressing the same basic truths.[99]

To me, he seems to be a vampire who feeds on religions or a gluttonous child bent on eating all of the cookies in the cookie jar.

Smith perfected, in essence, the individuation process Jung developed. Smith understands the importance of the word "ME." He strove to accommodate all of his whims, settling for nothing, a vacuum of self in the throes of actualization. In his opinion, nothing exists "that is greater than we are by every criterion of worth that we know."[100] The point of existence, from the opinion of those who hold a worldview in concert with Smith and Jung, is to know how important we are; religion is a function of our desire to feel a sense of moral conviction. Smith is the model of postmodern man and universalist doctrine of contemporary religion. We have been conditioned to believe that we are the center of the universe and reality is a construct of our own perception. The thrust of the secular humanist movement in society is that it promoted the idea that "all religions are equal and each individual is his or her own authority."[101] Secular humanism suggests that each individual him, her, zed, or zem is one's "own god."[102] The emergent church, influenced by secular humanism, promotes a god who is ambiguous, unknowable, and distant. This god is defined by the human "I" and bound by the "ME."

It is this false doctrine found in modern religious understanding that leads to the deconstruction of truth. A survey conducted by Ligonier Ministries in conjunction with Lifeway Research suggests that "the majority of the general U.S. population rejects the deity of Christ."[103] It is sad, but not surprising. However, what is surprising in this survey is the discovery of the perspective held by the majority regarding the divinity of Jesus. The survey suggest that "almost a third of evangelicals agree that He was merely a great teacher."[104] The first key word in this quote is "evangelicals." The second key word is "agree." Evangelicals are beginning to agree with the cultural position that Jesus is not divine, and they choose to reduce Him to a "great teacher." This unfortunate fact is partially due to the trend within the Church to progressively step away from the standard of truth in God's Holy Word. This survey also finds that many of those who participated in the survey "assume that truth is relative."[105] Religious expression is a personal choice, according to the majority of those surveyed, that has no basis in objective truth. Again, this false belief comes from the drive culturally to devalue external truth in exchange for personal preferences. The emerging church of secular humanism is a church filled with those who choose to worship the god of the self.

3

CRITICAL THEORY

Thus far, we have encountered mechanisms that contribute to the deconstruction of knowledge, identity, biology, and truth. Chaos in the tree has spoken deceit over humanity. It has woven threads of confusion throughout the tapestry of life. Confusion has contributed to the general sense of apathy that taints the beauty inherent in the larger picture. Rather than focusing our attention on the grandeur of the tapestry as a whole, we tend to focus on the minute imperfections. The serpent is adept at deceiving us to look at the problems so that our attention is brought low. We turn within ourselves, which causes us to turn on one another. The problems that affect our within are perceived to be caused by faulty systems originating from the without. Thus, any system of thought accused of being a form of oppression will fall victim to criticism and destruction. Both criticism and destruction take residence in the concepts brought forth by critical theory.

A core tenet of critical theory is deconstruction. Critical theory attempts to identify, dismantle, and abrogate anything that appears to be a function of the oppressor. Systems of governing a society are generalized as part of the controlling patriarchy. It is therefore the obligation of those who perceive themselves to be victims of the controlling minority to dismantle all forms of systemic order that has been built within a society. Thus, we see our cities burn in peaceful protest.

Critical theory is a psychosocial theory oriented to critiquing social order in an attempt to bring about systemic change as a whole. As a general definition, it "designates several generations of German philosophers and social theorists in the Western European Marxist tradition known as the Frankfurt School."[106] The Frankfurt School, founded in 1923 as an institute of Goethe University, was focused on the development and application of Marxist studies. The most prominent figures of the Frankfurt School were Max Horkheimer and Theodor Adorno. Horkheimer became the director of the school in 1930. He continued to lead through the lens of Marxist inspiration. Under Horkheimer's leadership, the school embarked on integrating Marxist philosophy through interdisciplinary approaches. The school sought to integrate socialist ideologies into the fabric of multiple educational disciplines in an effort to identify and dismantle elitist practices within a culture. In 1933 the Nazis forced the closure of the school. As a result, the school was relocated to the United States and found residence initially at Columbia University in New York City.[107] From this point of origin, we see the influence of critical theory scattered throughout our educational system and culture. Today we can see the influence of critical theory in our culture in ideologies identified as "critical race theory, cultural theory, gender, and queer theory as well as media theory and studies."[108]

Key issues at the core of the philosophy involve a "critique of modernity and capitalist society, the definition of social emancipation, as well as the detection of pathologies of society."[109] For critical theorists, a capitalistic government serves as an indicator of systemic oppression of the less affluent. Capitalistic governments are seen as a source of exploitation. Critical theorists seek to identify and apply remediation for systemic oppression within a governmental structure. When a contributor of oppression is identified, it is necessary to dismantle the source of oppression. In this chain of thought it becomes necessary to replace one human-conceived form of government led by the social elite for another human-conceived form of government that is also led by a social elite.

Those in charge remain in charge; they just use different words in their political pandering.

Social emancipation, another point of focus in this philosophy, is the drive to liberate social class through the redistribution of wealth. In other words, it is a form of socialistic government. Social emancipation seeks to liberate the individual from external mechanisms of control. Critical theorists reject the idea that knowledge is a mirror of reality, because they suggest that all knowledge conforms to preconceived notions of reality based on history, science, and social collectivism. To be emancipated from these perceived forms of control, it is necessary to reject an empirical understanding with existence replacing this mindset of the exaltation of consciousness and self-reflection. Critical theorists suggest that knowledge is manipulated in a given culture to conform to an agreed-upon set of standards defining how we see our world. Social emancipation requires liberation from the constraints of conformity to a projected understanding within a particular culture. Critical theory distinguished itself from scientific theory because "the latter understands knowledge as an objectified product, the former serves the purpose of human emancipation through consciousness and self-reflection."[110] The height of this ideology is the liberation of the self from all that is thought to be a mechanism designed to oppress the individual.

One of the most influential books defining critical theory came from the Frankfurt School of Critical Theory. The book was written by the earlier-mentioned Max Horkheimer and Theodor Adorno, both prominent professors of this philosophy. The book is titled *Dialectic of Enlightenment*, and it was originally published 1947. In this book, the authors postulate the demise of Western reason through a process of self-destruction. The authors suggest that the drive of knowledge acquisition and advances in technology have given rise to "disenchantment of the world."[111] As enlightenment increases, the myth of existence decreases. Scientific discovery provides answers to questions of existence, which replace the necessity of mythology. The authors suggest that enlightenment "has always aimed at liberating human beings from fear and installing them as masters."[112] The lust for knowledge has the potential to incite humanity to claim lordship of perceived lesser forms of existence. Atheistic enlightenment reduces humanity to the following two points: those being "*logos*—which, with the advance of philosophy, contracts to a monad, a mere reference point—and the mass of things and creatures in the external world."[113] The human is relegated to an expression of philosophy and matter. From this point of view, the authors suggest that "the world is made subject to man."[114] With the mastery over nature through the exaltation of the human intellect, the distinction between "the creative God and the ordering mind"[115] is nullified. Knowledge overthrows the fear of subjugation to a higher authority. From the view of the authors, knowledge replaces faith. They suggest that an intellectual examination of faith exposed that "faith repeatedly shows itself of the same stamp as the world history it would like to command; indeed, in the modern period it has become that history's preferred means, its special ruse."[116] Faith is a mechanism that has been used to subjugate the masses through fear, but in the pursuit of enlightenment we have the means to escape oppression. The dialectic of enlightenment is discovered in the presence of a dualistic human existence. To be known, there must also be the unknown. To be elevated, there must also be the oppressed. To be enlightened in contemporary thought requires the presence of those who cling to myth as an explanation of the world we inhabit. Reason and myth collide in the necessity of dualistic existence. The authors suggest that transcendence of the unknown is anchored to the known, "permanently linking horror and holiness."[117] That which remains beyond the grasp of understanding only remains there because of what is already understood. The horrors found in the sin of mankind are attached, fixedly, to the purity of holiness. The authors, from this perspective, relegate all religion to being founded from one point of origin. All are the same; all religion becomes fable built on the persistence of duality in human cognition.

The authors, in writing about systems of governmental control over the masses, suggest that "each human being has been endowed with a self of his or her own, different from all of the others, so that it could all the more surely be made the same. But because that self never fitted the mold, enlightenment throughout the liberalistic period has always sympathized with social coercion."[118] I agree with this statement in that the ruling elite seek to gain control over the people by allowing the chaos that we can see in our society to spiral toward self-destruction. People strive in vanity to find an identity that is unique to themselves. The authors continue: "The peculiarity of the self is a socially conditioned monopoly commodity misrepresented as the natural."[119] The variety on perversion in self-identity noted in contemporary culture is a result of the controlling state attempting to manipulate the individual. It is apparent that a motivator of the gender movement generates a way to self-identify according to a definition that is so abstract that no other person can share this same identity. This is why we currently have the plethora of genders, pronouns, and sexual perversions expressed by individuals who are trying desperately to be unique. In this struggle to be an individual, the extremity of the diversity always reverts to the same thought. The extent of the effort to be different eventually circles back upon itself. The puppet masters revel in the chaos, knowing that as we writhe on the ground kicking our feet to try to get the attention of others, they quietly gain control. The coils of the serpent draw that much more tightly around the neck of the lost. They are so consumed with discovering a unique expression of the self that they pay no attention to the death slowly crushing their neck. There are many who have become a perpetual Narcissus drowning in their own reflection. Those who choose not to identify as a child of God redeemed by the blood of our Savior will continually be in a cycle of self-reinvention, satisfied only at the cost of the self. The ruling elite know this and coerce culture toward calamity in order to solidify control. The motto of Freemasonry in its efforts to manipulate society to succumb to world order is *ordo ab chao*, a Latin phrase meaning "order out of chaos." From the ashes of chaos in the culture, the ruling class grasps at further control over the lesser. The authors comment on this phenomenon, writing: "The distance of subject from object, the presupposition of abstraction, is founded on the distance from things which the ruler attains by means of the ruled."[120] The ruled are oppressed by the distance created by the ruler. Chaos in society causes a chasm between the everyman and the enlightened. There are rules for thee but not for me. We now have those in charge who are unreservedly lording over the lesser, flaunting their authority in their threats and arrogant behaviors. Critical theory calls for the dismantling of perceived systems of oppression in order to bring rise to change. Again, the ruling class knows this. Those in charge allow for periods of deconstruction because they recognize that from the rubble will rise a renewed, stronger hand of control. In the plight of our world as we see it this day, we discover the definition of dialectic reasoning. As suggested by the authors: "The concept, usually defined as the unity of the features of what is subsumes, was rather, from the first, a product of dialectical thinking, in which each thing is what it is only by becoming what it is not."[121] *Ordo ab chao*, the chaos we feel in our world, is identified as chaos during the transition. Order, control, is chaos only during the fortification of dominance. The cities burn chaos in the streets, but behind these scenes, the serpent coils itself around those who slumber in the shade of the tree.

The deconstruction of a civilization involves removing the old and manipulating what is considered new. Again, deconstruction of perceived systems of the controlling class is a tenet of critical theory. The authors note this pattern historically, stating, "As a rule, whenever a new religion and a new mentality have won place in world history, bringing a new mode of social existence, the old gods have been cast into the dust together with the old classes, tribes, and peoples."[122] In order to bring about a new paradigm, the old must be let go. The letting go of the old is facilitated with distance. It is easier to forget something the farther away from the something one gets. Our world is striving to erase the memory of faith from the minds of humanity. The enemy employs smoke and mirrors to arrest the attention of the masses as the world drifts farther from the biblical standard of truth. There are many who claim to be enlightened. They claim to know better, to be too intelligent to fall victim to old fables.

Advances in understanding our world have caused many to reject the necessity of God because the answers are perceived to be supplied through human endeavor. But they are blinded to the reality that they simply fall victim to the cycle of deception. Even those who claim to be in control, those who work to design the new order, cannot escape. The Ouroboros consumes itself as it plods along the course of time. The cycle of deception repeats, continually employing the tactics used since the beginning. The serpent entices humanity to grasp the fruit of enlightenment, exalting the self. Thus, the new religion, the new mentality that gains precedence in the new reality, birthed from the ashes of the deconstructed, is truly only a reimagining, a remodeling of the downfall of humanity—the downfall of humanity being pride, the religion of chaos.

Critical theory, in its various mutations, has claimed dominance in the perception of humanity worldwide. People around the world are being enticed to react in violence against any form of established government. This lashing out is not done in an effort to bring forth logical discussion to foster positive change. The anger so many people spout forth is an attempt only to destroy, to dismantle, to deconstruct whatever is deemed to be in the way of complete liberation of the self to one's own sinful demise. The arguments that incite anger need not hold any logic or legitimate basis in order to be perpetuated. Only accusation is necessary to fuel a fire that burns with such ferocity that reason itself bows to its wrath. It is also apparent that those in charge stir up chaos in the populace to grasp a deeper level of control. The promotion of ideologies such as critical theory, though adorned in the garb of compassion for the oppressed, serves only as a catalyst to grant the rulers distance between themselves and the problems they create to cause division. The greater the division or separation from objective truth, the greater the proposed, grandiose, yet never fully realized promises the political leaders can pledge but never intend to fully act upon. Critical theory takes its origin in Marxist communist ideologies designed to further increase the gap between the ruling elite and the common man. As people of God, it is vital that we use discernment, asking the Father for His witness in the earth.

In Defense of Freedom

Let me say this in defense of the freedom that all people should be granted as a right in any functional governmental structure. It is good to be able to have the right to criticize the government for functioning in a way that is beyond the scope of their authority. A tyrannical government strives to view its constituency as subjects. Tyrannical leadership works to deny its constituency the basic right to question leadership. In making the above statements regarding critical theory, I do not suggest that we should, as Christian individuals, neglect our responsibility to hold our elected leaders accountable. It is our obligation in a free society to defend what is ethical from a biblical perspective in our culture. We must not forget that our elected officials work for the populace. They are accountable to the common people who elected them into leadership. Yet, it appears that the tables have been turned, and they rule from the top down. We find ourselves in a dark place when free people lose the authority in a society to hold errant leaders accountable. It is, therefore, essential that we retain the right, using critical discernment to elect political leaders who will work toward justice founded on truth. The problem of critical theory is not found in the practice of identifying societal imperfections and calling for change, but in that it equates all perceived imperfections in a given system as a function of corrupt humanity. Therefore, all perceived imperfections in a society must be deconstructed, burnt to the ground so a new authority can rise to power. The argument comes from a place of destruction, division, and subjugation to those who shout with the loudest hate-filled voices. I write from the perspective of a Christian. My only interest in the subject of critical theory is how it affects faith. Critical theory categorizes, in its logically extreme expression, all aspects of a culture as being a promulgation of values defined only by a patriarchal, predominantly white ruling class that hungers to retain authority. The Christian faith has been deemed part of this privileged system that must be dismantled. It is here where I take my stand, as should the Church. I do not take offense to anyone calling a human-developed governmental structure corrupt. We should have the right to do so. I do not take offense to this because, in any system developed by humanity, there will be inherent corruption because we function from a sinful condition. Unless we fall under the authority of our Savior, Jesus Christ, all of our efforts will be tainted with the stain of sin. But we have an alternative to the corruption of human government. We have the right to choose to be citizens of an eternal Kingdom ruled by a Divine Ruler who is beyond corruption. We have the ability to choose freedom in a Kingdom ruled by God. We must therefore defend the right of people to choose citizenship in this Kingdom.

4

INTERLUDE

Today Is Still Called "Today"!

In the book of Exodus, we read that Moses comes down from Mt. Sinai and sees the people of God worshipping a golden calf. Because of the lackluster leadership of Aaron, the people fell victim to old patterns of behavior. Egypt was still alive and active in them. The voices of those who allowed corruption into their hearts overshadowed the voices of those who stood to defend the name of God. The people, therefore, fell victim to weak leadership and a minority of aggressive individuals with loud voices. Sounds familiar to our ears, does it not? The Holy Word of God gives account of this event as follows:

> It came about, as soon as Moses came near the camp, that he saw the calf and the dancing; and Moses' anger burned, and he threw the tablets from his hands and shattered them at the foot of the mountain. He took the calf which they had made and burned it with fire, and ground it to powder, and scattered it over the surface of the water and made the sons of Israel drink it.
>
> Then Moses said to Aaron, "What did this people do to you, that you have brought such great sin upon them?" Aaron said, "Do not let the anger of my lord burn; you know the people yourself, that they are prone to evil. For they said to me, 'Make

a god for us who will go before us; for this Moses, the man who brought us up from the land of Egypt, we do not know what has become of him.' I said to them, 'Whoever has any gold, let them tear it off.' So they gave it to me, and I threw it into the fire, and out came this calf."

Now when Moses saw that the people were out of control—for Aaron had let them get out of control to be a derision among their enemies—then Moses stood in the gate of the camp, and said, "Whoever is for the Lord, come to me!" And all the sons of Levi gathered together to him. He said to them, "Thus says the Lord, the God of Israel, 'Every man of you put his sword upon his thigh, and go back and forth from gate to gate in the camp, and kill every man his brother, and every man his friend, and every man his neighbor.'" So the sons of Levi did as Moses instructed, and about three thousand men of the people fell that day. Then Moses said, "Dedicate yourselves today to the Lord—for every man has been against his son and against his brother—in order that He may bestow a blessing upon you today." (Exodus 32:19–29)

We find ourselves, as people of faith in the One True God, at this very juncture. The people are out of control due to the veracity of unrepentant sin. Egypt burns brightly in the desires of the hearts of mankind in our day. The sin nature has been allowed to go unchecked due to the lackluster leadership. The Word of God has been permitted to be criticized as mere fiction in the eyes of the deceived. We find ourselves, like Moses, looking upon a people who have gone out of control both in and out of the Church. The Word of God tells us the response of Moses in verse 26: "Moses stood in the gate of the camp, and said: 'Whoever is for the Lord, come to me!'" Moses called for those who were willing to defend the name of God to take a stand against the evil who had been allowed to run rampant in the camp. Unfortunately, only a few were willing to stand. Only the sons of Levi had the courage to stand in defense of the Lord.

Because of this, God brought judgment upon those who refused to stand. My question to you, then, is this: Will you stand? Will you defend the name of your Savior in a world that chases after the unbridled imaginings of the sin nature? Let me be clear: I in no way advocate violence in making these statements. In our defense of God, we can never act in violence toward another. What I do advocate for is that we become a people who are willing to pick up the sword of the Word. We must place this sword upon our mouths and speak truth over the people. We must place this sword upon our hearts so that we can be guided by His will, determined to preserve faith in God Almighty for those of worth. Will you, like the sons of Levi, fight for your King?

I leave this subject for now, as we will come back to it later. I know that what has been written thus far can feel overwhelming or portray a sense of foreboding when considering the scale of the fight of faith we find ourselves laboring within. But I do not write with the intent to frighten anyone. My intent is not to discourage, but to warn and encourage His Church to walk in His authority. My intent in writing what has thus far been stated is in an attempt to expose the treachery of our enemy. Our common enemy works tirelessly to speak the enchantment of chaos over those who close their ears to the Word of truth. I do not write to scare, but to warn. God is not surprised by any of this. God knows the plight we suffer through to walk out our faith. God knows our struggles, both internally and externally, as we interact with the world. God knows. We are not alone. The Almighty God, the Author of the universe, the Father of salvation, fights for us. Fight therefore! Fight the good fight of faith with the Spirit of the Living God dwelling in your heart. Fight, for He is with you. Fight to be a true witness of the gospel of salvation in a world that desperately needs hope. But especially fight for those who come after you. Fight for those of worth. Fight for our children, for they are worthy. With these words we have come to the premise of this writing. Knowing the chaos that is unfolding before our very eyes, I ask: Are you willing to fight? Is the next generation valuable enough to motivate you to stand in your God-given authority and push back against the serpent who whispers lies? Do you love the Lord your God enough to respond when He calls forth: "'Whom shall I send, and who will go for Us?' Then I said, 'Here am I. Send me!'" (Isaiah 6:8). He is calling for you. He is calling for you to defend the faith:

> Take care, brethren, that there not be in any one of you an evil, unbelieving heart that falls away from the living God. But encourage one another day after day, as long as it is still called "Today," so that none of you will be hardened by the deceitfulness of sin. For we have become partakers of Christ, if we hold fast the beginning of our assurance firm until the end. (Hebrews 13:12–14)

Today is still called "today"! Hold fast to the hand of our Savior. He is our assurance and ever-present source of hope. Participate in your walk of faith for the promise of Christ.

Before closing this section, I want to give one final warning. I do not want to dwell on the difficulties we face regarding faith, but, as I stated earlier, a herald who offers warning without the weight of evidence finds no listeners. The warning without evidence becomes an empty cry blown asunder by the wind of chaos. I, therefore, and we, as the people of God, must take our faith seriously. We cannot afford to simply wear the appearance of a Christian externally while disregarding the responsibility of internal submission to the will of the Father. Our faith must be internal, resulting in transformation. Our faith is a choice we must make leading to the circumcision of the heart (Deuteronomy 30:6). The gospel of salvation is transformative. Especially in the times in which we live, we cannot afford to stagnate into complacent acceptance of a world that actively seeks to suppress truth (Romans 1:18). Our enemy seeks to destroy the knowledge of God. The enemy wants to quench the fire burning within those of faith so that we do not pass on the knowledge of God to those who come after. The enemy wants to distract us from passing the fire to our children. This vile creature wants to remove the name of Salvation from the lips of our children. The serpent thirsts to deceive the pure of heart in an effort to control the masses. Hitler shared a similar opinion as he fought to bring about German totalitarianism: "He alone, who owns the youth, gains the future."[123] The enemies of God's family strive to gain the future through the destruction of the present. If you will not fight for your children, there is One who will. He stands as King of Mount Zion waiting to return to in order to put an end to lies. I implore you, therefore, to take your stand as God's Kingdom priest and defend the faith, for the time is short. Hold your ground. Fight for faith. Fight for the next generation. Fight, because we bear the name of a King!

PART TWO

THE SPIRIT SPEAKS
The Word, the Sword of Our God and King

In this section, we will shift focus from evidences in our culture that point to the lies spoken by the serpent to the instruction God gives us in His Holy Word. We will look at a few passages of Scripture that provide encouragement for His people. Not only will we find encouragement, we will also find wisdom:

> For the word of God is living and active and sharper than any two-edged sword, and piercing as far as the division of soul and spirit, of both joints and marrow, and able to judge the thoughts and intentions of the heart. And there is no creature hidden from His sight, but all things are open and laid bare to the eyes of Him with whom we have to do. (Hebrews 4:12–13)

The Word convicts. It convicts those who are His to turn from sin in repentance. As a father who disciplines a child, the Lord disciplines those who are His (Hebrews 12:3–12). Count it joy what God speaks into your heart. It is proof that you are considered a child. The Word lays bare all things. Nothing is hidden from His sight. The Lord is laying bare the works of the enemy. He does this so we can know how to respond. He shows us the traps before they are sprung. Trust, therefore, in the provision of our God Most High. Heed the warning of God given through the prophet Isaiah:

> Therefore My people go into exile for their lack of knowledge; And their honorable men are famished, And their multitude is parched with thirst. Therefore Sheol has enlarged its throat and opened its mouth without measure; And Jerusalem's splendor, her multitude, her din of revelry and the jubilant within her, descend into it. (Isaiah 5:13–14)

In this context, the people who were led into exile did not heed the warning of God. They did not listen to the cries of the prophets. Unlike the sons of Issachar, they did not discern the times, nor did they know what to do in response. God warns us. God gives us recourse. God gives us hope. God goes with us in this fight (Deuteronomy 31:8). We do not have to fear falling into exile because the Lord has shown forth His glorious light.

5

LUKE 23:27-32

Behold the Days Are Coming

We begin our series of chapters of exposition on selected Scripture by looking at a few verses found in the book of Luke. In context, Luke is writing about the events leading up to the crucifixion of Jesus. Luke gives insight into the hearts of the crowds chanting to punish Jesus even though He was found innocent. These verses are heart-wrenching. On the surface, they can appear grim, without hope. But take heart; we serve a Risen Lord. The grave was not able to contain Him. He has overcome. In these verses, we are given a dire warning from the mouth of our Savior. The warning is frightening, but know that we are His. He speaks these things to us so that we can know how to respond. He tells us these things not to frighten us, but to draw us closer to Him. Luke writes of these events beginning in verse 13 of chapter 23:

> Pilate summoned the chief priests and the rulers and the people, and said to them, "You brought this man to me as one who incites the people to rebellion, and behold, having examined Him before you, I have found no guilt in this man regarding the charges which you make against Him. No, nor has Herod, for he sent Him back to us; and behold, nothing deserving death has been done by Him. Therefore I will punish Him and release Him."

Now he was obliged to release to them at the feast one prisoner.

But they cried out all together, saying, "Away with this man, and release for us Barabbas!" (He was one who had been thrown into prison for an insurrection made in the city, and for murder.) Pilate, wanting to release Jesus, addressed them again, but they kept on calling out, saying, "Crucify, crucify Him!" And he said to them the third time, "Why, what evil has this man done? I have found in Him no guilt demanding death; therefore I will punish Him and release Him." But they were insistent, with loud voices asking that He be crucified. And their voices began to prevail. And Pilate pronounced sentence that their demand be granted. And he released the man they were asking for who had been thrown into prison for insurrection and murder, but he delivered Jesus to their will.

When they led Him away, they seized a man, Simon of Cyrene, coming in from the country, and placed on him the cross to carry behind Jesus.

And following Him was a large crowd of the people, and of women who were mourning and lamenting Him. But Jesus turning to them said, "Daughters of Jerusalem, stop weeping for Me, but weep for yourselves and for your children. For behold, the days are coming when they will say, 'Blessed are the barren, and the wombs that never bore, and the breasts that never nursed.' Then they will begin to say to the mountains, 'Fall on us,' and to the hills, 'Cover us.' For if they do these things when the tree is green, what will happen when it is dry?" (Luke 23:13–31)

"Weep for yourselves. Weep for yourselves and your children. Weep, for behold the days are coming. Weep." This is a paraphrase of the words of our Lord as He was led to His death on the cross. His warning given to those who had ears to hear was that the days are coming when the land will be dry. Jesus tells those who followed the procession of the cross to stop weeping for Him. He has come to fulfill His purpose in this First

Advent of our Messiah. That purpose was to go to the cross, suffer, and die as our propitiation for sin. He gave His very life, a sacrifice eternal, for the redemption of sin. Our Messiah says, "Weep not for Me." Jesus triumphant. Jesus eternal: "Weep not for me, but weep for yourselves. Weep because your King is now going back to His throne awaiting the day for His final return. Weep because the tree is about to wither and dry."

Jesus spoke to those who were there watching this tragedy unfold, but this warning transcends time. It is also meant for us, this day. He tells us to weep because there are many living in this world who cannot see truth while the tree was green; what hope do they have to see it when it is dry? He tells us the land will suffer drought due to the hearts of the people. The Word of the Lord will be rejected as the standard for salvation. The source of nourishing life will be trampled by the incessant drive of carnal lusts. Because the Word of truth is rejected, each one will turn to the truth that is found only in their own eyes (Judges 17:6). In the time of the judges, there was no King in the land. The people turned inward to embrace the king of self. There was no King in the land or in their hearts, so the people became carnal, as is our cursed nature without the knowledge of truth.

The book of Judges does not seem so foreign as we consider the plight of mankind in the scope of our current society. We have become, as the Apostle Paul warns, lovers of self and evil in thought, turning to folly and chasing what is fleeting (2 Timothy 3:1–9). The people will turn from the mercy of our Savior. They will reject the love of God. They will not have the heart to hear His message of mercy. They will be dry, cracked, and barren. It will be like in the day when they led Him to the cross. Violence erupted from the tongue of those who hated. The tongue lashed out against hope. Violence, manifested from the heart of fallen mankind, spurred on the crowds who chanted, "Crucify, crucify!" Barren and dry are the hearts of those who hate good and chase evil; barren and dry. Their hatred, all-consuming, left them with no other recourse but to embrace the hopelessness that is prevalent in their heart. So were the people who hung the King of Glory on the cross.

So are the people in our day who harden their hearts to the victory in the cross. The pride of mankind continues to curse the heart, making it callous. Unfortunately, many choose to harden their hearts to the mercy of Jesus. They chase what is fleeting; they cherish the temporal pleasures of a cursed existence. Like the dry, cracked ground always thirsting for the next quick drink, they deny the power of Living Water and seek after momentary relief. They are barren, a salt flat harboring no life, giving nothing back to the environment, which through their rejection of Messiah they become. Hopeless and lost are they who cry out for the mountains to fall upon them. Our Lord tells us:

> Then they will begin to say to the mountains, "Fall on us," and to the hills, "Cover us." 31 For if they do these things when the tree is green, what will happen when it is dry? (Luke 23:30–31)

The people seek cover in their nakedness before the Lord. He has exposed their sin. They cannot bear to be seen in the fullness of the horror sin wreaks upon the unrepentant heart. They think it is better for us to be buried under rubble than to contend with the chaos that sin brings upon us. They think it is better to be buried than to address the responsibility of bearing the name of salvation. They run and hide in the hope of escaping the conviction of the Lord. They hide due to fear of the landscape—the barren, cracked landscape of the human heart that has been given over the imaginings of the flesh. We walk upon this landscape. It is upon this field that He has called us to labor for His Kingdom (Matthew 9:37–38). We walk a barren landscape as His people.

The book of Luke continues in verse 27:

> And following Him was a large crowd of the people, and of women who were mourning and lamenting Him. But Jesus turning to them said, "Daughters of Jerusalem, stop weeping for Me, but weep for yourselves and for your children. For behold, the days are coming when they will say, 'Blessed are the barren, and the

wombs that never bore, and the breasts that never nursed.' Then they will begin to say to the mountains, 'Fall on us,' and to the hills, 'Cover us.' For if they do these things when the tree is green, what will happen when it is dry?" (Luke 23:13–31)

These words of our Savior are only found in the book of Luke. He tells the women who were weeping for Him to weep for themselves, because there will be dire days ahead. Jesus tells us that there will be people in those dire days who proclaim: "Blessed are the barren, and the wombs that never bore, and the breasts that never nursed" (Luke 23:29). Blessed are the barren; blessed are they who bear no life. Jesus speaks of this time when people will proclaim a blessing over those who have no children. He does this to offer warning. He warns of a time to come when the hearts of mankind will be stricken with the fear not of God, but of this fallen world. Jesus warns that there will be a day when men will seek to hide under the rubble of fallen earth rather than address the problems on the surface. They fear persecution. They fear judgment by others. They choose to hide rather than to fight. Jesus offers this grim warning in an attempt to revive the hearts of His people to be bold in the day. Be bold in faith and the fear of the Lord. Be bold for our children. It is for them that I write these words. It is for my children. It is for the children who fall under our leadership as parents, grandparents, and people of faith who have the responsibility to train a child in the way he should go (Proverbs 22). It is for them that I fight. It is for those who are with us now and for those who are yet to enter this life. We must prepare the way for the coming of the Lord (Isaiah 40:3).

Jesus warns that there will be days ahead when people will proclaim, "Blessed are they who are barren." This implies that the barren will be seen as blessed by the people because they do not bear the responsibility of upholding the gospel. This blessing for those who are barren is not one spoken by God. This blessing comes from the mouths of men who recognize in their heart that they have failed to embrace the commission of Jesus. They have failed to proclaim the gospel. This blessing spoken by those who failed is directed to those who are without children. Those who will speak this blessing do so in an attempt to alleviate the responsibility for failing to pass on the faith to those who come after. This is why the people run for cover under the mountains. They see it as a better fate than to fall into the hands of an angry God. They recognize that they have failed. They have failed to proclaim the victory of our Messiah to the next generation. Jesus warns of a day to come, but the fullness of this day is not yet. Jesus warns of a day when the barren will be considered blessed. While the realization of this day is not yet, His words should resound clearly in the now. It is now that the people of God must prepare the hearts of our children for the not yet. While this day of trouble is yet to come, its bleak shadow can clearly be seen on the horizon. As God's people, we are called to proclaim the truth of salvation in boldness. Let it never be said of any of us that we have neglected this call.

Jesus, as He labors under the weight of the cross, calls out to a group of women referred to as the daughters of Jerusalem:

> And following Him was a large crowd of the people, and of women who were mourning and lamenting Him. But Jesus turning to them said, "Daughters of Jerusalem, stop weeping for Me, but weep for yourselves and for your children."

He calls out to these women, calling them daughters of the city of peace as the blood of His scourging stains the streets of this same city—the city of peace turned red by the blood of God. "Daughters of Jerusalem, city of peace, cry not for me, but for your children" is the directive of Messiah. Jesus suggests that tears should not be shed for Him, because He looks forward. He looks forward and warns of a day when His Church chooses to be weak. "Cry for the children, because the children will be those who suffer from a complacent, anemic church." He says, "Cry not for me, but for those who will unfortunately suffer under the weakness of the Church in days ahead. Our Messiah sees through the course of time and He speaks of the deterioration of the Church."

It is clear that we can see this iteration of the Church taking form in our culture. The foundation was laid when we allowed the whims of the culture to begin to hold influence over the Word of God. The walls were erected as the people sat down, turning deaf ears to the lies creeping into faith. Complacently, they watch the roof being lowered, shading the lazy sinbathers from the vibrancy of the Son. It is this Church that our Messiah warns about and for which we are to shed a tear. As difficult as it is to read the words of our Savior suggesting that we cry for our children, it is all the more difficult to recognize that He is warning us: **"Cry for your children, for they reap what YOU have sown."** But even behind this somber warning there is hope. Jesus says, "Cry or fight." He says, "Cry or do something." We can cry and be resolved to defeat or stand in the victory of Christ, who is risen. He gives us this choice. Not only does He give us this choice, He equips us with the authority to make the choice aligned with the heart of God bringing about change. Revival in the hearts of mankind—our Lord calls for it.

With Revival Comes Responsibility

The prophet Malachi, through the inspiration of God, writes of revival in the midst of trouble. He writes of revival in the hearts of humankind as the Day of the Lord draws near. He writes these words to encourage us that the Lord will make a way for His people. The Lord will preserve those who have chosen to be His. Malachi wrote:

> Then those who feared the Lord spoke to one another, and the Lord gave attention and heard it, and a book of remembrance was written before Him for those who fear the Lord and who esteem His name. "They will be Mine," says the Lord of hosts, "on the day that I prepare My own possession, and I will spare them as a man spares his own son who serves him." So you will again distinguish between the righteous and the wicked, between one who serves God and one who does not serve Him. (Malachi 3:16–18)

Malachi gives us this word from the Lord in a time when the hearts of the people turned from God. The people questioned the necessity to serve God. The people suggested that the wealth and prosperity they longed to return to would only be realized through their own determination. Therefore, God was without worth. The hearts of the people grew cold, devoid of the love of God. They forgot what God had done for them. Even during this dark time, those who feared the name of the Lord began to speak to one another. I can only imagine that they spoke of the blessings of knowing God. They must have spoken about the love God has poured out upon them as He preserved them. Because they feared the Lord, the Lord remembered them. The Lord declares that there will be a book of remembrance for those who fear His name. Oh, how we should all long to be remembered in this book. The Lord commands that those written of in the book of remembrance will be His! Those who fear His name will be His cherished possession. The Lord, Himself, calls us His crown possession! He declares in the day He judges evil; He will spare those who are His. **We are His.** Not only are we His, we are the crown of His possession. In humility I write these words. What a blessing to know that we are the cherished possession of an eternal God. We are the chosen people of an all-loving Creator. Hallelujah and amen, for the Lord is the King of Kings!

Malachi goes on to say that in this day of judgment, God will distinguish between the righteous and the wicked, between those who serve Him and those who do not. This is the day of judgment. This day God will differentiate between the righteous and the wicked; this day is today. This day is now. It is clearly happening in our day. If we look at our world, it is evident that God is drawing a line in the sand. He is exposing deception. He does this so we can make a choice: Fear the Lord or fear the world that has fallen victim to the wiles of the devil. The choice is clear, but the choice is yours.

The prophet Malachi wrote of the Day of the Lord in chapter 4:

"For behold, the day is coming, burning like a furnace; and all the arrogant and every evildoer will be chaff; and the day that is coming will set them ablaze," says the Lord of hosts, "so that it will leave them neither root nor branch.

"But for you who fear My name, the sun of righteousness will rise with healing in its wings; and you will go forth and skip about like calves from the stall. You will tread down the wicked, for they will be ashes under the soles of your feet on the day which I am preparing," says the Lord of hosts.

"Remember the law of Moses My servant, even the statutes and ordinances which I commanded him in Horeb for all Israel.

"Behold, I am going to send you Elijah the prophet before the coming of the great and terrible day of the Lord. He will restore the hearts of the fathers to their children and the hearts of the children to their fathers, so that I will not come and smite the land with a curse." (Malachi 4:1–6)

The Day of the Lord will be like a burning furnace destroying those who reject His mercy. He will utterly remove the presence of evil. But for those, but for those who fear His name, He will bless. Those who fear His name will burst forth with joy as they are healed, purified by the Son of Righteousness. Revival. Revival in the hearts of the people. Revival comes amid the movement of God to judge evil.

There are many in this life who possess a dismal outlook for the Church. They presume that the Church is dead. They argue, suggesting the Church possesses no influence over the culture. The lustfulness of the culture therefore swallows up the Church in its gaping maw of deception. They assume the presence of evil in the thoughts of men has gained victory over the people of God. The serpent has caused the Church to grow silent as the world outside grows dark. I remind you and I remind those who scoff at the Church of this promise spoken by the Lord God Almighty:

"But for you who fear My name, the sun of righteousness will rise with healing in its wings; and you will go forth and skip about like calves from the stall. You will tread down the wicked, for they will be ashes under the soles of your feet on the day which I am preparing," says the Lord of hosts. (Malachi 4:2–3)

Revival. Revival of the people of God. Revival of His Church. Revival causing His people to once again walk in the authority of God, trampling the presence of evil underfoot. The Church belongs to God. The Church, His people, revived again to stand firm until His return.

The work of God's people is far from complete. We are called to stand firm on faith, declaring the holiness of God and the mercy of salvation to those who have ears to hear. The Lord declares:

Behold, I am going to send you Elijah the prophet before the coming of the great and terrible day of the Lord. He will restore the hearts of the fathers to their children and the hearts of the children to their fathers, so that I will not come and smite the land with a curse. (Malachi 4:1–5)

As the Day of the Lord draws near, the Church will prepare the way for the coming of the Lord. Our witness of grace and love for our neighbor founded on repentance will be the message proclaimed until His return: "Thus says the Lord of hosts, 'Return to Me,' declares the Lord of hosts, 'that I may return to you'" (Zechariah 1:3). The Lord of angel armies declares that His people return to Him. Return to Him and He will restore the broken. He will restore the lost. He will restore so that His witness can be heard.

With revival comes responsibility. When we are made alive in Christ through faith, we must recognize our responsibility to cherish the newness of life that God has poured into us. It is our responsibility, as individuals, to cling to the hands of our Savior. But it is also the responsibility of the Church to instruct the people of God how to walk in a faith that is in keeping with the will of God. We can have revival, but if there is no responsibility, revival fades again into the backdrop of the theater of life.

Recognizing the fragility of revival in the hands of man, I want to return for a moment to the book of Luke. We looked at these verses earlier, but I want to draw out another point to bring attention to the futility of the human mind. I remind you of the writing of Luke. He writes of the events leading to the crucifixion of our Savior, stating:

> Pilate summoned the chief priests and the rulers and the people, and said to them, "You brought this man to me as one who incites the people to rebellion, and behold, having examined Him before you, I have found no guilt in this man regarding the charges which you make against Him. No, nor has Herod, for he sent Him back to us; and behold, nothing deserving death has been done by Him. Therefore I will punish Him and release Him." Now he was obliged to release to them at the feast one prisoner.
>
> But they cried out all together, saying, "Away with this man, and release for us Barabbas!" (He was one who had been thrown into prison for an insurrection made in the city, and for murder.) Pilate, wanting to release Jesus, addressed them again, but they kept on calling out, saying, "Crucify, crucify Him!" And he said to them the third time, "Why, what evil has this man done? I have found in Him no guilt demanding death; therefore I will punish Him and release Him." But they were insistent, with loud voices asking that He be crucified. And their voices began to prevail. (Luke 23:13–23)

These events took place a few days after Jesus entered Jerusalem. As our Messiah rode into the city upon a donkey, the people shouted exaltations of joy. They threw palm fronds at His feet, shouting, "Hosanna! Blessed is He who comes in the name of the Lord, even the King of Israel" (John 12:13). The word "hosanna" in the Greek (G5614: ὡσαννά - *hosannah*) has adopted the meaning "to praise." It is often used as an exclamation of adoration. As Jesus rode into the city, they shouted words of adoration, exalting Him as King. The word "hosanna" is based on a Hebrew word on which the Greek translation was based, the word (H3467: יָשַׁע - *yasa*). This word means "to save and deliver." The people shouted, "Save, save us. Deliver us from our enslavement to Rome." They saw Jesus in this moment as a deliverer. They declared that salvation rode into the city and He would set them free. The problem is that the freedom they sought in this moment was freedom from the Roman occupation. They wanted Jesus to deliver them from the oppression of a foreign government and reestablish the nation of Israel to a position of prosperity once again. We know this was not the intent of Jesus on this First Advent. He came to deliver from the enslavement of sin, setting us free from its bondage. Jesus is our Deliverer who brings about a much greater liberation. He offers liberation from the sin nature.

Unfortunately, the people who praised Jesus on the day the Church remembers as the triumphal entry did not recognize the purpose of His coming. In only a few days, the declarations shouted forth by those who welcomed Jesus into the city were forgotten. The exclamation, "Blessed is the King who comes in the name of the Lord" (Luke 19:38) turned into, "We have no king but Caesar" (John 19:15). The shouts of "Hosanna, our deliverer has come!" regressed into words of rejection as the people turned their backs on Jesus and suggested that He save Himself (Luke 23:25). A King upon a donkey who rode into the city bringing the promise of peace is now a criminal who incites hatred in those who look upon His face. As Jesus was declared innocent by Pilate, who could find no guilt, the people choose death. They shout in condemnation of Jesus: "Away with this man, and release for us Barabbas!" [19] (He was one who had been thrown into prison for an insurrection made in the city, and for murder). The people chose to condemn the source of redemption, calling forth, in preference, for the release of murder. How quickly the hearts of the people changed. How quickly they were influenced by the loud minority of those who spoke words of chaos. How convincing the whispers of the serpent can be if we do not guard our hearts.

Once a King, now a criminal, Jesus in the hearts of a people who fail to cling to revival. It is striking to read of the events leading up to His crucifixion. It is remarkable to note the dramatic change in behaviors of the people who initially praised Christ. Within just a few days they rejected Him. It is easy to read this account and blame those who were present for the tragedy. It is easy because of the distance afforded by time to place blame on the past. We often point to others in their failings while proclaiming that we are innocent. But we who claim faith in Jesus our Savior possess the proclivity to fall victim to the same failure. Once a King, Jesus in the hearts of those who are roused to claim salvation proclaim this truth spurred on by the emotional impact of the moment. In the moment of revival, Christ can be King and He can be all. But as the lights are dimmed following the zenith of the great act of deliverance when we sing "Hosanna, I have found my King," the silence can be deafening. The great emotion of the moments leading to revival is often bookended by the remembrance of the mundane. Following the emotional high, we face the return of the normal. Jesus the King can become the criminal. What I mean by this statement is that when we return from what I call "great moments in our faith walk" wherein we feel emotionally exhilarated, the struggle of life remains. When we return to the regular patterns of our daily lives, the "great moments in our faith walk" can become less vibrant. Revival can fade. Jesus can become the criminal. His presence in our lives brings conviction directing us to reject sinful desire. The conviction of sin we feel through the presence of His Holy Spirit in our hearts can be interpreted as a burden. I do not want to imply that He is a burden; the point that I am trying to make is that our faith in the everyday can become a challenge if we are not intentional.

We are creatures of habit. The routine of daily life is often a much more attainable standard than that of intentionality in the application of faith. Not only this, but we are sinful by result of the Fall (Genesis 3). The sin nature is easy to embrace if we do not choose, with determination, to avoid its influence. In the moments when we feel the strings of temptation pulling at our heart, Jesus can become criminal. He can become one we wish to forget. He can become the burden of conviction as we desire to embrace the temptation. One day He is a King, the next He is a culprit. We are no different than those who shouted for His crucifixion. There are times for all of us, if we are honest, when we would rather have Jesus be put away. We would rather not deal with what we know is right, because what we desire to do, knowing that it is wrong, is much easier to attain. This is the difficulty we all face. The pull of temptation contrasted with the draw of the Lord is the dilemma of humanity. We all struggle with this great battle in our minds to: Succumb to the flesh or rise above in recognition of our responsibility to the Lord. The choice is ours. And in our own strength, we will fail. Praise be to God that He has given us the power to overcome through the outpouring of His Holy Spirit. He gives us the authority to reject temptation. He gives us the opportunity to be delivered by the blood of the Lamb. It is, therefore, a matter of utmost importance that we cling to those moments of revival in our hearts. We must cling to those times when we have felt close to God, remembering that He is always with us. The moments of remembrance can be a catalyst to bring about victory in those times of regression. When we feel compromised by whatever difficulties life is placing in our path, the love of God is always there. He will always lift us up (James 4:7–10). He will always comfort us in our time of need (Matthew 11:28–30). He is the immoveable foundation upon which we must be set (Psalm 62:5–7).

With revival comes responsibility. To neglect the responsibility of allowing the Lord to transform your heart in those moments of revival leads only to regression. I am reminded of the account recorded in the book of John. In chapter 6 of this book, we are given insight into the futility of the human heart. The chapter opens with Jesus feeding the five thousand. The people who were benefactors of this miracle, seeing what He was able to do, declared that He must be "the Prophet who is to come into the world" (John 6:14). They believed Jesus to be sent by God because He had the authority to heal the sick and feed those who were in need. When they were fed, when they were the recipients of the blessing, they believed. John goes on to write about the crossing of the sea of Galilee, where Jesus walked upon the water. Following this crossing, the people again find Jesus and are astonished by the miracles He performed. As Jesus is with them, He begins to teach them, saying:

Truly, truly, I say to you, you seek Me, not because you saw signs, but because you ate of the loaves and were filled. Do not work for the food which perishes, but for the food which endures to eternal life, which the Son of Man will give to you, for on Him the Father, God, has set His seal. (John 6:36–27)

Jesus is teaching about responsibility. He is charging those who have ears to hear with the directive to walk in responsibility following moments of revival. He instructs the people to seek after a depth of faith that comes only when we choose to accept the responsibility of knowing Him. The people in this account given by John are walking in superficial faith. They are chasing the miracles. They are chasing the times when Jesus was blessing them with food or healing them from affliction. They were chasing a feeling, an emotional response. It is easy to blame them. It is easy to point out the fault of the people in these verses, but we are the same. We are no different. We chase after the blessing. We chase after the emotional high. We chase after an experience. We chase after the feeling we get in those "great moments of faith" when we feel close to God. But when those experiences are over, when we find ourselves alone on the shore of the Galilee, reeling in the wake of the experience, the vibrancy of revival tends to fade, giving way to the fog of personal responsibility. I equate personal responsibility with fog for this reason. When we find ourselves in a natural fog, it can be disorienting. Fog is limiting, meaning it restricts our view. It closes us off to the larger picture. In a fog, it becomes more difficult to discern what is coming and which direction we should go. The emotional impact of revival fades over time as a result of our unwillingness to cling to the transformation of the gospel. The fog of the norm clouds our perception, causing us to focus once again on the daily activities that all too often grab our attention. Remember revival. Remember the hope of God that will enable you to see through the fog.

Our Messiah was with the people on the shores of the Galilee. While He was with them feeding them, caring for them, leading them, the people were more than willing to follow. They held out their edacious hands toward Christ, content to perpetually receive. But the moment Jesus taught them of the personal responsibility inherent in faith, many people retracted their outstretched hands, claiming that was too difficult. They enjoyed the blessings. They eagerly awaited the miracles. They selfishly followed in the hope of receiving. The moment Jesus required them to walk in personal responsibility, they claimed it was too difficult (John 6:60). They chose to walk away (John 6:66). They chose to focus on the fog rather than the Light. They chose to look at what surrounded them as opposed to focusing on the Light, who has the authority to empower them to overcome. Because of this choice, they lost sight of the truth. They lost their way.

With revival comes responsibility. Do not be like those in the Galilee who fell away when the Master instructed them to carry forth the message. Do not be like those who exalted Jesus as King only to condemn His as a criminal. It is our responsibility, even in the fog, to cling to faith. He will never leave us or forsake us (Deuteronomy 31:6–8). This is true and this is eternal. We can trust our God, *Elohim*, the Almighty Creator who has spoken the universe into existence. He will keep His Word to us. The question is: Will we do the same? Will we, when we find ourselves in those moments of difficulty, seek out the One who walks with us? With revival comes responsibility. I repeat this phrase because it is vital to remember. There has been, there is, and there will be revival in His Church because the Church belongs to Him. Along with revival, we know that there will be trial. Will you choose, even in the trial, to cling to Jesus? Will you remain in Him so that His presence can bring you peace? You are not alone. He is always with you. Choose, therefore, to never squander the blessing of knowing Him.

6

EPHESIANS 4:17-19
Those Who Walk in Futility

In those great moments of faith, times of revival when we feel an emotional exhilaration, God is drawing us closer to Him. He is revealing to us the importance of fellowship with Him. He is expressing to us who He is and how we are to respond to Him. Our responsibility in faith requires that we hold onto those moments as points of remembrance. We must hold onto those times when God is speaking into our hearts. It is in these moments when God can bind us together as His people. The Apostle Paul addresses this subject in His letter to the church at Ephesus. He wrote:

> Therefore I, the prisoner of the Lord, implore you to walk in a manner worthy of the calling with which you have been called, with all humility and gentleness, with patience, showing tolerance for one another in love, being diligent to preserve the unity of the Spirit in the bond of peace. There is one body and one Spirit, just as also you were called in one hope of your calling; one Lord, one faith, one baptism, one God and Father of all who is over all and through all and in all. (Ephesians 4:1–6)

The responsibility of revival is to make the choice to walk in a manner that is worthy of your calling. Paul encourages us to recognize the work of the Lord in your life, embrace it, and choose to walk it out in the everyday. Revival is not intended to remain in the church pew and be picked up only when needed. Revival is intended to ignite a fire within the heart so that the Word of the Lord brings about transformation into the newness of life. We are the people of God, called to unity of faith, founded on the preservation of love in our hearts as we serve our neighbor for the purpose of expressing the testimony of truth. The old self must die and the new must come (2 Corinthians 5:14–17). Our responsibility is to allow Christ, dwelling in us, to draw out the old self, the sin nature, and transform us into His likeness. This is how we walk in a manner worthy of our calling. Just think about those words for a moment. We are called by His name (2 Chronicles 7:14). We are called to repent, seeking God for help to remove any obstacle that potentially causes us to stumble (Isaiah 57:14). You are called to walk as His witness in the earth. He chose you! Is He worthy? Is He worthy to bring about change in your life? And are you willing?

Returning to what the Apostle Paul wrote in the book of Ephesians, in chapter 4 of this letter, he writes of the responsibility inherent in knowing Jesus as Lord. Paul exhorts his listeners, writing:

So this I say, and affirm together with the Lord, that you walk no longer just as the Gentiles also walk, in the futility of their mind, being darkened in their understanding, excluded from the life of God because of the ignorance that is in them, because of the hardness of their heart; and they, having become callous, have given themselves over to sensuality for the practice of every kind of impurity with greediness. But you did not learn Christ in this way, if indeed you have heard Him and have been taught in Him, just as truth is in Jesus, that, in reference to your former manner of life, you lay aside the old self, which is being corrupted in accordance with the lusts of deceit, and that you be renewed in the spirit of your mind, and put on the new self, which in the likeness of God has been created in righteousness and holiness of the truth. (Ephesians 4:17–24)

As the traditional saying goes, "This is where the rubber meets the road." This is where faith comes to action. Paul is speaking to a people who have found Christ. Paul is speaking to a group of people who have felt revival. He is speaking to those who have heard the message of salvation and believed. He is speaking to people who find themselves at a crossroads. He is speaking to people of faith who are torn between a life of faith and the enticement of the world. He is speaking to you and to me. Paul is addressing the newness of life born of those who find salvation on our Redeemer. No longer are they—or we—slaves to the futility of our minds. We have found freedom and deliverance from worthlessness through the promise of Christ, our King. Paul addresses a church, a people who should know better than to allow the temptations of this world to draw them into sin. Yet, he writes to the church. He writes these words because the Ephesian church needed to hear and be delivered from the old self. They needed to be delivered from the sinful self. The church of Ephesus struggled; so do we.

The contemporary Church struggles, as did Ephesus, to step fully into the promises of God. Too often we straddle the boundary between the desert and the promise. Like Israel, looking upon the land of their inheritance, they doubted the Word of God (Numbers 13). They saw the giants who, in their perception, could not be defeated, and they chose to remain in the desert. They believed the lies; they rejected the responsibility. We, too, struggle to step into His promise. It is often much more convenient to remain in the desert because it is familiar. In the desert, we do not look different. We look just like everyone else, those who the Apostle Paul suggests have given themselves over to the "futility of their mind." We often want to remain firmly planted in the desert of the old self while receiving the blessings of the promise found in the land that flows with milk and honey. In the desert, we can reject the responsibility of walking in faith. In the desert, we have no expectations. Futility is a viable option—futility being a pointless life, focused on the self. No one in the desert will question this choice. No one in the desert will question why those who are called "His Church" look just like the unrepentant world surrounding. To dwell in the desert promotes anonymity among conformity. We don a ghillie suit fashioned to allow us to blend into the background and go unnoticed by potentially unfriendly onlookers. We become anonymous through conformity to the unrepentant culture. So many people choose to dwell in the chasm between the land of promise and the wilderness of sin. Straddling the chasm between the desert and the promise offers safety in our self-centeredness and non-committal. We find it more comfortable to remain ignorant of the will of God drawing us into a deeper relationship with Him. If this is you, then your testimony is a pointless witness. If these words offend you, then take action to discover the source from which the offense originates. Ask the Lord God to reveal to you the things that you hold onto in your life that cause you to falter in your calling to walk with Him. Repent and be made whole in the mercy of our Savior Christ Jesus.

Paul encourages the Church to walk in a manner that is fitting to our calling. A manner fitting to our calling suggests that we have a part to play. We are responsible to carry our faith with integrity. It is imperative that we humble ourselves before the Lord, submitting to His will. In our humility, He can work in us, allowing us to grow in faith (Romans 12:2). Paul laments in his letter that there are many who have been given over to the futility of their minds. They are "darkened in their understanding," a result of rejecting the light of truth. Because they have rejected the light, they suffer from "hardness of their heart; and they, having become callous, have given themselves over to sensuality for the practice of every kind of impurity with greediness" (Ephesian 4:18–19). Regrettably, many in our world have chosen this path. It is with little effort that I can point to countless examples of those embracing deception. Many have rejected truth and embraced a lie. Because they have rejected the power of Christ to overcome sin, they have hardened their heart to God. The hearts become callous and thick, dense and dry. This is a tactic of our enemy. If he cannot have us through deception, he will submit to causing the hearts of the people of God to become hard and dry toward walking in the fullness of salvation. Our faith then can become just another event to attend amid the countless other events on the calendar of life. The result of a calloused faith may not be greatly significant in your life, but it will be of remarkable consequence to those who follow. A calloused heart leaves only a bitter witness strewn along the path. The bitter witness serves as errant trail markers leading others to barren destinations. Moses warns of roots of bitterness springing up in the hearts of God's people:

> But I am not making this covenant and this oath only with you. Rather, I am making it both with him who is standing here with us today before Adonai our God and also with him who is not here with us today. For you know how we lived in the land of Egypt and how we came directly through the nations you passed through; and you saw their detestable things and their idols of wood, stone, silver and gold that they had with them. So let there not be among you a man, woman, family or tribe whose heart turns away today from Adonai our God to go and serve the gods of those nations. Let there not be among you a root bearing such bitter poison and wormwood. If there is such a person, when he hears the words of this curse, he will bless himself secretly, saying to himself, "I will be all right, even though I will stubbornly keep doing whatever I feel like doing; so that I, although 'dry' [sinful], will be added to the 'watered' [righteous]." But Adonai will not forgive him. Rather, the anger and jealousy of Adonai will blaze up against that person. Every curse written in this book will be upon him. Adonai will blot out his name from under heaven. (Deuteronomy 29:13–19 CJB)

Moses reiterates the covenant that God maintains for His people. It is a covenant of welcome for all those who are willing to accept and walk in it. However, the covenant, while upheld by God Almighty, requires our participation. God declares that those walking in this covenant must reject the negative influences of the culture around them.

> For you know how we lived in the land of Egypt and how we came directly through the nations you passed through; and you saw their detestable things and their idols of wood, stone, silver and gold that they had with them. So let there not be among you a man, woman, family or tribe whose heart turns away today from Adonai our God to go and serve the gods of those nations. (Deuteronomy 29:15–17 CJB)

When we are awakened to faith in Christ, He leads us on a path toward a Kingdom that is for the now and the not yet. We are justified to find residence in this Kingdom upon our declaration of faith in the now. But the fullness of the Kingdom will only be realized in the not yet, the life to come. We pass through many kingdoms born of the heart of fallen man, kingdoms conceived in the imaginings of the sinful heart: kingdoms of pride, lust, greed, jealousy and unbelief. All of these kingdoms require payment or penalty for the unfortunate travelers who darken the doors. The Lord your God commands that as you walk through the path of life, passing through the kingdoms of man, you reject the temptation to take up residence. **Do not allow the influence of the temporal kingdom to entice you to wander from the path of the eternal.** Do not be tempted to comingle the detestable things of the kings of men with the holiness of the Kingdom of God. For God warns us through Moses of those who try to hide the detestable while claiming membership in the covenant:

> If there is such a person, when he hears the words of this curse, he will bless himself secretly, saying to himself, "I will be all right, even though I will stubbornly keep doing whatever I feel like doing; so that I, although 'dry,' [sinful,] will be added to the 'watered' [righteous]." (Deuteronomy 29:18 CJB)

Moses states that these people produce bitter poison in the camp. They function with a self-centered heart, serving God only to remain in the blessing (watered) and clinging to sin because they choose to do what they want, rejecting the transformation of faith (sinful). They have one foot in the promise while keeping the other firmly planted in the desert. Moses stated, "Let there not be among you a root bearing such bitter poison and wormwood" (Deuteronomy 29:17 CJB). Moses warns us of the people who produce bitter poison in the camp, because the bitterness has the capacity to contaminate others and create discord.

This warning given by God through Moses is the catalyst for what Paul writes to the church in Ephesus. Paul instructs that those of faith reject the poison of the world, which can cause the heart that has been softened by the Lord to grow hard. Paul states that when we come to Christ in faith, we are to cast off the old self (Ephesians 4:22). Our faith in Jesus gives us the opportunity to remove the old and be adorned with the new. The new self is a likeness made in the image of God in holiness and righteousness (Ephesians 4:24). Paul wrote to the church of Ephesus, but he also write to us. We must hold fast to revival. We must hold fast to the blessing of knowing God so that our first love does not grow cold (Revelation 2:4). This was the unfortunate result of the church at Ephesus whose love for the Savior faded. Put off the old self and embrace the new. Cast aside the futility of this world and choose to embrace the eternal. Again, this warning is not only for then, it is for the now. Seek God with purity of heart, allowing Him to correct you in times of error. This, truly, is the only response toward an Almighty, all-loving Father.

We are blessed to live in the age of grace. We live in the revelation of our Savior who pours out His grace upon us allowing us to be recipients of His salvation. Because we are to walk in grace though Jesus, He calls us to carry forth the message of salvation to the nations. Now is the time that we have the opportunity to be fishers of men, drawing others to the saving knowledge of Jesus. Now is the time when we must live up to the call on our lives to be:

...a chosen race, a royal priesthood, a holy nation, a people for God's own possession, so that you may proclaim the excellencies of Him who has called you out of darkness into His marvelous light; 10 for you once were not a people, but now you are the people of God; you had not received mercy, but now you have received mercy. (1 Peter 2:9–10)

It is now that God has sent out fishermen to draw people into faith. Now is the age of mercy, but this age is coming to an end. God foretold, through the prophet Jeremiah, of a day when He will send out the hunters.

7

JEREMIAH 16:16-18
I Will Send Out Hunters

Chapter 16 of the book of Jeremiah is a warning. God warned, in this chapter, that His people have forsaken Him (Jeremiah 16:10–13). The people have gone after false gods, worshipping them, forsaking the covenant of God Almighty. Because they have forsaken the covenant, the Lord will bring judgment upon the people. The beginning of the chapter foretells the judgment that will befall the people because they have turned away from their God. The Lord brings a charge against the people, stating:

> You too have done evil, even more than your forefathers; for behold, you are each one walking according to the stubbornness of his own evil heart, without listening to Me. (Jeremiah 16:12)

This is a tragic statement pointing to the evil of the prideful heart. God charged the people for not listening to His warnings to repent. God provided warning and correction as the people tended to waver walking in their own way, but they chose to ignore the counsel. They chose rather to walk in the stubbornness of the calloused heart fueled by self-serving pride. Not only were the hearts of the people stubborn, but

God also judged that their hearts were also evil. The hearts of the people were judged as evil because they "have done evil, *even* more than your forefathers." God charged the people with not listening, but ultimately, judgment is a response to the reality that the people have committed a greater sin than their forefathers. The evil they have committed was forsaking the covenant. They relinquished their responsibility as inheritors of the covenant. They did not keep the commandment of the Lord.

The greatest commandment for the people of God, as spoken by Jesus our Messiah, is: "'You shall love the Lord your God with all your heart, and with all your soul, and with all your mind.' This is the great and foremost commandment" (Matthew 22:27). Jesus quotes, in His response to the Pharisees, from the book of Deuteronomy. Jesus teaches, in these verses, the standard required of all people of faith in that we are to make fellowship with God the central aspect of our being. Beginning in chapter 6 of the book of Deuteronomy, Moses reminded all of us of our responsibility toward God. Our first responsibility is to love the Lord our God with all of our being. As a result of loving God with all of our being, we should naturally respond with a determined effort by teaching the ways of the Lord to our children and those who follow after. Moses wrote of our responsibility to proclaim the Word of the Lord:

> Teach them diligently to your sons and shall talk of them when you sit in your house and when you walk by the way and when you lie down and when you rise up. You shall bind them as a sign on your hand and they shall be as frontals on your forehead. You shall write them on the doorposts of your house and on your gates. (Deuteronomy 6:4)

The truth of God should fill our homes, hearts, and heads. We should be conversing with our families about the blessings of God, teaching our children how to appropriately walk in faith with our loving Father. The Word of the Lord should be a central, unifying aspect in our homes. Our response is not out of obligation to a dictator, but out of love for a Savior.

Think back to the judgment against the people found in the book of Jeremiah. God brought charges against the people for doing "evil, even more than your forefathers" (Jeremiah 16:12). This judgment fell upon the people because they failed to uphold the covenant. The responsibility of walking in covenant with God is found in the verses from Moses. We are to make our faith central in our lives. We are to talk about our faith with our children, teaching them to use discernment as they make decisions. The people mentioned in the words of Jeremiah failed because they did not uphold their responsibility. They failed to pass on the love of God to their children. They failed to teach their children to respond to God with integrity. They failed to expose sin, calling it for what it is and casting it out of their lives. They failed to teach their children to walk. Instead, the children fell. They fell from responsibility. They fell from God's grace, and they landed in condemnation because they turned to false gods to find comfort—or should I say to find liberty to sin without penalty.

Will you be held accountable before God with the charge that you have done "evil, even more than your forefathers" (Jeremiah 16:12)? As a people who have received the mercy of salvation being made alive in Christ, will you fail? Will you fail to teach the next generation how to walk?

With revival comes responsibility. I continue to return to this thought. When delivered from the grave through faith in Jesus, we must hold firm to the promises of God. He has done it all for us. He has provided a propitiation for the wrath poured out on sin. Our response must be to accept that gift of grace, remembering that He has done it all for us. Our part of this covenantal relationship is in the remembering. We are called to remember our God, our deliverer. He is the only authority we can call upon to save us from sin. It appears as if we find ourselves, as the contemporary Church, in a position similar to that of those who were condemned in the book of Jeremiah. We have allowed the culture to gain influence in what should be set apart. We have allowed the influence of the snake in the tree to cause us to forget our responsibility in keeping covenant with God. We failed to keep His covenant. As a result, He is calling us to remember or be judged. Jeremiah told us of the right, just response of an Almighty God toward those who reject His covering of provision. Jeremiah writes in chapter 16:

You too have done evil, even more than your forefathers; for behold, you are each one walking according to the stubbornness of his own evil heart, without listening to Me. So I will hurl you out of this land into the land which you have not known, neither you nor your fathers; and there you will serve other gods day and night, for I will grant you no favor.

"Therefore behold, days are coming," declares the Lord, "when it will no longer be said, 'As the Lord lives, who brought up the sons of Israel out of the land of Egypt,' but, 'As the Lord lives, who brought up the sons of Israel from the land of the north and from all the countries where He had banished them.' For I will restore them to their own land which I gave to their fathers.

"Behold, I am going to send for many fishermen," declares the Lord, "and they will fish for them; and afterwards I will send for many hunters, and they will hunt them from every mountain and every hill and from the clefts of the rocks. For My eyes are on all their ways; they are not hidden from My face, nor is their iniquity concealed from My eyes. I will first doubly repay their iniquity and their sin, because they have polluted My land; they have filled My inheritance with the carcasses of their detestable idols and with their abominations." (Jeremiah 16:12–18)

Because of the evil committed against God in the fact that some forgot His covenant, the judgment will be to hurl the disobedient out from the land of promise. God will hurl those who forget to walk in responsibility in faith out of the covenant, causing them to serve other gods. They will serve the gods of the sinful desires they have allowed to fester in their heart. The judgment upon those who reject God's covenant will be found in a place of desolation where there is no hope beyond the confinement of the human mind. They are judged and sentenced to be a means of hope unto themselves. The judgment is that God gives them what they want. The judgment of God toward those who turn a deaf ear to His Word is to be given over to the desires of their heart (Romans 1:24)—the disobedient given to disobedience. The sinful given over to fulfill their sin. The Apostle Paul explains this judgment in the book of Romans:

> And just as they did not see fit to acknowledge God any longer, God gave them over to a depraved mind, to do those things which are not proper, being filled with all unrighteousness, wickedness, greed, evil; full of envy, murder, strife, deceit, malice; they are gossips, slanderers, haters of God, insolent, arrogant, boastful, inventors of evil, disobedient to parents, without understanding, untrustworthy, unloving, unmerciful; and although they know the ordinance of God, that those who practice such things are worthy of death, they not only do the same, but also give hearty approval to those who practice them. (Romans 1:28–30)[124]

This is why we see so much confusion in our world. So many people have rejected the standard of truth, causing them to be given over to lies. They have chosen to be given over to a depraved mind striving for the things that are not proper. Sin causes the mind to be filled with all that is unrighteous; therefore, those who reject God become gods unto themselves. They become gods of pride who are consumed with elevating the self.

What is astounding in the verses found in Jeremiah is the realization that, even in judgment, God desires to call His people to remembrance. He desires to call us back to Himself. The Lord promises to restore the people to the land of promise. The invitation to repent and be restored to God is always available. He corrects us to spur us to remember and turn to Him. His discipline is an act of grace.

Jeremiah tells us that the Lord will send out fishermen: "'Behold, I am going to send for many fishermen,' declares the Lord, 'and they will fish for them'" (Jeremiah 16:16). The fishermen will cast the net of the gospel of salvation upon the waters of the nations. The fishermen seek to catch the wayward fish, drawing them to peace with God. When Jesus called His first disciples to follow Him, He called fishermen.

As Jesus walked along the shore of Lake Galilee, he saw two brothers who were fishermen, Simon (called Peter) and his brother Andrew, catching fish in the lake with a net. Jesus said to them, "Come with me, and I will teach you to catch people." At once they left their nets and went with him.

He went on and saw two other brothers, James and John, the sons of Zebedee. They were in their boat with their father Zebedee, getting their nets ready. Jesus called them, and at once they left the boat and their father, and went with him. (Matthew 4:18–22)

"Poetic" is not the word for such beauty in the unfolding of God's plan. Maybe the word "sublime" is more appropriate. The word "sublime" connotes a sense of awe, grandeur, or exaltation in thought. The thought that God declared that He will send out fishermen to catch the hearts of mankind is beautiful. To connect this declaration with the account told in Matthew, where our Savior calls upon fishermen to walk with Him and become fishers of men, is awe-inspiring. Not only did Jesus call Peter, Andrew, James, and John to be fishermen, He calls us. He calls you and me. This thought, in reflection of God's Word in Jeremiah, is beyond enumeration. I cannot find the words to appropriately express how amazing God is. Maybe the best we can do is exclaim, "Hallelujah, praise be to God!"

The Lord called forth fishermen to carry out His message of salvation. Jesus fulfilled this promise of God in the calling of the twelve, as well as in the imperative directed to all people of faith in the Great Commission. We live in the age of the fishermen. We live in the age when God is casting His net upon the waters to find those who are lost. We live in the age when God's grace is poured out for all those who are in need of reprieve. We are all called to be fishermen. Without the fishermen, the lost will have no opportunity to hear the good news. As the Apostle Paul instructs us in the book written to the church in Rome:

> For the Scripture says, "Whoever believes in Him will not be disappointed." For there is no distinction between Jew and Greek; for the same Lord is Lord of all, abounding in riches for all who call on Him; for "Whoever will call on the name of the Lord will be saved."
> How then will they call on Him in whom they have not believed? How will they believe in Him whom they have not heard? And how will they hear without a preacher? How will they preach unless they are sent? Just as it is written, "How beautiful are the feet of those who bring good news of good things." (Romans 10:11–15)

Salvation has come for the whosoever. Salvation has come; God's grace is a gift granted to those who believe. The fishermen are the messengers of the gospel of salvation, for "how will they hear without a preacher?" How will the lost find hope if the Word of truth is not extended to them? Paul wrote these words as the Church was expanding. The message of salvation was being taken out into the nations. Paul writes these words to us, the Church. We are to stand firm upon the Word of God, proclaiming sight to the blind (Isaiah 42:7).

Knowing that this is a directive sent by God to His people, I cannot help but wonder where all the fishermen have gone. Where are the people proclaiming the eternal truth of salvation to the nations? Jesus, Himself, expounds upon this thought:

Jesus was going through all the cities and villages, teaching in their synagogues and proclaiming the gospel of the kingdom, and healing every kind of disease and every kind of sickness.

Seeing the people, He felt compassion for them, because they were distressed and dispirited like sheep without a shepherd. Then He said to His disciples, "The harvest is plentiful, but the workers are few. Therefore beseech the Lord of the harvest to send out workers into His harvest. (Matthew 9:36–38)

The harvest is plentiful, but the laborers are few. The task in addressing the needs of the people is extensive, but the laborers willing to address the task are lacking. I am not suggesting that we cannot find any fishermen in our day; we do benefit from many people who are willing to serve the Church for the glory of God. Praise be to God for placing the drive to serve within the hearts of His people. What I am suggesting, as did Jesus, is that given the scope of the task, we are lacking in fishermen who are willing to get their hands dirty. Where have all the fishermen gone? Have they been frightened by the sharks in the water? There was once a day when the Church walked in the authority of God. Mistakes were still made, as we are human, but at the least God's Word was a starting point for appropriate social conduct. The Church commanded that the culture be cognizant of the Word of the Lord. Decisions were made based on this perspective; laws were passed and judgments levied through the lens of the Bible. For the most part, society attempted to adhere to a standard of behavior that was founded on biblical truth. The reason this was the case is due to the fact that the fishermen were willing to stand upon the Word no matter the conditions of the sea. They were willing to fish in any condition. If the sea be turbulent, the nets were cast. If a struggle presented itself, the Word of God was utilized to try to find a solution. God's Holy Word was the standard that was applied to direct society.

Looking at the plight of our world contemporaneously, we see chaos. We see strife. We see discord. We hear the cries of those without hope. We hear the gnashing of teeth as people lash out against God. The culture is upside down, as the prophet Isaiah foretold ages past:

> Woe unto them that call evil good, and good evil; that put darkness for light, and light for darkness; that put bitter for sweet, and sweet for bitter!
> Woe unto them that are wise in their own eyes, and prudent in their own sight! (Isaiah 5:20–21 KJV)

Evil is called good and things that are sweet, bitter. Darkness of human sin in the fallen states is exalted as the Light of Life is suppressed in the thoughts of mankind. Woe to those who are wise in their own eyes; they are being made into fools. Pride of a sinful heart blinds the eyes. All of this is a result of the snake in the tree. Since the Fall, we reel in the wake of destruction spewed forth by the father of lies. The people of God, since the Fall, have been staggering through the course of history mustering up only enough strength to avoid suffering complete disillusion. We suffer from weakness; the weakness of the Church, the people of God, to stand against the influence of the serpent is the catalyst that has allowed the enemy to deceive so many. We forget that God did not give us a spirit of fear, as the Apostle Paul reminds us in his letter to Timothy:

> For God has not given us a spirit of timidity, but of power and love and discipline.
> Therefore do not be ashamed of the testimony of our Lord or of me His prisoner, but join with me in suffering for the gospel according to the power of God, who has saved us and called us with a holy calling, not according to our works, but according to His own purpose and grace which was granted us in Christ Jesus from all eternity, but now has been revealed by the appearing of our Savior Christ Jesus, who abolished death and brought life and immortality to light through the gospel, for which I was

appointed a preacher and an apostle and a teacher. (2 Timothy 1:7–11)

We are given the authority of Christ to stand in strength, discipline, and love as we walk out a pure witness of faith in God. But so often we forget. We forget, because so much chaos has been allowed to germinate in the fabric of society. We forget who we are, but we are not forgotten. God remembers His covenant with His people. Praise be to God for the salvation poured out through Jesus the King. It is only by His strength that we continue to find hope. If it were not for His mercy, we would surely be lost.

The prophet Jeremiah wrote of the age of the fishermen. The Lord will send out the fishermen to cast the net of mercy over the people. A fisherman typically does not see the catch prior to bringing it to the boat. Nor does the fisherman know the exact location of the fish before being caught. The fisherman simply casts the net and is overjoyed in the provision of the catch. Utilizing this method is effective to cover the most area. The largest areas could be covered in the shortest amount of time. Not only this, but potentially the most fish could be caught using this method. While effective for covering the most territory, this method of fishing does not require the fishermen to expose the fish that choose to remain hidden in the clefts of the sea floor. Some fish do, however, evade the net. These fish are left to grow unnoticed in the dark depths of the sea.

Jesus uses the analogy of the fishermen to serve as an example of how the message of the gospel was sent into the world. The truth was cast; the fish were wrangled. On the boat, the fish were processed, secured, and gathered together awaiting the next destination. We know the literal destination of the fish that were caught on a fishing boat. We must therefore use our imaginations to extend the figurative language used in this example. In keeping with the analogy given by Jesus, the fish caught by the net are brought together to form the Body of Christ. When we, as the fish, find security on the boat of Jesus, we enter fellowship with Him as well as others. All those on the boat are then called to become fishermen themselves. We are to cast the testimony of God's grace to those with whom we come into contact in an effort to bring them onto the safety of the boat. Fishers of men, we all are. But, we are at the end of the age of the fishermen. Jeremiah writes of the day when the Lord will send out the fishermen. And He has. However, the age of casting out the net of God's grace is drawing to a close. I remind you of the words of the Lord through the prophet:

> "Behold, I am going to send for many fishermen," declares the Lord, "and they will fish for them; and afterwards I will send for many hunters, and they will hunt them from every mountain and every hill and from the clefts of the rocks. For My eyes are on all their ways; they are not hidden from My face, nor is their iniquity concealed from My eyes. I will first doubly repay their iniquity and their sin, because they have polluted My land; they have filled My inheritance with the carcasses of their detestable idols and with their abominations." (Jeremiah 16:16–18)

In the afterwards, the Lord will send out hunters. The Lord will send out hunters who will search for those who seek to remain hidden in the darkness. The Lord will find them, expose them, and judge them. They will be judged because they have polluted the land—not with refuse, but with idolatry.

The Hebrew word used in Jeremiah 16:16 is, צַיָּדִים (H6719- *sayyadim*: "hunters"). This word is the plural form of the word צַיִד (H6718- *sayid*: "hunting, game, provision, food supply chain"). In most instances when this word is used in Scripture, it refers to the act of hunting or the provisions secured through the hunt. A few references that use the word in this way include Genesis 27:19; Leviticus 17:13; Joshua 9:14; Job 38:41; Psalms 132:15; and Proverbs 12:27. The word is only used in the plural once in Scripture, in Jeremiah 16:16. The Lord declares He will send out hunters. In context, the word is not referring to the act of hunting in order to secure food. The context of Jeremiah 16:16 suggests *hunters* who will be sent out to track down and dispose of those who attempt to deceive God's people. The hunted attempt to hide from God in the clefts of the mountains as they perform the despicable deeds of sin. Jeremiah wrote:

> I will send for many hunters, and they will hunt them from every mountain and every hill and from the clefts of the rocks. For My eyes are on all their ways; they are not hidden from My face, nor is their iniquity concealed from My eyes. (Jeremiah 16:16–17)

The Lord will send for many hunters. The hunters will search out for the "them." We are not given a specific name for "them," but it is not too difficult to discern who or what the Lord is referring to in this verse. "Them" in this context refers to the people, systems, and/or evil spiritual entities influenced by the serpent in the tree. These people, systems, and wicked spiritual entities have been enticed to rebel against the Lord Most High. They attempt to deceive the innocent, preventing them from coming to a saving knowledge in Christ. The Lord, after the age of the fishermen, will send out the hunters. The hunters will expose the works of evil and dispose of those who pervert purity. The consequences of those who pervert purity is clear. Jeremiah wrote of those who are hunted:

> I will first doubly repay their iniquity and their sin, because they have polluted My land; they have filled My inheritance with the carcasses of their detestable idols and with their abominations. (Jeremiah 16:18)

The iniquity of the hunted is not hidden from the face of the Lord. Iniquity is willful sin. The hunted commit acts of willful sin in the eyes of the Lord. The Lord will judge them with a double portion of wrath because of their wickedness. He will judge because the wicked have polluted His land. The wicked have caused purity to be tainted with sin. The wicked manipulate the culture to turn from God. They deceive the people into allowing sin the comingle with the holy. They cause the hearts of mankind to be double-minded. The hunted do this, in a sense, to bring about a spiritual abortion in the faith of the children who are the next generation. The hunted attempt to corrupt the Lord's inheritance and joy. They "have filled My inheritance with the carcasses of their detestable idols and with their abominations" (Jeremiah 16:18). Chaos in the tree. The serpent's influence crept into the ears of the people because the people were too busy sinbathing to take a stand. We and our children are the Lord's inheritance. It is for this reason that the Lord determines to send out the hunters.

Jeremiah gives us an ominous Word from the Lord. The Lord speaks a direct threat to those entities who seek to take away His children. They will be hunted. They will be hunted to the ends of the earth. They will be found, and they will be judged. Woe to those who try to corrupt a child with the candy of sin. Woe to those who pervert purity with lust. Woe to those who cause a child of the Lord to stumble. Woe, woe, woe. A better fate for them would be to be cast into the sea adorned with a large millstone (Luke 17:2).

We can clearly see the Lord working this way in our world. He is casting light upon the darkness that has been hidden for countless years. The Lord is revealing the deception found in our political, entertainment, and educational systems. The idolatry, perversion, and wickedness are being brought into the light. The wicked are being hunted. The Lord has exposed them for what they are. God does this not to scare us, but to reveal to us the ways of the enemy. God exposes sin so we can make a choice between ignoring the sin, allowing it to thrive and bringing further deception, or rejecting sin, allowing God to judge it and creating within us a pure heart through Jesus. Which do you choose?

Jeremiah tells us the Lord will raise up hunters in the last days. It is difficult to define who the Lord intends to be His hunters. It is difficult because the word, צַיָּדִים (H6719- *sayyadim*: "hunters"), is only used once in Scripture. It can only be found in the plural and in the context of Jeremiah 16. It is therefore difficult to know exactly who the Lord intends to serve as His hunters. In the context of the passage, it appears as if the hunters will be the Lord's angelic army coming to the aid of the people, the angels sent by God to fight off the influence of the wicked. They pull back the curtain of deception, allowing humanity to see the wicked acts of the unrepentant. This is grace, an act of grace by God who gives us insight into the battle that wages just beyond our perception.

To interpret the hunters as being angelic warriors is the safest interpretation. But I do believe the Lord calls each of us to act as hunters under His authority. I do not suggest that we engage in spiritual battle with fallen angelic beings. This would be folly. We must call on the Lord and the Lord alone to rebuke the evil ones (Jude 8–10). What I mean by suggesting that we are all called to be hunters is that we are called to seek out sin. We are to seek out the influence of sin in our lives and ask God to remove it. We are to find the sin hidden in the clefts of the mountains, repent, and call on the Lord for strength to overcome. The Lord wants us to walk in this authority. He encourages us to stand upon His Word to be empowered to expose sin and remove its negative influence. We are to do this in our hearts, homes, and fellowship. Too often we forget, neglect, or even refuse to walk in authority over sin. Too often it is much more convenient to go the ways of the world. We do this out of ignorance. We fail due to poor leadership in the Church. The shepherds have failed to uphold the Lord's standard.

8

ZECHARIAH 10

Weak Shepherds and a Wandering Flock

I have included the entirety of Zechariah chapter 10 below. I included this passage of Scripture because it directly addresses the struggle the modern Church faces. The people wander because the shepherds cannot be found.

Ask rain from the Lord at the time of the spring rain—
The Lord who makes the storm clouds; And He will give them
    showers of rain, vegetation in the field to each man.
For the teraphim speak iniquity,
And the diviners see lying visions
And tell false dreams;
They comfort in vain.
Therefore the people wander like sheep,
They are afflicted, because there is no shepherd.
"My anger is kindled against the shepherds,
"And I will punish the male goats;
"For the Lord of hosts has visited His flock, the house of Judah,
"And will make them like His majestic horse in battle.
"From them will come the cornerstone,
"From them the tent peg,
"From them the bow of battle,

"From them every ruler, all of them together.
"They will be as mighty men,
"Treading down the enemy in the mire of the streets in battle;
"And they will fight, for the Lord will be with them;
"And the riders on horses will be put to shame.
"I will strengthen the house of Judah,
"And I will save the house of Joseph,
"And I will bring them back,
"Because I have had compassion on them;
"And they will be as though I had not rejected them,
"For I am the Lord their God and I will answer them.
"Ephraim will be like a mighty man,
"And their heart will be glad as if from wine;
"Indeed, their children will see it and be glad,
"Their heart will rejoice in the Lord.
"I will whistle for them to gather them together,
"For I have redeemed them;
"And they will be as numerous as they were before.
"When I scatter them among the peoples,
"They will remember Me in far countries,
"And they with their children will live and come back.
"I will bring them back from the land of Egypt
"And gather them from Assyria;
"And I will bring them into the land of Gilead and Lebanon
"Until no room can be found for them.
"And they will pass through the sea of distress
"And He will strike the waves in the sea,
"So that all the depths of the Nile will dry up;
"And the pride of Assyria will be brought down
"And the scepter of Egypt will depart.
"And I will strengthen them in the Lord,
"And in His name they will walk," declares the Lord.
(Zechariah 10:1–12)

The prophet Zechariah opens this chapter by alluding to the root cause that has enticed the sheep to wander. Zechariah points to the teraphim and the diviners who speak lies. "Teraphim" is a word that suggests idols or false gods. Some translations may use the term "household gods" in place of teraphim. The people were turning to household shrine worship rather than seeking the Lord. They also consulted diviners who look to signs to foretell the unfolding of events. In both cases, the people were led astray. They turned from the promises of God. They forgot who they were in the presence of the Almighty. They forgot the provision of the Lord as He continually led them through difficulty.

Zechariah charges the shepherds for failing to protect the sheep from this calamity. It is because the shepherds neglected their responsibility to properly prepare the sheep to withstand trial that they have been led astray. The shepherds allowed deception to enter the hearts of the sheep. One of the responsibilities of the shepherd was to keep watch over the flock. They were to be aware of the predators that attempted to enter the sheep pen. The shepherd was responsible to identify the threat and then eliminate the threat before it had the opportunity to attack the sheep. If a threat did enter the sheep pen, the shepherd must then rally around the sheep who are in danger, equipping them to overcome the attacker. As suggested by the prophet, the shepherds are failing to walk in their authority as they have charge of the sheep. The result of weak shepherds is a flock that wanders.

This Word of God through the prophet Zechariah was given around the year 480 BC. Zechariah spoke in the period following the return from exile in Babylon. He warned the returning remnant of Israel to not fall into the same patterns that had brought about their torment. While these words were written thousands of years ago, they resonate with exhortation for those who have ears to hear. I have been speaking about the inferred weakness in the contemporary Church. I use the word "inferred" because the weakness that is often associated with the contemporary Church is not actually absolute. The weakness is a placebo administered by the enemies of God in order to sedate the Church. The sedated Church ingesting this placebo believes the lies about weakness and therefore neglects walking in the full authority of God. The sheep, the Church, have been led astray by the placebo engineered by the culture because the shepherds fail to defend the flock. Not only do the shepherds fail to defend the flock, but, woefully, they fail to defend the Word of our God. The Church suffers from weak shepherds who are willing to defend the Word in the face of trial. Because the shepherds choose to be weak, the Church struggles with division, deception, and confusion.

Zechariah continues in chapter 10, stating that God's "anger is kindled against the shepherds. And I will punish the male goats" (Zechariah 10:3). The anger of the Lord burns against the shepherds who have allowed the sheep to fall prey to deception. The Lord burns with wrath toward those who did not rise to defend the purity of fellowship in the flock. He will punish the "male goats." The Lord will punish the leaders who have allowed the wolves to walk among the sheep. God will judge those leaders who have abused their authority. He will remove them from their responsibility and replace them with shepherds who are determined to fight for the sheep. The Lord will preserve those who are His because He loves us.

Zechariah chapter 10 verses 3–5 five warn:

For the Lord of hosts has visited His flock, the house of Judah,
And will make them like His majestic horse in battle.
From them will come the cornerstone,
From them the tent peg,
From them the bow of battle,
From them every ruler, all of them together.
They will be as mighty men,
Treading down the enemy in the mire of the streets in battle;
And they will fight, for the Lord will be with them.
(Zechariah 10:3–5)

These verses ring with jubilation in my ears. They speak peace and comfort to my heart. This is where we are in our day. This is the promised condition of the modern Church. The Lord of Hosts cares for us. The Lord who has command over the armies of Heaven watches over us. If the Lord be for us, who can stand against us? I am reminded of the Apostle Paul's word to the church in Rome:

> What then shall we say to these things? If God is for us, who is against us? He who did not spare His own Son, but delivered Him over for us all, how will He not also with Him freely give us all things? Who will bring a charge against God's elect? God is the one who justifies; who is the one who condemns? Christ Jesus is He who died, yes, rather who was raised, who is at the right hand of God, who also intercedes for us. Who will separate us from the love of Christ? Will tribulation, or distress, or persecution, or famine, or nakedness, or peril, or sword? Just as it is written,
>
> "For Your sake we are being put to death all day long; We were considered as sheep to be slaughtered."
>
> But in all these things we overwhelmingly conquer through Him who loved us. For I am convinced that neither death, nor life, nor angels, nor principalities, nor things present, nor things to come, nor powers, nor height, nor depth, nor any other created thing, will be able to separate us from the love of God, which is in Christ Jesus our Lord. (Romans 8:31–39)

The Lord watches over us, extending to us the remedy for sin. God gave us Jesus to redeem with a promise that carries the weight of the eternal in its wings. Nothing can separate us form the love of Christ Jesus our Lord. Therefore, we are more than conquerors. We can be more than victorious in the fight of faith. We can revel in the victory of Christ our Messiah, who has put all things under His feet (Ephesians 1:22).

The Lord will make the Church like "His majestic horse in battle" (Zechariah 10:3). He will prepare us for war. He will equip us with strength to overcome sin. He will steady us in the fight as we walk toward victory. This is the promise for the Church. This is the promise for you as you choose to take your stand for the Lord. **We are to be His horses who enter the battle fray. Majestic and mighty are we, as He is our God, the Overcomer. Know this Church!** Know this and be not dismayed at the struggle before you. The battle is the Lord's. The victory is already sealed. The Lord's promise to His Church in victory:

They will be as mighty men,
Treading down the enemy in the mire of the streets in battle;
And they will fight, for the Lord will be with them.
(Zechariah 10:5)

He calls us to be mighty. He lifts us, strengthening us to be mighty people determined to stand firmly on the promises of God. By His authority we have the power to tread down the enemy in the streets of battle. We have the authority to stand behind our God as He fights for us. We are overcomers! **Because He has overcome, fight then for your faith.** The enemy is already defeated; our task is to remember. We must remember that we already possess the power within us to reject the influence of the ramblings of the defeated. Stamp out the voice of deception tempting you to sin and fight. Fight for your faith. Fight for those of worth. For valor we fight. For valor we defend the faith. For valor in defense of those of worth, our children, we take our stand in Jesus our King!

The Lord is with us in the battle. He equips us with the confidence, in Him, to withstand tribulation. In our determination to stand, our "children will see *it* and be glad" (Zechariah 10:7). Our children will be glad because they will recognize that love prevails. The love of God prevails. The love of parents for their children prevails. The love for those who are lost, lonely, or languid drawing them to repentance prevails.

The Lord's promise to us continues in the passage of Scripture given by Zechariah:

"And they will pass through the sea of distress
"And He will strike the waves in the sea,

"So that all the depths of the Nile will dry up;
"And the pride of Assyria will be brought down
"And the scepter of Egypt will depart.
"And I will strengthen them in the Lord,
"And in His name they will walk," declares the Lord.
(Zechariah 10:1–12)

He will give us safe passage through the sea of distress. He will walk with us as we traverse the difficulties of this life. He is with us. He strikes the waves of the sea, causing them to lose their potency to topple us. He dries up the pride of those who stand against us. In His strength we walk. In His strength we become mighty warriors of God. He calls forth hunters (Jeremiah 16:16). He calls for hunters to eliminate deception, and hunters we will be.

AMEN!

as he sinks to the depths of the sea. Enraptured by the wants of the flesh, so many are blinded to reality.

The Apostle Paul confirms this unfortunate reality in his letter to the church in Ephesus:

> So this I say, and affirm together with the Lord, that you walk no longer just as the Gentiles also walk, in the futility of their mind,
>
> being darkened in their understanding, be excluded from the life of God because of the ignorance that is in them, because of the hardness of their heart;
>
> and they, having become callous, have given themselves over to sensuality for the practice of every kind of impurity with greediness. (Ephesians 4:17–19)

Paul spoke of the futility of the mind apart from God. The term "futile" means "worthless, without hope, without peace." Clinging to the promises of a dying world, those filled with rage toward God choose to suffer Ahab's fate and be dragged to the depths of their own lust. Their hearts are hardened by sin. They lash out at God. They fight against the Holy Spirit; their minds are futile.

We see the response of those who are condemned in futility of thought in verse 3 of Psalm 2: "Let us tear their fetters apart and cast away their cords from us." The kings of the earth who rise up against God are speaking in this verse. They strive to remove the fetters they perceive to be restraining them from reaching their full potential apart from God. These earthly rulers were driven to remove the chains that bound them. They claim God restricted them from fully embracing fleshly desires. It is the same evil lie found in the Garden of Eden. The serpent deceived Eve by saying that if she eats of the fruit, she will be like God. This lie implies that God was restricting knowledge. In this lie, God was holding something back that was not allowed. The psalmist tells us that the kings of the earth removed the fetters to escape bondage, because they claim God was keeping something from them. We can also see this drive in our culture today. Many claim that tradition is limiting. Religion, faith in the Living God, is meaningless and restraining. Therefore, many seek to remove the shackles they perceive to be applied by God. Removing the shackles, in their view, will liberate them from the slavery of a tyrant God. They want the freedom to sin by removing the definitions. They want the freedom to live vulgar lives. God is the enemy in this worldview. God is the enemy because He is holy and calls for people to repent of sin in the pursuit of purity.

Verses 4–6 provide the Lord's response as He looks upon His unruly creation: "He who sits in the heavens laughs, the Lord scoffs at them" (Psalm 2:4). This is the right response of an all-powerful God looking upon His Creation that is in rebellion. God is filled with wrath—scornful anger at the dissent of His children. But what can those who rise in rebellion against the Almighty actually do? What power do they have over God? None. None but to voice hatred to the wind. Anger against God is a vain thing.

The Lord speaks to those who rebel in His anger:

> Then He will speak to them in His anger and terrify them in His fury, saying, "But as for Me, I have installed My King Upon Zion, My holy mountain." (Psalm 2:5–6)

The Lord responds in anger toward the pride of humanity. He declares terror as He moves in fury stoked by the arrogance of those who lash out against the Creator. Again, this is the right response for the God of the universe. As God declares terror to befall the people, I want you to note the source of the terror. The source of the terror that strikes the hearts of those who practice evil is found in verse 6. **The Lord declares, "But as for Me, I have installed My King upon Zion, My holy mountain."** Terror fills the hearts of those who practice evil because the King has been installed on His holy mountain. Jesus is that King! Jesus strikes fear into the hearts of those who fight against God because He is our eternal King.

He is coming back to rule with an iron rod to rule and reign forever. He is coming back to pour out judgment upon all those who hate God. Judgment will be levied upon those who cause His children to turn from grace. Our Savior, our King, will return to put an end to weeping and the gnashing of teeth (Revelation 21:1–8). He will put an end to suffering as He establishes His throne.

This is an amazing promise that we look forward to receiving in the coming Kingdom. Praise be to our God who upholds us with His mighty hand (Psalm 139:9–10)! Praise be to our God!

Before moving to the next verse, there are two more thoughts I want to elaborate on. First, the Lord declares that He has installed His King upon His mountain. Symbolically in the Bible, mountains often refer to places of authority. An example of this symbolism can be found in the following passage. Isaiah 2:2–3 reads:

> Now it will come about that
> In the last days
> The mountain of the house of the LORD
> Will be established as the chief of the mountains,
> And will be raised above the hills;
> And all the nations will stream to it.
> And many peoples will come and say,
> "Come, let us go up to the mountain of the LORD,
> "To the house of the God of Jacob;
> "That He may teach us concerning His ways
> "And that we may walk in His paths."
> For the law will go forth from Zion
> And the word of the LORD from Jerusalem.

Isaiah wrote of the mountain of God being the chief of mountains. God's dwelling place, in these verses, is a figurative mountain indicating His position of authority. From this mountain, the command of the

141

Lord will emanate. The use of the symbolism of a mountain in Psalm 2 suggests that God has determined His place of authority, and has installed a King to have charge.

The second thought I want to bring out in verse 6 deals with the location of the holy mountain. God declares that His holy mountain will be in Zion. We typically think of Zion as being the location of the city Jerusalem. The Bible does use the term "Zion" to refer to Jerusalem; this is a correct association. But what is interesting about the word "Zion" is found when we look into the original meaning of the word. Its etymology is difficult to trace, as there are two commonly held definitions. The first word suggested as the Hebrew root word for "Zion" is the term צִיּוֹן (tsion). This word is interpreted to imply a dry, parched place. In using this word, the picture we are given is that God chooses to set up His Kingdom in a dry place, making it fertile. He has the authority to establish beauty in the things we perceive to be dry and dead. God fulfills this promise in the physical through the providence of the land of Israel. He brought the dry bones back to life in the land of promise (Ezekiel 37). But what is more astonishing is that God chooses to establish His Kingdom in the most arid, dry place. God chooses to establish His Kingdom in the human heart. Verses 1–3 speak of this. The kings of the earth take council together and, in the word of the psalmist, devise a vain thing. The vanity devised is hatred against God. There is no more striking desolation than the heart of mankind turned enemy of God. Only in the unfettered sinfulness of the fallen state can we become a natural enemy of God. But in our faith, He makes this dry place in our heart fertile. He breathes life into the lifeless giving hope to the hopeless. Not only does He enliven us to repent of sin, but He says He will dwell within our hearts. Amazing!

As I expressed earlier, the term "Zion" is difficult to define, as the etymology of the word leads to two conclusions. The second interpretation of this word is based on the Hebrew, צוּן (tson). This word can carry the following meanings: "set up, refuge, asylum, signpost." God tells us, in this word, that He will set up a signpost on Zion, His holy mountain! God will give us a sign. The cross is a signpost leading to refuge. The cross is a signpost set up in this dry place of our heart. It is only the cross that possesses the power to lead us to peace and security amid turmoil. The cross is the signpost given on His mountain of refuge. The King established on the holy mountain of God Jesus our Messiah!

Verses 7–9 of Psalm 2 give us the decree of the Anointed Son. Beginning in verse 7, we read: "I will surely tell of the decree of the LORD: He said to Me, 'You are My Son, Today I have begotten You." This is the voice of the Anointed, the One who has been installed as King over Zion. This is the voice of our Savior, Jesus. He is the King of Zion! Jesus, in this verse, is repeating His commission. He reminds us that He is the Begotten Son of God.

The voice of the Anointed continues in verse 8: "Ask of Me, and I will surely give the nations as Your inheritance, And the very ends of the earth as Your possession." Jesus repeats the promise of the Father. Jesus came to take His people as His inheritance. He came to establish His authority on the earth.

Verse 9: "You shall a break them with a rod of iron, You shall shatter them like earthenware." Jesus again repeats His commission. He came to rule with a rod of iron. His authority will not fail. He will shatter the enemies of God like earthenware.

In verses 10–12 we have a word of advice given to those who lash out against God:

Now therefore, O kings, show discernment; Take warning, O judges of the earth. Worship the LORD with reverence and rejoice with trembling. Do homage to the Son, that He not become angry, and you perish in the way, For His wrath may soon be kindled. How blessed are all who take refuge in Him!

The voice speaking in these verses appears to be the same voice, the one of the Anointed, the voice of Jesus. But this time, rather than reiterating His purpose for coming into this world, He offers warning to the kings who plot against Him. The warning of Jesus is to the leaders of the earth who rise against the grace of God. He warns them to use discernment: "Wake up! Think about what you are doing." Jesus offers them recourse, suggesting that they worship the Lord in reverence rather than fight against His sovereignty; turn in submission to God's authority and the wrath of God will be withheld. Worship the Lord and rejoice with trembling. Notice the cause for the trembling of those who possess so much pride in their sinful hearts. The source is Jesus. They tremble at the warning spoken over them. They tremble at the wrath that God will pour out upon them lest they repent. Be warned therefore, judges of the earth, rulers of this present age. Be warned those who take their stand against the Lord; be warned because our King reigns! He will return to silence the mouths of liars. The psalmist tells us to rejoice! Rejoice because Jesus sets us free! Rejoice because He will return to defeat His enemies! Rejoice with trembling for this will be a day of AWE!

The psalm continues in verse 12, "Do homage to the Son, that He not become angry, and you perish in the way, For His wrath may soon be kindled. How blessed are all who take refuge in Him!" Do homage to the Son. Honor, respect, and show reverence for our King! The word translated as "homage" in the English is taken from the Hebrew word נַשְּׁקוּ (H5401: *nasaq*). This more accurately translated means "to kiss." Kiss the Son. It is an act of love, an act of intimacy. The psalmist exhorts us to love Jesus. Reciprocate the love that He has for you. Our love for our Messiah saves us from His wrath. Don't be an enemy of the Savior. Take refuge in Him. He is our shelter. He is our protection. He is our source of peace. Take refuge in Him. The King will take His throne on Zion, the holy mountain. Be encouraged, children of a King. Be encouraged, even as we face so much in this life. Take heart that your Savior watches over you. He is with you in trial and hardship. Take your stand with Him. He is your refuge and strength. I close this section by quoting Psalm 46:

God is our refuge and strength,
A very present help in trouble.
Therefore we will not fear, though the earth should change

And though the mountains slip into the heart of the sea;
Though its waters roar and foam,
Though the mountains quake at its swelling pride. *Selah.*

Do not fear, beloved, the Lord is with you. *Jehovah Ezer*, "the Lord our Help," walks with us. *Jehovah Roi*, "the Lord our Shepherd," guides us. *El Shaddai*, "the Almighty," calls you His child. Be encouraged. Do not fear. God Almighty reigns!

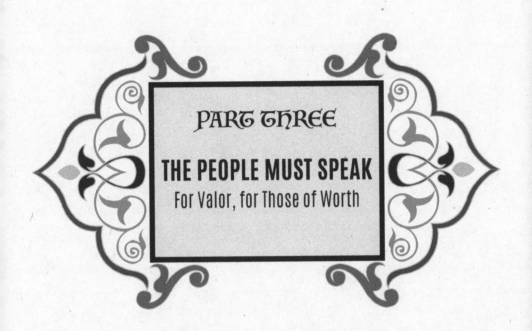

PART THREE

THE PEOPLE MUST SPEAK
For Valor, for Those of Worth

10

THE GLASS DIVIDE

U pon reflecting on what has been written thus far, we find ourselves at a place of division. We find ourselves at the place of choice, a place of separation determined by our choice. I often refer to this place of choice as the glass divide. On one side of the glass, chaos. On this side of the glass resides disorder, confusion, the world fallen victim to the curse of sin. This is a place in the wilderness outside of the promises of God. It is a carnal place of unrepentance. This place adheres to the whispers in the tree. The deception we have briefly examined at the outset of this writing is evidence of the voice of chaos making itself known. Chaos is in the tree, pining for the attention of humanity. Like a great parasite, the chaos must have a host in order to thrive. Therefore, chaos clamors to latch onto any source of sustenance too feeble to reject the unsolicited intrusion. It is on this side of the glass divide that the world suffers in torment.

A choice must be made in order to move away from chaos and cross the divide to enter the peace of the Lord. Our Father, God the Almighty who pours forth His provision, offers us peace under His hand of protection (Isaiah 41:13). When we choose to accept the gift of grace revealed through the shed blood of Jesus, the Lamb of God, we enter His peace. We can rejoice with God, *Jehovah Shalom*, "the Lord of Peace." It is from this side of the glass divide that we can find hope in turmoil. We can find truth amid lies. We can rest in the security of a future apart from death (Matthew 25:46). We are made new, becoming a new creation in our Savior (2 Corinthians 5:17). In faith, we are a new creature imparted by the Holy Spirit with the ability to choose. In our new status as a child of God, we have the choice. It is a choice between life and death, sin and holiness. We are no longer held captive in the slavery of sin. In salvation, we have the freedom to choose (Galatians 5:1). It is for freedom that we have been set free from the yoke of slavery to sin by our Lord and Savior Jesus.

We are secure with the Lord. Have confidence in this, beloved. We are secure in the Lord; this is a truth that has no rival. Yet He allows us to see the world across the divide. We can look at the world of chaos from the security of God. From this perspective we are able to discern the turmoil that has befallen a world that refuses to repent of sin and turn to God for deliverance. We can see the chaos. We can feel and hear the reverberations of calamity pounding on the glass, a vast ocean of torment rhythmically droning its whispers of poison upon the glass divide. From a vantage point grounded on the Word of God, we are able to resist the incessant drone of the snake of deceit. It was by choice that we are able to enter this place of peace. By His blood we were granted access, but it took the choice of a slave to walk into His freedom. It was the choice of a slave, who, while still in slavery, perceived himself to be free to take hold of the promise of truth leaving bondage. We who have made that choice to enter the mercy of God were once slaves. We suffered under the bondage of sin until our Messiah liberated us through His mercy. Praise be to God that we were able to see the state of our being and have the fortitude to choose.

The glass divide, the place of choice, is a dividing line between peace and catastrophe. It is the point of division separating the holy from the profane. From the side of chaos struggles a people who are able to look across the glass divide and peer into the promises of hope. From chaos there are people too hard of heart to let go of their own sinful desire to fully cross into the land of promise. The division of glass is fragile, yet unfathomably formidable. How easy it is to accept the gift of grace in our Savior, yet how impossible it can be. For those dwelling, willfully, in the land of tragedy, crossing the divide of glass is a bewildering concept. They cling to the empty promises of the dying god. The serpent in the tree generously lavishing the deceived with gifts that have no substance. "You will be like God," the serpent exclaims from its perch. "You will know the hidden secrets of good and evil" (Genesis 3:5). The gift of the snake is a vain promise of knowledge that, when found, is unwanted. When the knowledge is gained, it only becomes poison in the mind. Existing in this reality, in the chaos side of the glass divide, requires conformity to an existence at odds with holiness. Submission to confusion is demanded. To think beyond the scope of bondage to the sinful self is seen as intolerant. To long for the view just beyond the glass is to dream of a fable that has long been proved false. This is why it is so hard for those willfully dwelling in chaos to cross into the promise of the Lord. All that is manifested in the land of chaos speaks against this hope in deliverance. The curse of sin inherent in our flesh pulls against the nudging of the Holy Spirit. It is an act of determined effort on the part of those who break the chains of sin, allowing our Messiah to set them free. The chaos, a great parasite, cleaves to the deceived with its black tendrils, unwilling to surrender its grasp. The glass divide is so fragile, yet so formidable.

From the side of God, for those set free of sin, there is joy. There is joy because they are liberated from chaos. On the side of the promise, we can dwell in peace. With humble confidence in the covenant that God Himself upholds, we find stability. We can find hope as the torrent of chaos swirls just beyond the divide. We are called "chosen" and we are called "children" (Deuteronomy 14:2; 1 Peter 2:9; 1 John 3:1). Sons and daughters of an eternal King we are. It is from this side of the divide that we can find joy.

Joy in the Lord is our strength (Nehemiah 8:10). From the side of promise, we can rest in His peace, but He allows us to look back at the chaos of our past so that we do not forget. It is important that we do not forget the chaos from which we have been delivered. It is important so that we do not return. We have been delivered and our sins are forgiven as far as the east is from the west; this promise is true (Psalm 103:11–12). He allows us to remember our sinful past lest we repeat it, but it is sometimes in the remembering that we suffer the greatest threat of temptation. Even on this side of the divide, the glass remains fragile in our perception. The chaos is dangling its false promises before our eyes in an attempt to entice the old self to bow to temptation. There are times when we all press our faces against the glass of the divide, thirsting after the savor of the sinful self. It is during these times that we wish the glass to crack, allowing the poison to seep through. The choice to reach across the divide and grab onto sin remains so close and dismally within the grasp of the unchecked sin nature. The chaos sells its wares with such fervent persistence. It is in these times when we need God the most. It is in our time of need that we must remember to call upon the name of the Lord. When the glass between chaos and hope seems about to break, we need our Savior to remind us that He holds us in the palm of His hand (John 10:28). No one will take us out of the hands of our King. In our weakness, He can make us strong.

We have a choice: remain in the land of chaos, a stranger to God, cursed to bear the weight of sin without redemption or choose freedom in Christ our Savior. There are only two choices. We cannot live a life of the in-between. As Joshua pronounces this charge over the people:

> Now therefore fear the Lord and serve him in sincerity and in
> faithfulness. Put away the gods that your fathers served beyond the
> River and in Egypt, and serve the Lord. And if it is evil in your eyes
> to serve the Lord, choose this day whom you will serve, whether
> the gods your fathers served in the region beyond the River, or the
> gods of the Amorites in whose land you dwell. But as for me and
> my house, we will serve the Lord. (Joshua 24:14–15 ESV)

Choose this day whom you will serve. Again, the choice is ours to make. In this hour God is calling for a people who have made the choice. Serve the gods of chaos or serve the One God of an eternal truth. Will you have the courage to stand for what is true? Will you rely on the strength of the Lord to give you boldness to stand in the face of adversity? Today is still called "today." I remind you of the words written in the book of Hebrews:

> Take care, brethren, that there not be in any one of you an evil, unbelieving heart that falls away from the living God. But encourage one another day after day, as long as it is still called "Today," so that none of you will be hardened by the deceitfulness of sin. (Hebrews 3:12–13)

Encourage one another in the strength of the Lord so that we all have the hope to endure. In our weakness He will be made strong. Let us all rest in the power of the Living God. As the Apostle Paul writes in his letter to the church in Corinth:

> And He has said to me, "My grace is sufficient for you, for power is perfected in weakness." Most gladly, therefore, I will rather boast about my weaknesses, so that the power of Christ may dwell in me. Therefore I am well content with weaknesses, with insults, with distresses, with persecutions, with difficulties, for Christ's sake; for when I am weak, then I am strong. (2 Corinthians 12:9–19)

It is our time. It is the time of His Church to rise in boldness proclaiming His salvation to a world starving for truth. In the hope of our Savior, we can be made strong to stand against the tide of deceit. For the sake of Christ, choose this day to serve the Lord.

Dancing in the Shadow of the Golden Calf

In faith, you have been set free by Jesus. Our freedom requires willingness to allow Him to guide us in our walk. When God set the Israelites free from captivity in Egypt, He led them by cloud in the day and by fire at night (Exodus 13:21). The Israelites were required to follow. To receive the blessings of being in fellowship with God, it was a necessity for the people to be willing. However, their determination to follow waned. When they came to the foot of the mountain, the voices of a few who were discontent swayed the masses to worship a golden calf. Additionally, because of the lackluster leadership of Aaron, the people were allowed to fall into deception, turning their backs on God, who had delivered them from captivity. I now return to the thought that we left earlier in this writing. I remind you of the account of the events described in the book of Exodus:

> It came about, as soon as Moses came near the camp, that he saw the calf and the dancing; and Moses' anger burned, and he threw the tablets from his hands and shattered them at the foot of the mountain. He took the calf which they had made and burned it with fire, and ground it to powder, and scattered it over the surface of the water and made the sons of Israel drink it.
>
> Then Moses said to Aaron, "What did this people do to you, that you have brought such great sin upon them?" Aaron said, "Do not let the anger of my lord burn; you know the people yourself, that they are prone to evil. For they said to me, 'Make a god for us who will go before us; for this Moses, the man who brought us up from the land of Egypt, we do not know what has become of him.' I said to them, 'Whoever has any gold, let them tear it off.' So they gave it to me, and I threw it into the fire, and out came this calf." (Exodus 32:19–24)

The people camped at the foot of the mountain. Moses met with the Lord on the mountain. God gave Moses the words of the testimony to bring to the people. These words established His covenant with His people. Upon descending from the mountain, Moses drew near to the camp and he saw the golden calf and the revelry. He addressed Aaron, inquiring about what led up to the creation of the false god of gold. Aaron immediately blamed the people. He accused them of being prone to evil. Aaron suggested that the people suspected Moses to have died because he was gone for so long up on the mountain. The people, according to Aaron, asked him to make an image of another god so they could worship. Aaron, in his weakness, obliged their request. Herein lies the failure of Aaron and others in the camp who were placed into positions of leadership. They failed to keep the people focused on truth. They failed to redirect the people when they wavered. They failed to demand that the deliverance from slavery brought about by God be remembered. They failed to lead, correct, and teach the people with integrity. Rather, the leadership allowed the voices of the people to have precedence over the promises of God. The leadership conformed to the whispers of deceit spoken from the tree—the same whispers that have been slithering through time since the garden. How quickly the people fell when the leadership cowered.

We find ourselves, as the contemporary Church, at the foot of the mountain. We find ourselves at the place of meeting. We stand at the foot of the mountain waiting for the return of our King. The camp is growing restless due to poor leadership. Whispers of corruption have been allowed to pass from one ear to the next without consequence. The Church is waiting and watching at the foot of the mountain. In the waiting, the shadow of deceit dances across the landscape. Darkness flickers over the faces of the crowds gathered who are gazing up toward the peak of the mountain. The people question the return of the King, concocting all sorts of convoluted hypotheses to vie for attention in the camp. I ask you, is the Church doomed to make the same mistake as Israel when they were led out of captivity in Egypt? Will we erect golden calves proclaiming that the image made of gold was that which delivered us from bondage? As we await the Lord's return, many grumble. Many accuse the Lord of being gone too long, so they look for other "gods" to worship in the meantime. Many suggest (amillennialism) that He has already come and the world we live in, and all of its depraved splendor, is a result of His millennial reign. Is the Church therefore doomed to repeat the mistakes of the past?

Unfortunately, the answer is a resounding "yes." We have, in many ways, taken our eyes off of the Lord and have devised our own "gods" of conformity to quell the complaints of the masses. The golden calf has been erected in varying forms. Denominations have been formed to dance around the image of a calf that takes the shape of our personal preferences. The shadow of the calf cast upon the foundation of God's Word, enthralling the people who respond by dancing in darkness. They dance in this shadow by choice and by failed leadership. They choose the dark because the dark invites doctrine that tickles the ears. The leadership fails because it offers no correction. The leadership of the Church at large has bowed the knee to the drone of deception, allowing the carnal drive of the sin nature to mingle the holy with the profane. The whims of the culture season the fervor of the people of God with the taste of compliance. God's clear standard, preserved in the revelation of His Word, is found to be out of fashion for those in contemporary culture. They have taken a liking to standing in the shadow of the calf. The praises upon the voices of the people are lifted up to false promises of fake gods, praises given to gods of our own design that suit our own desire. The Word of truth is comingled with a self-serving, pretentious façade. The definition of the contemporary Church, in the eyes of the sinbathing churchgoers, is best summarized with the letter "I." Faith has become about the all-important "I." Our focus has turned inward; often we worship the golden calf of the self. The Church, in modernity, has become a vehicle to satiate the ego. Therefore, we have failed. We have failed to stand firmly upon the eternal Word of God. We failed to be led by the Word of truth. We have failed to cull the calamity creeping through the cracks we allow to take shape in our faith. The enemy seeks a foothold through which he can exert his perverse influence. The Church, due to a plethora of reasons, has allowed the influence of the enemy to invade. The invasion is intended to persuade the people of God to step away from the exclusivity of His Word. God's Word is exclusive. Faith is exclusive. Jesus Himself states that there is only one way into His eternal Kingdom: through the door of salvation in His name (John 10:9–16).

I speak of extremes in these statements. Not everyone, nor are all churches, suffering from what I have expressed. I therefore, do not want to convey pessimism, but hope. I speak in the extremes to warn. In the extreme, we can see the shadow of the things to come cast upon the now. The warning is to discern truth so that we do not follow. We have failed because we have allowed the integrity of faith to be strewn across the landscape of human endeavor. However, in our failure, God promises hope. God will bring revival for His remnant. He promises restoration for His people for the sake of His great name. Here are the Lord's promises recorded by the prophet Ezekiel:

"And I will set My glory among the nations; and all the nations will see My judgment which I have executed and My hand which I have laid on them. And the house of Israel will know that I am the Lord their God from that day onward. The nations will know that the house of Israel went into exile for their iniquity because they acted treacherously against Me, and I hid My face from them; so I gave them into the hand of their adversaries, and all of them fell by the sword. According to their uncleanness and according to their transgressions I dealt with them, and I hid My face from them."

Therefore thus says the Lord God, "Now I will restore the fortunes of Jacob and have mercy on the whole house of Israel; and I will be jealous for My holy name. They will forget their disgrace and all their treachery which they perpetrated against Me, when they live securely on their own land with no one to make them afraid." (Ezekiel 39:21–26)

The Church finds itself in a place of exile. I do not mean exile to a foreign land. Nor do I mean exile from the presence of God; He dwells with us forever (John 2:1). The exile I speak of is an exile into prosperity. We are well fed. We are rich with the things of this world. The desires of our every need and want can be attained with relative ease. We are in exile to luxury and complacency. Will the Church awaken or drift perpetually toward the fog of deception?

The Lord tells us, in the verses given by Ezekiel, that the people went into exile because of their iniquity. The acted "treacherously against" God. The purpose of Israel's exile was to awaken them so they would turn back to God. The Father sought to restore integrity in their hearts. Exile, in this context, was a judgment of grace. God exerted judgment because of His grace. He wanted a people of repentance. He wanted a people who would recognize their mistakes and turn to Him for correction. Exile into Babylon, for the people dwelling in the day of Ezekiel, served as a wake-up call designed to prompt the people to bow in humility for how far they had drifted from the authority of God. Like Israel, who was prompted by God through exile to return to Him, will the Church hear and act? Will we return? Will the Church awaken, turning in repentance to God our King?

The Lord, in His mercy, provided us with an example of what is required: if the Church would hear, repent, and turn toward God in this day. We can find the promise of God for a people who are driven to restore the integrity of faith in the book of Exodus. After the events of the golden calf took place at the foot of Mt. Sinai, Moses called for a people who were willing to stand in defense of the Lord:

> Now when Moses saw that the people were out of control—for Aaron had let them get out of control to be a derision among their enemies—then Moses stood in the gate of the camp, and said, "Whoever is for the Lord, come to me!" And all the sons of Levi gathered together to him. He said to them, "Thus says the Lord, the God of Israel, 'Every man of you put his sword upon his thigh, and go back and forth from gate to gate in the camp, and kill every man his brother, and every man his friend, and every man his neighbor.'" So the sons of Levi did as Moses instructed, and about three thousand men of the people fell that day. Then Moses said, "Dedicate yourselves today to the Lord—

for every man has been against his son and against his brother—in order that He may bestow a blessing upon you today." (Exodus 32:25–29)

The people were out of control. Aaron allowed this to take place. Aaron permitted the people to be disgraced among the nations. They became a laughingstock. Nations would have heard of the miraculous account of Israel. They would have heard that God, Himself, walks with them delivering them from Egypt. Israel made themselves a disgrace in the eyes of other nations because of how quickly they chose to forget God and turn back to idolatry. It took fewer than forty days for the people to forget their God. Though God delivered them through His mighty works in Egypt, now the very people of deliverance returned to worship the idol they had just left. The people of Israel were renowned as a people whose God walks with them. But now they look to a calf of gold, worshipping it as their deliverer. They turned from God, choosing rather to adhere to a lie. Because the many people had fallen into deception, Moses called for anyone remaining in the camp who held fellowship with God as a priority. He called for a remnant of people who were willing to reestablish order. Of the multitude camped at the mountain, only the sons of Levi had the courage to stand with the Lord. Moses called for a people to stand in defense of the Lord's integrity, but only the tribe of Levi saw fit to come to his side. The rest of the camp found comfort in the conformity. The gleam of the golden calf proved too difficult to resist.

I must remind you that God did not need help to defend Himself that day. He could have wiped out the entirety of the earth with the breath of His mouth. The Lord does not need help, but He wants it. He allows us to help, if we can even be considered a help, as a way to bless us. God opens the door for us to defend His Word not for Him, but for us. He blesses us with the opportunity to be witnesses of His grace. He provides us with an avenue where we can stand in holiness and integrity as we proclaim the truth. In our willingness to stand firm on the Word, we draw closer to God. The Lord calls for a people to come to Him in defense of His great name; are you willing to take your stand by the side of your King?

Moses instructed the Levites to take their swords upon their sides and essentially clean house. The Levites exterminated those in the camp that brought about dissention. They hunted those with the desire to listen to the voice of chaos. The Levites removed those who brought confusion into the camp. They rid the camp of the voices of division so that the Lord could bring unity once again. There was no discretion in whom or what the Levites judged by sword that day. No one who spoke out against God or Moses was allowed to remain alive no matter their position. The Levites removed sin indiscriminately.

An Example Given by the Good Teacher

I must pause for a moment to clarify my intent before any misinterpretations can be levied against the purpose of this writing. I emphatically remind the reader that I in no way promote violence of any sort as we walk out our faith. The example given in the book of Exodus was a physical example of a spiritual truth. Many times in the First Testament, God gives us illustrations to aid in our understanding. He shows us a picture in the physical that ultimately is meant to be a spiritual reality. Like a good teacher, God provides multiple examples in order that we can understand difficult concepts. The spiritual reality in the account of Moses and the Levites found here in these passages gives an illustration of the veracity to which we are to identify and eradicate the influence of sin in our own lives. Our call, as the people of God, is to exterminate sin within ourselves as well as within the camp, His Church. Like the tribe of Levi, we are to search out those things that are allowed to creep into faith and destroy it before it can take root. The leadership of the Church must stand guard, watching over the people so that the voice of chaos does not influence them to erect any golden calves. The people, likewise, must be accountable unto themselves as they serve their individual families offering discernment according to the standard of His Holy Word. Sin must be eliminated indiscriminately.

No trace can be allowed to remain. We must, therefore, be like the tribe of Levi, standing alongside the leadership as we serve God in humility. Place the sword of the Word upon your side with firmness of faith. Defend the truth for the preservation of the saints. *For valor*, defend the integrity of His Word.

Returning to the thought regarding the tribe of Levi, it is imperative that we adopt a similar attitude. It was because the tribe of Levi was willing to fight for the integrity of the Lord that they were blessed. They were willing to take a step of faith in boldness to come alongside Moses as a representation of the Lord's truth. Not only were they willing to be identified as servants of the Lord, they were willing to put their words into action. They acted upon their confession of faith, defending the good name of the Lord. In their diligence, they were blessed. Verse 29 of chapter 32 in Exodus reads:

> Then Moses said, "Dedicate yourselves today to the Lord—for every
> man has been against his son and against his brother—in order that
> He may bestow a blessing upon you today." (Exodus 32:29)

The Levites were blessed even in the horror of this day. They were blessed by God to be called His priests. God chose them because they chose God. The Levites were willing to defend the name of the Lord. The Levites were willing to hunt sin and eradicate it from within the midst of the people. Because of their willingness to obey the will of the Lord, they were called priests. They were chosen to bear the testimony of the Lord. Moses gives account of this in the book of Deuteronomy:

> Now the sons of Israel set out from Beeroth Bene-jaakan to
> Moserah. There Aaron died and there he was buried and Eleazar
> his son ministered as priest in his place. From there they set out to
> Gudgodah, and from Gudgodah to Jotbathah, a land of brooks
> of water. At that time the Lord set apart the tribe of Levi to carry
> the ark of the covenant of the Lord, to stand before the Lord to

serve Him and to bless in His name until this day. Therefore, Levi does not have a portion or inheritance with his brothers; the Lord is his inheritance, just as the Lord your God spoke to him. (Deuteronomy 10:6–9)

In this passage, Moses tells us of the events after the rewriting of the tablets (Exodus 34:1). During the incident with the golden calf, Moses broke the tablets of stone containing the ten words. The covenant established between God and the people of Israel was shattered due to their idolatrous heart. The Lord's anger burned against the people, and He sought to wipe them out. But Moses made intercession with the Lord on behalf of the people. The Lord relented and the tablets of stone were rewritten. The covenant relationship was reestablished. Aaron, the brother of Moses, died shortly after these events. Aaron served as priest among the people. After his death, Aaron's son Eleazar inherited the role. Additionally, the Lord set apart the tribe of Levi to carry the Ark of the Testimony. God chose them because they were willing to carry it with integrity. They proved that they were willing to defend the witness of God Almighty. They were chosen to be priests unto the Lord because of their willingness to fight for the honor of God. As a result of their determination, the Lord gave Himself to the tribe of Levi as their inheritance. This tribe would not be given a portion of the Promised Land as a possession, they became the possession of the God, Himself.

The Levitical priesthood, in its ordained form, functioned according to God's design as a model for all people who choose to enter into covenant with the Almighty. I use the phrase "ordained form" in reference to the Levitical priesthood in this context to confer the purity of the office before the weaknesses that plague humanity gained influence over the honor of the position. We know from the biblical account that the Levitical priesthood failed to function according to God's standard. The office of the priest fell to temptation, lust for authority, and greed (1 Samuel 2:22–25). They neglected to humble themselves before the Word of God, choosing rather to present themselves as whitewashed tombs (Matthew

23:27–28). They looked the part on the outside, but on the inside, they were full of death. They allowed the weakness of human flesh to take hold of what was to be set apart for God. The priesthood descended into the fate that so often befalls all of us: pride. They began to serve themselves, reaping the privileges of the position, gleaning for themselves what belonged to God.

Before the Levitical priesthood succumbed to the weakness of the human condition, the office served as an example. The Levitical priesthood is a picture of the role that was designed to be the identity of all people who come to faith in God. The Lord offers to deliver us from the slavery of sin. Upon our delivery from sin, we enter into covenant with God. We are thus designated His royal priesthood. By God's design, we take up citizenship as members of a kingdom of priests. The intended standard revealed in the Holy Word of our God:

> In the third month after the sons of Israel had gone out of the land of Egypt, on that very day they came into the wilderness of Sinai. When they set out from Rephidim, they came to the wilderness of Sinai and camped in the wilderness; and there Israel camped in front of the mountain. Moses went up to God, and the Lord called to him from the mountain, saying, "Thus you shall say to the house of Jacob and tell the sons of Israel: 'You yourselves have seen what I did to the Egyptians, and how I bore you on eagles' wings, and brought you to Myself. Now then, if you will indeed obey My voice and keep My covenant, then you shall be My own possession among all the peoples, for all the earth is Mine; and you shall be to Me a kingdom of priests and a holy nation.' These are the words that you shall speak to the sons of Israel."
>
> So Moses came and called the elders of the people, and set before them all these words which the Lord had commanded him. All the people answered together and said, "All that the Lord has spoken we will do!" And Moses brought back the words of the people to the Lord. (Exodus 19:1–8)

After God delivered Israel from slavery in Egypt, He led them to the foot of Sinai. God reminds the people that they have seen His mighty works as He humbled the enemy, which allowed Israel to be set free. He brought them to Himself, by His authority. Because God delivered them out of oppression, He offered them a covenant. If the people were willing to hear the Lord's voice and obey it, they would become His own possession. If they were willing to remember the grace of the Lord that was poured out for their benefit, they would become a distinct people group among all the earth. All the people who were willing to remember His covenant are a kingdom of priests and a holy nation. The people were to be a priesthood unto the Lord. This designation was initially intended to be for all those who were willing to keep covenant with God. Those whom God delivers are to become His priests. It was only because the people rejected this calling, as evidenced in the veneration of the golden calf, that God called forth the tribe of Levi. As I stated earlier, during this unfortunate event, God called for a people to stand against the idolatry of the camp. Only the tribe of Levi, along with Moses, was willing to defend the integrity of God at that moment. As a result, God designated the tribe of Levi to be His priesthood resulting from their willingness to keep His covenant. The rest of the people rejected this call. Had others stood up alongside Moses, strapping their swords to their side, they too would have stepped into the role appointed for all those who come to faith.

The call that was accepted by the tribe of Levi is the call that falls upon all those of faith. It was the call that was offered to the camp as they waited at the foot of the mountain. It is the call that is still extended to believers this day. We are all to function as His priests, serving as a holy nation. I ask you, then, will you take your stand? Will you defend the name of the Lord? The Lord continues to ask these questions to us as we await His return. It is from this general calling that we discern the doctrine of the priesthood of believers. Those who know Jesus have a responsibility to function as His priesthood.

In context of what God intends for His people—found in the book of Exodus (19:1–8)—He calls the people of faith a "kingdom of priests."

We are to function as citizens of His Kingdom, upholding the truth of His Word. In the original Hebrew, the word translated to "kingdom" is מַמְלָכָה (H4467- *mamlaka*). This word means "kingdom, dominion, reign, sovereignty, and rule." Upon our declaration of faith in our King, Jesus, we enter a Kingdom that is distinct. We gain entrance to a dominion that is set apart from sin. It is a Kingdom that is holy, distinct, and unlike that which we commonly know in this fallen world.

Our faith grants us citizenship in His Holy Kingdom. Along with this citizenship comes the responsibility to function as priests. The term "priest" comes from the Hebrew word כֹּהֵן (H3548- *kohen*). The term means "priest, principal officer, or chief-ruler." All who look to the Lord as Savior are therefore installed into the office of priest. We all bear the responsibility of applying the Word of God to our personal lives. As members of this Holy Kingdom bearing the responsibility of an individual priesthood, we are to strive to emulate Jesus. We are to adopt His character, choosing daily to be led by His Spirit as we walk in faith. As the Apostle Paul instructs us in the book of Ephesians:

Now this I say and testify in the Lord, that you must no longer walk as the Gentiles do, in the futility of their minds. They are darkened in their understanding, alienated from the life of God because of the ignorance that is in them, due to their hardness of heart. They have become callous and have given themselves up to sensuality, greedy to practice every kind of impurity. But that is not the way you learned Christ!—assuming that you have heard about him and were taught in him, as the truth is in Jesus, to put off your old self, which belongs to your former manner of life and is corrupt through deceitful desires, and to be renewed in the spirit of your minds, and to put on the new self, created after the likeness of God in true righteousness and holiness.

Therefore, having put away falsehood, let each one of you speak the truth with his neighbor, for we are members one of another. Be angry and do not sin; do not let the sun go down on your anger, and give no opportunity to the devil. Let the thief no longer steal, but rather let him labor, doing honest work with his own hands, so that he may have something to share with anyone in need. Let no corrupting talk come out of your mouths, but only such as is good for building up, as fits the occasion, that it may give grace to those who hear. And do not grieve the Holy Spirit of God, by whom you were sealed for the day of redemption. Let all bitterness and wrath and anger and clamor and slander be put away from you, along with all malice. Be kind to one another, tenderhearted, forgiving one another, as God in Christ forgave you.

Therefore be imitators of God, as beloved children. And walk in love, as Christ loved us and gave himself up for us, a fragrant offering and sacrifice to God. (Ephesians 4:17–5:2)

The Apostle Paul instructs those who enter covenant with God that they are to put away the desires of the old self. No longer do those who trust in Jesus as their Savior and Lord identify with a kingdom that is fallen, enveloped in chaos. We are of a distinct Kingdom, an eternal one identified by purity of heart and compassion. Walk therefore, in this authority. As His priests who have gained victory by His blood, we stand in the authority of our Savior. We are born anew in His Kingdom, set free from the bondage of sin. We have the responsibility to stand in this authority as we proclaim truth to a corrupt world. Our call as His Kingdom of priests is to declare that the Lord reigns!

PRIESTHOOD OF BELIEVERS

To better understand our calling as His people, let us examine what the Lord states about the function of the priesthood. The priesthood that was defined during the time of the wilderness wanderings served a number of functions. In the book of Numbers, chapter 3, the Lord gives instruction on some of the responsibilities of the priesthood:

> And the Lord spoke to Moses, saying, "Bring the tribe of Levi near, and set them before Aaron the priest, that they may minister to him. They shall keep guard over him and over the whole congregation before the tent of meeting, as they minister at the tabernacle. They shall guard all the furnishings of the tent of meeting, and keep guard over the people of Israel as they minister at the tabernacle. And you shall give the Levites to Aaron and his sons; they are wholly given to him from among the people of Israel. And you shall appoint Aaron and his sons, and they shall guard their priesthood. But if any outsider comes near, he shall be put to death." (Numbers 3:5–10 ESV)

The priests were to minister to Aaron. They were to attend to Aaron as he watched over the people. This is a biblical principle that is consistent throughout Scripture. Luke addresses this standard of practice in the book of Acts. In chapter 6 of this book, we find the account of the calling of a group of individuals to work alongside of the twelve disciples. Those called to minister alongside the disciples were required to attend to the needs of the people, which allowed for the twelve to focus on study and the ministry of the Word (Acts 6:1–7). Paul suggests, in a number of his letters, that there are those who are called to serve in a specific purpose for the preservation of the saints (1 Timothy 3:1–13; Titus 1:6–9; Ephesians 4:11–16). Those called to serve in the capacity as elder or deacon of a church assume the role of shepherd alongside the minister. The elders and deacons attend to the daily activities of the church. They attend to church business and minister to the needs of the congregation in tandem with the minister. While there are some whom God calls to serve in this capacity, all believers share a personal responsibility to attend to their faith and to encourage the faith of their brothers and sisters.

Doctors Uche Anizor and Hank Voss expound upon the concept of the priesthood of believers in their book, *Representing Christ: A Vision for the Priesthood of Believers*. Upon writing about the distinction and commonality surrounding both official clergy and the general calling of individual believers, they suggest that "both official leadership and the priesthood of all believers are necessary for Christ's body to grow into maturity."[126] The Church ordains called-apart ministers to serve as overseers of the flock. Working in tandem with the set-apart ministry is the priesthood of all believers. All people of faith receive a general calling to be ministers of the Word for the purpose of promoting the gospel message. Anizor and Voss suggest: "Being a priest is at the core of what it means to be a Christian. It is an identity, not simply a set of lofty but optional tasks one might perform should he or she choose."[127] The centrality of our calling as His people is that of being a priest. All those of faith share the responsibility of the office in all of its nuances. The role of ministering to the flock is a shared responsibility. The requirement to keep the Word is essential for the people of faith. The commission to share the gospel falls to all who claim Jesus as Messiah. Anizor and Voss continue to express the inherent importance of recognizing our own individual responsibilities of our faith. They write: "Priesthood connotes a dignity before God and a responsibility to creation."[128] Our identity as those saved by faith in Messiah brings with it an obligation to dignity. It is not for frivolity that we claim Jesus as Lord. Our faith is not and can never become just another activity that we participate in alongside the mundane. Our position as His people, sanctified by His blood, demands dignity. It demands respect. It requires our attention to integrity for the sake of His name. We bear the name of Christ in our faith. How powerful is this thought! In our salvation, we bear His name. For His glory and the propagation of His grace, we bear the name of our eternal King! What a blessed gift this is that He calls us by His name. We have the privilege of representing our Savior!

Anizor and Voss bring forth a powerful reminder that our priesthood did not start at Sinai, it started in Eden. They write of Adam's priesthood as he was instructed to work and keep the garden. God placed Adam in the garden with the responsibility to bring under the subjugation of the Lord's will all of creation. Adam was a priest unto the Lord as he was to walk in the authority given him by God in order to express the dominion of the Almighty. God could have done this Himself, of course, but He chose to enlist humanity. Anizor and Voss write:

> Humanity is *representational* and *representative*, being like God in exercise of rule over the earth while delegating authority. There is both royal dignity and responsibility in the *imago Dei*.[129]

God chose to create humanity in His image, imparting upon us dignity in relation to Him. We, therefore, inherit—through Christ—the authority to speak order into chaos. We represent His attributes of mercy and grace in our created likeness to His image while administering those attributes, with His authority, speaking truth to the lost. Like Adam, who was to keep the garden from being overrun by intruders, we, the people of God, wear the same mantle. We bear the responsibility of maintaining the garden. Our responsibility as a priesthood of believers is to guard the flock from the intrusion of sin. We are to defend the sanctuary of God as

His ambassadors on earth. Let our prayer then be to find success in this endeavor. Let us pray that, unlike Adam, we hold fast to the Word of truth, allowing it to empower us to withstand the trials that will inevitably befall us for His glory.

Anizor and Voss explain the roles of the priesthood in context to Exodus chapter 19. I mentioned these verses earlier. To simply remind the reader of the context in which the priesthood of believers was spoken by God, I will briefly summarize the event. God assembled the people of Israel at the foot of Sinai. The Lord called Moses forth to ascend the mountain to meet with Him. God calls out to Moses and the people recounting what He has done to deliver them from slavery. God offers a reminder outlining the details of rescue from the hands of slavery delivering them to freedom. Because God showed favor to His people through the deliverance, He required them to keep covenant with Him. God declared that, because He served as their deliverer, they are to keep His Word. In response to their willingness to keep the Word of the Lord and remain in covenant with Him, God pronounced that they will be unto Him a kingdom of priests and a holy nation. This becomes the designation of those rescued by God. The Almighty claims those who trust in Him as His own possession, a royal priesthood. Doctors Anizor and Voss emphasize an important point of clarification. They explain:

> …this early episode calls attention to the fact that the privilege and calling of royal priesthood is not something procured by one's desiring, but finds its roots in divine initiative. God establishes the priesthood; we do not.[130]

The priesthood was established by God's design in His directive and to serve His purpose. Those who claim faith in the Lord enter this inheritance as His nation of priests because, and only because, of the favor of the Lord poured out upon those of faith. The authors continue the discussion of the priesthood:

This conditional promise does not suggest that Israel must earn their status as royal priests, but that they will live out their status by fulfilling their end of the bargain.[131]

The priesthood of believers is a responsibility given by position, not personal drive. We enter this covenant with God by position in our redemption. Upon receiving forgiveness from sin through faith in Messiah, we find ourselves positioned with Christ, restored unto God (Colossians 3:1). However, status does not always predict reliability of response.

The responsibility of responding to God through a desire to keep His Word is a difficulty for many in faith. By our declaration of trust in our Savior, we become priests in His Holy Kingdom. Our status as His priests is determined by God through faith. It is a position given, not earned. Although we do not need to do anything to earn our position, we are required to respond in faith. This requirement of response does not harbor the threat of losing our position as His people if we choose to neglect our responsibility. But, nonetheless, we as the people of God, should, in loving response to His mercy, *choose* to act as His people serving as a priesthood of believers declaring truth. It is with this thought that we draw close to the heart of this writing. We are His. We have been won, delivered from death resulting from sin by His sacrifice. He calls us His own treasured possession, a holy nation, and a kingdom of priests (Exodus 19:5–6). If this is the perspective of God as He looks upon His creation, let us then respond to this love through our diligence to keep His Word. Let us respond by continually striving to remain in covenant with Him. *For valor*, for integrity, and for Him, we are His. Be that, then. Be His.

Though the choice to be His seems obvious, attainable, and right, chaos lingers. Chaos is a complex, unwanted visitor. It is birthed of subtility, originating as an unnoticed breeze slithering through the boughs of the tree. Like dogs returning to their vomit (Psalm 26:11), we allow ourselves, as His people, to dabble in the filth of sin. Herein lies the plight of mankind, which lazily sinbathes under the tree. We enjoy reprieve from the Son, thinking to ourselves, "better to be ignorant than to be responsible." Do you not despise how we have responded to our God? Do you not detest how we have behaved as His royal priesthood? Are we not a holy nation, too caught up in selfish ambition to be considered anything less than rife with holes in efforts, leading toward dedication and falling far short of anything close to a unified, under the direction of God, nationhood. We, like those crying out for a calf, are no different. Our leaders, no different than Aaron avoiding responsibility for allowing the people to fall into chaos. The Church has been allowed to veer, recklessly, off the rails.

Professor William Barclay, in his book titled *Ethics in a Permissive Society*, warns that "a subservient church is a national disaster."[132] A society loosed from the ethic of morality grounded on the Word of God is destined for unrelenting chaos, with each man given to the whims of his own desire, unfettered from purity. A man given over to his own lustful imaginings is a man cast to the vilest sin. The individual becomes the ethic for the individual. A standard of ethical thought, for the benefit of a society, becomes abhorrent to the ears of those who strive for self-actualization. The desire of those who reject the truth of God's Word is to find temporal pleasure in the fleeting things of this world. Morality is only in the pursuit of personal happiness. Dr. Barclay continues: "The nation which has no independent church has lost its conscience."[133] It is clear that we can see this trend in the world and, unfortunately, in our own country. Governments are limiting the influence of the Church. Those who stand for a common ethical paradigm are beginning to be labeled as radicals or extremists. Unabashed individualism is being promoted as the world loses its collective conscience. Dr. Barclay suggests that, as the Christian ethic decreases in society, it becomes more difficult to govern the people according to law and order. Chaos results when people are loosed from morality founded on an eternal truth. Dr. Barclay states in this circumstance that "the sword is necessary."[134] As Moses instructed the tribe of Levi to take up their swords in an effort to eradicate sin from the camp, in this hour, we the people of God must bear arms to defend the honor of the Church. I do not suggest violence toward another human, nor would I ever do so. I suggest that it is time to act. It is time to stand in our authority. It is time to call upon the Lord to expose sin, making it abundantly clear in an effort to separate those who are His from those who are in bondage to the sin nature. It is beyond time to stifle the influence of sin in the Church and in our homes. It is time to recognize that we do not have to allow our children to be left without recourse as the serpent in the tree attempts to draw them away from a biblical worldview. We can fight for His good name! We can fight for our children. We can fight for the truth to abound, bringing light in the darkness. I ask you then, as His people, where is valor? Where is integrity? Where is our love for God? For too long His Church has pretended to be His people. We have forgotten our purpose. It is time to remember. *For valor.*

Doctors Anizor and Voss in their earlier-mentioned book, *Representing Christ: A Vision for the Priesthood of All Believers,* delineate the responsibilities of the priesthood. They offer a reminder of the responsibilities of a functioning priesthood, stating that "priests were to guard holy space (tabernacle, temple), holy time (sabbath, holy days) and the covenant holiness of all God's people."[135] Priests stand guard over holy space. They defend the sanctity of God's Church. They defend the right to assemble as a free people to worship. They fight for this right for others. They carry the gospel with diligence to bring truth to those who have ears to hear. They set God's standard, claiming territory for the Kingdom! They claim God as sovereign King over their individual homes. They place God on the throne of their heart. Priests remember the covenant. They remember the responsibilities of keeping the covenant. They expose sin in the camp and strive to eradicate it from the presence of His people. They call upon the Lord for help and encouragement in their quest. They seek out chaos and speak order, quieting the storm. By His authority, we have the responsibility to walk out this purpose. Therefore, take your stand, Oh men and women of God our King! Men and women of valor, stand in defense of His good name. **You are called a "priest," and you are called His. Be what you have been called to be, by His help and for His glory!**

12

A CALL TO ARMS FOR THE
PRIESTHOOD OF FLINT

The prophet Isaiah encourages us to walk in our calling as the people of God. Isaiah reminds us to hope in the Lord as we strive to proclaim His Word of truth. Isaiah writes:

> For the Lord God helps me, Therefore, I am not disgraced; Therefore, I have set my face like flint, and I know that I will not be ashamed. (Isaiah 50:7)

These words rang forth in my spirit as I began to dwell upon the responsibilities of the Lord's priesthood of believers. The imperative is set forth through the prophet Isaiah as a declaration of the Lord to be resolute in faith. We are to set our faces like flint, without disgrace. We are to put away shame, disgrace, and reluctance for the sake of bearing the name of salvation. Our directive as His people, to be His priesthood, is that we are resolved to stand firm in His truth. Help us, oh Father. Help us to be your people, bearing your name with purpose and serving with integrity. For we walk in the shadow of giants who snarl words of contempt against purity. A call to faith, a call to action, a call to arms for the priesthood of flint are the marching orders for God's people in this hour.

I want to examine, briefly, the encouragement given by Isaiah in chapter 50. Isaiah begins this chapter by declaring the message he is recording is from the Lord. The first few verses call the people of God into question:

Where is the certificate of divorce
By which I have sent your mother away?
Or to whom of My creditors did I sell you?
Behold, you were sold for your iniquities,
And for your transgressions your mother was sent away.
Why was there no man when I came?
When I called, why was there none to answer? (Isaiah 50:1–2)

God is posing rhetorical questions to those who have called themselves His people. The line of questioning implies that though the people were once obedient, they are now falling short. The people are acting in ways that are not pleasing to God. The Lord reveals that although they are acting like they have become divorced from God, He is still upholding His covenant. The unfaithful behavior of the people is not a result of God forgetting about them, but a result of the people forgetting God. The charge against the people is that they have sold themselves for the price of their own iniquity. Lest they remember, they are lost.

God transitions in verses 2 and 3 by describing His ability to redeem those who repent and turn back to Him, in faith:

Is My hand so short that it cannot ransom?
Or have I no power to deliver?
Behold, I dry up the sea with My rebuke,
I make the rivers a wilderness;
Their fish stink for lack of water
And die of thirst.
I clothe the heavens with blackness
And make sackcloth their covering. (Isaiah 50:2–3)

God reminds them that there is nothing that will prevent Him from restoring the broken relationship. Nothing will or can come between the covenant promises upheld by the Father and His people. He is the sole authority keeping watch over the covenant that has been established. By the power of His rebuke, the earth itself responds. The Lord reminds those that are His of the power of deliverance. His mighty hand is not too short to bring deliverance of His people. By His Word, the earth itself will be humbled before His outstretched hand.

Moving on to verse 7 of chapter 50, Isaiah shifts focus. I am purposely avoiding verses 4, 5, and 6 for now. A discussion on the implications of this part of chapter 50 will be better served later in this writing. Verse 7 reads:

> For the Lord God helps Me,
> Therefore, I am not disgraced;
> Therefore, I have set My face like flint,
> And I know that I will not be ashamed. (Isaiah 50:7)

We read in verse 7 that the voice of the one speaking is from a different source. Previously, in verses 1 and 2, the voice was clearly of God. But now, in verse 7, the voice is from one who knows God and understands His covenant. The voice in verses 7–11 resounds with the confidence in knowing that when one is in covenant with God, that covenant will not be broken. God will help, encourage, restore, vindicate, and sustain those who walk in confidence and hold to His promises. The voice speaking in verse 7 resolutely states that, because of God's immutable nature, he will set his face like flint. The voice will not be ashamed of anything that comes against him, because he knows the covenant of God.

Following verse 7, the chapter concludes with a warning. The warning is directed to those who choose to reject the light of God. The warning is addressed to those who decide to walk according to the light they have made for themselves. They reject the provision of God and choose to follow selfish idols. Isaiah warns that unless these individuals turn to trust

177

in the Lord, they will suffer torment at His hand. Chapter 50 concludes with verses 8–11:

> He who vindicates Me is near;
> Who will contend with Me?
> Let us stand up to each other;
> Who has a case against Me?
> Let him draw near to Me.
> Behold, the Lord God helps Me;
> Who is he who condemns Me?
> Behold, they will all wear out like a garment;
> The moth will eat them.
> Who is among you that fears the Lord,
> That obeys the voice of His servant,
> That walks in darkness and has no light?
> Let him trust in the name of the Lord and rely on his God.
> Behold, all you who kindle a fire,
> Who encircle yourselves with firebrands,
> Walk in the light of your fire
> And among the brands you have set ablaze.
> This you will have from My hand:
> You will lie down in torment. (Isaiah 50:8–11)

The Lord's vindicator is near His people. Isaiah rests in the promise that no one will be able to contend with the vindicator of God's people. Those who bear false testimony against the people of God will wear out like a garment tormented by moths. Isaiah encourages those who do not know God to turn from their own deceived ways. He warns the deceived to turn from the light produced by the fire of deception that they themselves have kindled. The fire kindled by the whims of mankind serves only as a firebrand, a form of bondage to the self-will. The Lord rebukes those deceived to glory in the pride of the false light ignited by the imaginings of fallen humanity. The consequence for those enthralled in this light is the torment at the hand of the Almighty. God will not share His people with that of a lie.

To summarize, the encouragement we find in these verses is about resolve. It is about the resolve of God to accomplish His Word. Nothing will stand in the way or alter His perfect plan. The chapter is about the resolve of the voice speaking in the middle of the text. It is the resolve of this voice to be obedient to God at all costs. The obedience is driven by a recognition of the covenant that God shares with His people. Those who are His will be His and He will restore them though any circumstance. The resolve of God is both steadfast and true. He will accomplish what He has promised. The resolve of His people should be in confidence, knowing that He is Lord.

At this point, I want to discuss more deeply verse 7, specifically the phrase, "I have set my face like flint." It is essential to understand what this phrase suggests. Additionally, it is striking to discover who is the one making this statement. Let us begin by describing flint.

According to Dictionary.com, flint is:

1. A hard stone, a form of silica resembling chalcedony but more opaque, less pure, and less lustrous. 2. A piece of this, especially used for striking fire. 3. A chunk of this used as a primitive tool or as the core from which such a tool was struck. 4. Something very hard or unyielding. [136]

I assume that we most often associate flint with fire-starting. Most Boy Scouts or survivalists are adept at striking a fire using a flint and steel. Primitive cultures also used flint in weapon and tool-making. Flint can be broken along what is called a conchoidal fracture. [137] This trait in the rock causes "it to break into sharp-edged pieces." [138] Early people recognized that the rock can be used to make knife blades, spear points, and other sharp tools. Flint was a valuable resource to early culture because of its dense nature. When shaped through a process called "flint knapping," [139] the rock retains its form throughout many demanding uses.

As I have written earlier, flint can be employed to strike a fire. In this process, a steel striker is used to hit a piece of flint, which causes sparks. I have always mistakenly assumed that when the flint is hit with the steel, small flakes of flint are broken off and heated because of the force of the strike. However, this is actually the opposite of what happens. I refer to an article published by Quirky Science to explain:

> When a piece of steel is dragged quickly across a fresh flint surface, very tiny pieces of metal are heated by the friction to a temperature above the ignition point of iron. Iron is the main component of steel. In the presence of oxygen, the steel particle burns at white heat to produce a brilliant spark and a burned-out cinder![140]

Rather than breaking the flint rock, the steel is actually flaked off. Shards of steel are sheared off due to the hardness of the flint rock. The small flakes of steel are ignited by the force of the blow, facilitating the ability to kindle a flame.

Knowing, now, how the phenomenon of flint and steel works, I want to go back and look at who makes the statement "set my face like flint," in verse 7 of Isaiah chapter 50. Whose voice utters these words? Is it God, Isaiah, or someone else? Let me build back up to this point in the chapter in order to bring back remembrance of the context in which Isaiah speaks. Chapter 50 opens with a clear declaration of the voice of God. It is God Almighty speaking. There is no mistaking that it is the Lord making the statements that open the chapter. But when we read down to verse 4 and then to the end of the chapter, the voice of the one speaking changes. God is no longer referenced from a first-person perspective. He is now referred to in the third person. The voice is no longer of God, but another who is speaking about God. This voice claims to be in covenant with God, but he also claims that, because of his position with God, many people have come against him. The voice states that many strike him, pluck out his beard, humiliate him, and spit at him. Through all of this, the voice declares that he will not cover his face or be ashamed, because God vindicates him. Most, if not all, Christians can see the clear connection between the voice in Isaiah 50:4 and our Redeemer, Jesus, the Holy Son of God. In this chapter we hear the voice of our Savior as He copes with the hardship and torture that He will suffer at the hands of those He calls children. We see the willingness to offer His body as the sacrificial Lamb that will cleanse us of our sins. We see the potential violence of those who despise Him. And we see our Redeemer's resolve to standing, unwilling to compromise covenant of God. He has set His face like flint. He will not be moved or shaken. He will accomplish the will of the Father at all costs.

In my research, I came across a sermon by Charles Spurgeon titled "The Redeemer's Face Set Like a Flint." I want to take a few moments to highlight the truths that Spurgeon discusses as he deals with this topic. Isaiah 50:7 is the central verse Spurgeon reflects upon for the sermon that was delivered on November 28, 1880.

In opening this sermon, Spurgeon declares in regard to Isaiah 50:7 that "these are, in prophecy, the words of the Messiah. This is the language of Jesus of Nazareth, the promised Deliverer, whom God has sent into the world to be the one and only Savior."[141] Clearly Spurgeon understood the voice speaking in Isaiah as our Messiah. Jesus set His face like flint in resolve to accomplish His purpose at any cost. This is the voice of verse 7; it is the voice of our Savior.

The sermon builds as Spurgeon records numerous accounts of men falling from their position with God. Though men fall, God has an incessant nature to be with the fallen in an attempt to restore them to a right relationship. God continually moves to work on the behalf of His children. Spurgeon ties all of the accounts of the mighty works of God to His ultimate work on the cross. Spurgeon states that Jesus "set His face like a flint upon the accomplishment of the task He had undertaken and He resolved to go through with it even to the end!"[142] Jesus was determined to accomplish the will of the Father, even to the sting of death.

From this point in the sermon, Spurgeon gives his listeners insight into the learning that is to be taken away from a study of this subject.

Spurgeon states: "My great objective is to lead you to love Him who so loved you that He set His face like flint in His determination to save you!"[143] It was the love of Jesus for us that put Him on the cross. How deep a love Jesus has for us in His resolution to walk, willingly, to Jerusalem in the full knowledge that He would become our Passover Lamb, His face like flint, determined to redeem His children. To God be the glory!

Paul writes in his letter to the Romans:

> For while we were still helpless, at the right time Christ died for the ungodly. For one will hardly die for a righteous man; though perhaps for the good man someone would dare even to die. But God demonstrates His own love toward us, in that while we were yet sinners, Christ died for us. (Romans 5: 6–8)

What more can be said? Jesus knew the depth of our sin. He understood, fully, just how far we have fallen. He saw the depravity of what dwells in the hearts of men, yet He still walked willingly to the cross:

> For this reason I bow my knee before the Father, from whom every family in heaven and on earth derives its name, that He would grant you, according to the riches of His glory, to be strengthened with power through His Spirit in the inner man, so that Christ may dwell in your hearts through faith; and that you, being rooted and grounded in love, may be able to comprehend with all the saints what is the breadth and length and height and depth, and to know the love of Christ which surpasses knowledge, that you may be filled up to all the fullness of God. (Ephesians 3:14–18)

The love that Jesus has for His people surpasses all understanding. As Paul writes, Jesus knew the depth of our sin, yet He chose to bear the penalty of our sin for us. He did this not for those who are "good" in the eyes of humanity. Jesus did this for the "whosoever" (Romans 10:13).

Salvation is gifted to those who call out in faith. He chose to endure wrath poured out as judgment of sin while we were yet in sin. Jesus loves us with such a deep love that humiliation, betrayal, rejection, and even death on a cross had not the power to dissuade His purpose. His face is like flint, resolute to bring victory. It is through the recognition of His love and the resolute nature of His character that we are to find strength. We are to walk in confidence in our faith due to the witness of Christ's own resolve. Because He was, and still is, unwilling to compromise the will of the Father, so should we carry that same resolve. Take up your cross daily and follow your Messiah (Luke 9:23). Find strength in your Savior and proclaim His good name.

In Spurgeon's sermon, he outlines three aspects of the resolute nature of our Messiah. Spurgeon encourages believers to recognize and embrace these aspects of our Redeemer in our own walk of faith. The first area of resolve that Spurgeon speaks of is what he calls "His steadfast resolve tested." Our Lord was tested in many ways during His incarnation on earth. Not only was He tempted by the devil in the desert, Spurgeon states that the very people that our Lord came to be a witness to "wanted to take Him by force and make Him a king."[144] Jesus could have easily been influenced to comply with this attempt of the people. They were looking for a king, but it was the will of the Father to give them a Savior. It was the resolve of Jesus to walk according to the will of the Father. When the people realized Jesus did not come to deliver them out of the hands of the Romans and establish an earthly kingdom, they rejected Him. The cries of the people went from "Hosanna in the highest!" to "Crucify Him!" in a matter of days.

Yet Spurgeon explains that this was not the most difficult trial of our Lord. He says, "A far worse trial, however, to Christ's steadfast resolve was furnished by the *unworthiness of those He came to help.*"[145] Jesus came to His own people and they rejected His offer of salvation. Spurgeon explains further that even the twelve who were closest to Him rejected Him when the situation was dire. Jesus again could have retracted His gift of the remission of sin and allowed us to flounder in the mire of our guilt, but He was resolved to be obedient to the will of God. Spurgeon states: "Yet He set His face like a flint to carry out His purpose—whatever His elect might do, He still determined to plead their cause and to support His plea even by the shedding of His own blood."[146] It was His love for His people and for God that directed the resolve to walk to the cross in victory. It was His will to take up the cross and allow His executioners to nail His body to the tree. It was His will, His determination that kept Him there. The nails had no power. Spurgeon explains:

> His steadfast resolve held Him to the cross. He might have leaped down in the midst of the ribald throng, like the destroying angel in Egypt, and have swept them all to hell in an instant! Yet there He hung in order that He might redeem men from destruction—and all their taunts could not make Him move from His purpose.[147]

I praise Jesus for the restraint He exerted in that moment. It is His resolve to accomplish the will of the Father that has saved us from wrath.

A second aspect Spurgeon would like us to understand is how Christ's steadfast resolve was sustained. Spurgeon points out that part of Christ's resolve comes from His consciousness of His innocence. Verse 8 of Isaiah 50 states: "He is near that justifies me; who will contend with Me?" Spurgeon explains: "Christ knew, all the while, that He was suffering for sin, that He had personally done no wrong."[148] Jesus knew that He possessed no guilt of sin, yet He took the punishment of our sin. Again, this was because of His obedience to the Father and His resolve to save those who are lost. Jesus was sustained by the strength of knowing the reality of God's plan during His time or duress. Spurgeon recognizes that, because Jesus lived a sinless life and was obedient to the will of God, He was fueled with courage to press into the task set before Him. His courage was found in understanding that the Father would be His help. Spurgeon writes:

> How greatly the Father strengthened Christ in lonely midnight hours, we cannot tell, for we have no records of the fervent prayers

to which the cold mountains could have borne witness. He went wearied to the mountainside—not to sleep, but to cry out to God—and He came back with the drops of dew still clinging to His locks, but He was strong to face the multitude, or to perform any task that might have been required of Him, for He had been with His Father in the midnight hour and often the whole night through! It was God's own Spirit that came upon Him, when He was weary and faint, and strengthened Him for further service.[149]

Just as Jesus relied on the ever-present help of His Father, so should we as believers come to confidence in this reality. Jesus was unwavering in His trust in the will of the Father. He understood that the Word of the Father will not be shaken. He found strength in the darkest of night, knowing the full reality of an everlasting covenant: "He who vindicates Me is near; Who will contend with Me" (Isaiah 50:8). Christ, Himself, is the vindicator. No one contends with Him, as He is Lord. His will is to bring forth His people out of bondage. His face was like flint, His back was shredded, His hands were pierced in order to accomplish this.

Like our Messiah, we too, as His children, should stand in the full understanding of the position we have within the covenant God has established. He is the author and the finisher of our faith. He is our vindicator. He is our hope and resolve in time of need. Look to Him as your help and encouragement. He will not fail.

One other aspect of the sustained resolve of Jesus that Spurgeon makes note of is that it was driven by joy. The joy of Jesus was in the knowledge of walking according to the plan of God in order to bring salvation to the lost. Spurgeon wrote:

One, whose joy it was to lift us up who were so low, to cleanse us who were so foul, to find us who were lost, and to save us who, without His saving grace, would have been cast away forever? There must have beamed, in our Savior's eyes, a light of supreme benevolence as He said to Himself in His last agonies,

"I am dying, but I am, by My death, redeeming My people from destruction. I am suffering more than tongue can tell, but, by means of My sufferings, they shall be rescued from the wrath to come. The pouring out of My blood is scattering seeds of bliss in the furrows of earth that once were cursed by sin, and from them a seed shall arise to serve My Father, and to be unto Him a chosen generation, a peculiar people. Multitudes of weary ones shall find rest by coming to Me, and troubled spirits shall be filled with joy as, by faith, they behold Me dead and risen again."[150]

Jesus suffered for joy, the joy of knowing that He will serve as our propitiation. For joy He endured the cross. He was unshaken by trial because of His joy to save the lost. Through His suffering, joy was released into the hearts of those who have found their faith in the Messiah. Joy in abundance. Joy in hope. Joy bringing peace to the faithful. The work of Jesus has redeemed the lost children of God. The face of the Father, looking down on the Son, speaks: "This is My Beloved Son, in whom I am well-pleased" (Matthew 13:17). No doubt, joy fills the face of God because of the completed work of His Son. Joy complete. Joy sustained. Joy eternal.

Truly we can see that Jesus set His face like a flint. He was resolute to bring salvation to His people. Unwavering in His resolve, salvation came. But what does it mean, to set a face like flint? How can one set their face like a rock? Let us consider this phrase for a moment. Throughout the Word, we read about God setting His face toward something. The understanding of this declaration is that His will has been determined. The course has been set, the heading decided. His will is going to come to pass; this is and always will be true. It is a truth that is more real than the very paper these words are written upon or the notion of your own existence. God will accomplish His purpose. But what is more fascinating than the fact that His will is going to come to pass is the implication that His will has already been accomplished. It is finished, complete, done. We happen, through the limitations of temporal nature, to be in the process of catching up. When He declares to set His face toward an objective, the intent of the declaration has already been fulfilled. God's Word, expressed, exacts that beginning and the accomplishment of the Word instantaneously. A few examples clarify the point.

> **Leviticus 20:6:** As for the person who turns to mediums and to spiritists, to play the harlot after them, I will also set My face against that person and will cut him off from among his people.

The language in this verse is an if-then statement. There is no grey area of confusion. If one turns from God, then He will cut that person off. God does not have to do anything further to accomplish His will, by the simple declaration that His will is accomplished. God speaks through time. He is not bound to a linear understanding of the unfolding of events like we are. His Word is like a sword that is capable of cutting through the linear thread of time. When He interjects His will, the interjection is active and alive in all contexts of reality, past, present and future.

> **Jeremiah 21:10:** "For I have set My face against the city for harm and not for good," declares the Lord. "It will be given into the hand of the king of Babylon and he will burn it with fire."

The actions of the people of Judah have caused God to set His face against them. The judgment is that God will allow an invading army to take the city. To the listeners of Jeremiah's prophecy, a complete understanding of what God meant by this judgment against them could not be understood until they actually witnessed the events taking place. To God, the judgment has been accomplished upon its utterance; the only thing left is to allow time to catch up.

In the words of Jesus, from the **Gospel of Luke 9:51–56:**

> And it came to pass, when the time was come that He should be received up, He steadfastly set His face to go to Jerusalem, and He sent messengers before His face: and they went, and entered a

village of the Samaritans, to make ready for Him. And they did not receive Him, because His face was as though He would go to Jerusalem. And when His disciples James and John saw this, they said, Lord, wilt thou that we command fire to come down from heaven, and consume them, even as Elias did? But He turned, and rebuked them, and said, Ye know not what manner of spirit ye are of. For the Son of Man is not come to destroy men's lives, but to save them.

Jesus recognized that it was time for Him to be lifted up as an atoning sacrifice for mankind. Due to this recognition, He set His face toward Jerusalem. He was determined to walk to His death on our behalf. He knew fully well the suffering He would endure. He knew the torture that would be inflicted upon Him, yet He walked steadfastly to His destiny. The disciples themselves tried to tempt Him into sending fire down to consume His tormentors, for even they knew the fate that was in store for Jesus in Jerusalem. Jesus rebuked them because His will was in line with the will of the Father. The Messiah, in His First Advent, has come to save, not to judge. In His eyes, the salvation of mankind was already complete. The suffering was already endured. The wrath was already quenched. It was just a matter of allowing time to catch up.

One of the definitions of flint is "something very hard and unyielding."[151] We see in the face of Jesus that He was as flint. He was unyielded to do anything that departed from accomplishing the will of God. I can only imagine that, as He crested the Mount of Olives and looked down upon the walls of city that held His death, He saw a fire blaze, the blaze that would be ignited in the hearts of mankind as the spark emanated from the strike against His face of flint. He knew that, just like flint rock, when He was struck, a flame of redemption would engulf all of time and space. The scourging He endured was a strike against His face of flint. The humiliation was another strike. The nails were yet another strike inflicted by the enemy. The pierced side again was a strike against the flint that sparked the flame of redemption. His death was the flashpoint of the inferno of His mission. The resurrection was the nail in the coffin of the enemy. It is when He rose that He was able to utter the words, "Who is My adversary? Let Him come near me" (Isaiah 50:8 KJV). No one dare come, for He is a consuming fire (Hebrews 12:29).

Salvation was ignited as the enemy smote His back. Redemption was kindled as the enemy plucked out His beard. Restoration was established as the violence of the enemy struck at the determined face of flint of our Savior, Jesus Christ. He set His face like flint, knowing the results of Jerusalem. He knew the fire that He would bring to the world. *Hallelujah, salvation has come!*

The last point Charles Spurgeon makes in his sermon is that of imitation. He exhorts believers to adopt the same demeanor as Jesus in His resolute drive to walk the will of God. His Church should carry the same determination as the very one we profess faith in. Spurgeon wrote:

> It behooves us to be faithful to Him and to partake as far as we can of His Spirit. Does He not seem to accuse us, without saying a word, for His face was set like flint—while our faces are often made to blush with shame when we are called upon to speak up for Him, or perhaps when we are ashamed to do so? O fickle Christians, hot in a revival service, and lukewarm afterwards, you sing—"Here, Lord, I give myself away"—and yet do nothing of the kind![152]

These are harsh words, but all too true. The Church Christ came to ignite has diminished to that of a flicker, a mere shadow of its potential. It is not for the want of a fuel source, but the lack of a willingness to attend to the flame. So often we allow our flame to burn away, our faith to be snuffed out by the weight of the world around us. So often we disgrace the holy and glorious flame of His presence. He is well beyond anything we can come close to imagining, yet we ignore the bonfire that He is and bring Him down to our level. We are but a candle struggling to stay aflame in the midst of the winds of progress. We bring Him low. We relegate our Savior to a place of inferiority to the pressure of our own being. He becomes a commodity we look to when we are in a dire condition. His name is one we call upon when we feel discouraged. We place our Savior on a shelf along with the plethora of self-help texts competing for our attention. The blaze of faith, set alight by the realization of salvation, has been allowed to dwindle. We allow the wind of change to influence the power of our faith. We forget that the light of our faith should be a beaming constant unaltered by the environment. The light of God should be a powerful brilliance that stills the storm and offers refuge to the weary. Too often we live in the midst of the downpour, and we try to keep our flame lit under our cupped hand. We neglect to step out of the storm and rest under the cupped hand of the Father. He is our refuge and strength (Psalm 46:1).

His face is like flint; ours is like miry clay. Jesus' face is full of the resolve to be unmoved by opposition and hardship. The hardness of the flint is unmarred by the barrage directed against it. Our faces of clay are pockmarked by the beatings inflicted against us by this cursed existence. Day by day we are disfigured to an unrecognizable state of submission by our tormentors. The enemy's desire is to mold us into the likeness of the world, marring the image of God. We stumble, with our mangled faces of clay, into church at the end of the week with the hope of restoring our appearance back to some semblance of the original design. We are then sent back into the world not knowing how to stave off further attack. The cycle repeats, and we never find victory over torment. The Church never stands against the torrent, but falls further into the flood of defeat until, at last, the attacks are too much and the effort to restore the image of God, whom we should emulate, diminishes. We find comfort in allowing the alterations made against our image to remain. The beatings will lessen, and we become indistinguishable from the enemies we are to be battling against. We wear the camouflage of sin with ease, as the disguise allows us to go unnoticed in the cursed world.

It is without difficulty that we are able to walk in the world while wearing the mask of sin. Our faith is not challenged. Our outward status in society is that of everyone else; just another face in the vast sea of life.

We are thrown to and fro by the currents of conformity. Many Christians today live this life. They claim the moniker of Christ to be redeemed by His blood and set apart for His Kingdom, yet they are content to swim within the current of the culture. Jesus walked on water. He walked above the influence of the masses, because He was from another Kingdom. He served another King. He walked above the influence of sin to show us how to live. He calls us to rise up from conformity and also demonstrate the delivering power of God.

> Peter said to Him, "Lord, if it is You, command me to come to You on the water." And He said, "Come!" And Peter got out of the boat, and walked on the water and came toward Jesus. But seeing the wind, he became frightened, and beginning to sink, he cried out, "Lord, save me!" Immediately Jesus stretched out His hand and took hold of Him, and said to him "You of little faith, why did you doubt?" (Matthew 14:28–31)

The problem for Peter was not the walking on the water. The problem was not that Peter did not have ability to walk on the water. Our Lord clearly directs Peter to step out and walk on the water by the power of his faith in the truth. The problem was not Peter's willingness. The problem was his resolve. He was eager to step out in faith, but when he took his eyes off of Hope, he was reminded of the power of the storm. The violence of the opposition to his faith got the better of him, and he began to be swallowed up by it. He did not set his face like flint in determination to walk to Jesus. Peter allowed the situation and the hardship to take center stage. Had he focused on the provision of Jesus, Peter would have walked jubilantly atop the raging waves and stood beside our Lord, in undaunted confidence amid the tempest.

But it is easy to be critical of Peter because we can view him through the lens of history. It is in the immediate present and remembering the lesson of faith learned in this passage of walking on the water that is the challenge. During our times of trial, we flounder in the effort of obedience.

We are overwhelmed by the opposition to walking above the influence of the world, and we quickly submit to the magnetism of temptation. Our Lord reaches down and pulls us from the miasma of corruption. But this is not His will. He would much rather have us stand with confidence in the full assurance that we have the strength given to us through His Spirit to be steadfast in trials. He allows us to go through trials to fortify our character. He wants to make us hard as flint. He wants to give us the resolve to set our faces toward Jerusalem, walking in determination to accomplish the will of the Father.

Jesus walked to Jerusalem to ignite the fire of both redemption and victory. Through His blood, we find redemption from our sins and a restored relationship to the Father. We also see victory in the blood. We see His triumph over the tyranny of lucifer. We see our Messiah risen as the true King. The punishment He bore caused a fire to fall from Heaven at Pentecost:

> And suddenly there came from heaven a noise like a violent rushing wind, and it filled the whole house where they were sitting. And there appeared to them tongues as of fire distributing themselves, and they rested on each one of them. (Acts 2:2, 3)

As the strikes of the enemy fell upon His face of flint, the resolute nature of the character of Jesus sparked a flame that fell from Heaven. The flame, napalm from God, ignited an inferno in the hearts of men—the inferno being the power of the Spirit to walk according to the ways of God in the full assurance of His forgiveness and protection. He is alive, and His Spirit burns within us. It burns with the desire to express the holy glory of our precious God to the earth. The only limitation is our resolve. Just like Peter, we doubt. Lord help us in our unbelief (Mark 9:23–25).

But it is in the understanding that persecution and trials are the catalyst to spark the flame. The call to arms for the priesthood of believers is to set our faces as flint, with unrelenting drive to speak fire into the world. It is through our resolve that God can use us as His warrior priests to build His Kingdom. We need to rekindle the flame within ourselves by staring into the eyes of our hardships, and in accordance to the character of our Messiah, use that which comes against us to spark a new flame. "No weapon that is formed against you will prosper" (Isaiah 54:17), for the very same weapon will be broken by our faces of flint.

The persecution strikes the fire as it hits our faces of flint. The weapons formed against us become the source of flame to spark a fire of salvation. When resolved to be as flint, we keep our form and we keep our edge. The unrelenting, dense nature of our resolve is only further refined by all that comes against us. We are not changed; the world around us is changed. The true duty of the Church, the Body of Christ, is to be forged in His likeness, fortified by the Spirit to strike fear in the faces of all those who dare stand against the Holy God. The priesthood of believers is a call to be set apart in obedience to follow the lead of our Rabbi. In this day and in this hour, God is calling His remnant to arms to be His priesthood of flint. We are to trod across the surface of the earth, leaving footprints of fire in our wake. Where we walk, so also does the Holy One of Israel walk. His presence within us brings His glorious light. Let our walk not be in vain, but in resolute submission to building the Kingdom. To God be the glory, forever and ever!

We Too Shall Run

For valor, defending the faith for those of worth, is our call as His people. Let us not shrink away from the responsibility. Let us not cower in fear at the trial that come before us. Let us not neglect our purpose to defend His holy name for the sake of His Church, for the sake of His people. Let us stand in His authority, commanding His presence to be known throughout the land and the hearts of humanity. God, He is our God. We stand as His people, bearing His name in honor of who He declares us to be. We are His. I am reminded of David as he looked upon the giant who cast insults upon the name of our God. The Word of our Lord in the book of 1 Samuel 17:

Now the Philistines gathered their forces for war and assembled at Sokoh in Judah. They pitched camp at Ephes Dammim, between Sokoh and Azekah. Saul and the Israelites assembled and camped in the Valley of Elah and drew up their battle line to meet the Philistines. The Philistines occupied one hill and the Israelites another, with the valley between them.

A champion named Goliath, who was from Gath, came out of the Philistine camp. His height was six cubits and a span. He had a bronze helmet on his head and wore a coat of scale armor of bronze weighing five thousand shekels; on his legs he wore bronze greaves, and a bronze javelin was slung on his back. His spear shaft was like a weaver's rod, and its iron point weighed six hundred shekels. His shield bearer went ahead of him.

Goliath stood and shouted to the ranks of Israel, "Why do you come out and line up for battle? Am I not a Philistine, and are you not the servants of Saul? Choose a man and have him come down to me. If he is able to fight and kill me, we will become your subjects; but if I overcome him and kill him, you will become our subjects and serve us." Then the Philistine said, "This day I defy the armies of Israel! Give me a man and let us fight each other." On hearing the Philistine's words, Saul and all the Israelites were dismayed and terrified. (1 Samuel 17:1–11)

King Saul and the rest of the camp of Israel cowered in fear at the words of the giant. Goliath proved to be a test too difficult for any of them to attempt to overcome. Israel forgot, in this moment, who they were. They forgot their identity as the people of God. They forgot that they bore the name of God Almighty. Unfortunately, they forgot God. They forgot His promises. They forgot that He is *Jehovah Nissi*—"the Lord is my Banner" (Exodus 17). They forgot that God is the one who goes before His people in the face of difficulty. God led the people through the wilderness in a pillar of cloud by day and a pillar of fire by night. He went before them, the banner of their defense. The people walked behind, bearing the name of their defense. King Saul and the camp of Israel forgot this promise as they cowered at the insults of the unrepentant. How often does this happen to us? We forget who we are in the eyes of God. We forget that He goes before us, leading and preparing the way. We, too, fall to the insults of this world far too easily. We fall to the pressures of conformity. We neglect our calling. We choose to forget that God calls us His priesthood, His chosen people. So we shrink away from responsibility. Fortunately, the Lord gives us the rest of the story carried out by His servant David. Samuel records the events this way:

Now David was the son of an Ephrathite named Jesse, who was from Bethlehem in Judah. Jesse had eight sons, and in Saul's time he was very old. Jesse's three oldest sons had followed Saul to the war: The firstborn was Eliab; the second, Abinadab; and the third, Shammah. David was the youngest. The three oldest followed Saul, but David went back and forth from Saul to tend his father's sheep at Bethlehem.

For forty days the Philistine came forward every morning and evening and took his stand.

Now Jesse said to his son David, "Take this ephah of roasted grain and these ten loaves of bread for your brothers and hurry to their camp. Take along these ten cheeses to the commander of their unit. See how your brothers are and bring back some assurance from them. They are with Saul and all the men of Israel in the Valley of Elah, fighting against the Philistines."

Early in the morning David left the flock in the care of a shepherd, loaded up and set out, as Jesse had directed. He reached the camp as the army was going out to its battle positions, shouting the war cry. Israel and the Philistines were drawing up their lines facing each other. David left his things with the keeper of supplies, ran to the battle lines and asked his brothers how they were. As he was talking with them, Goliath, the Philistine champion from Gath, stepped out from his lines and shouted his usual defiance, and David heard it. Whenever the Israelites saw the man, they all fled from him in great fear.

Now the Israelites had been saying, "Do you see how this man keeps coming out? He comes out to defy Israel. The king will give great wealth to the man who kills him. He will also give him his daughter in marriage and will exempt his family from taxes in Israel."

David asked the men standing near him, "What will be done for the man who kills this Philistine and removes this disgrace from Israel? Who is this uncircumcised Philistine that he should defy the armies of the living God?" (1 Samuel 17:12–26)

David recognized that Goliath stood against the armies of God. David recognized that Goliath profaned the holiness of God Himself through the blasphemous actions against the people of God. David chose to take action. He chose to stand in defense of the name of the Lord. David remembered his responsibility as a servant of the Lord. Not only this, David remembered the Lord as *Jehovah Nissi*. David knew God would go with him in battle. The Lord Himself would be David's strength and ever-present help (Psalm 46:1). David responded to the giant who defies the very name of the Lord.

David said to Saul, "Let no one lose heart on account of this Philistine; your servant will go and fight him."

Saul replied, "You are not able to go out against this Philistine and fight him; you are only a young man, and he has been a warrior from his youth."

But David said to Saul, "Your servant has been keeping his father's sheep. When a lion or a bear came and carried off a sheep from the flock, I went after it, struck it and rescued the sheep from its mouth. When it turned on me, I seized it by its hair, struck it and killed it. Your servant has killed both the lion and the bear; this uncircumcised Philistine will be like one of them, because he has defied the armies of the living God. The Lord who rescued me from the paw of the lion and the paw of the bear will rescue me from the hand of this Philistine."

Saul said to David, "Go, and the Lord be with you."

Then Saul dressed David in his own tunic. He put a coat of armor on him and a bronze helmet on his head. David fastened on his sword over the tunic and tried walking around, because he was not used to them.

"I cannot go in these," he said to Saul, "because I am not used to them." So he took them off. Then he took his staff in his hand, chose five smooth stones from the stream, put them in the pouch of his shepherd's bag and, with his sling in his hand, approached the Philistine.

Meanwhile, the Philistine, with his shield bearer in front of him, kept coming closer to David. He looked David over and saw that he was little more than a boy, glowing with health and handsome, and he despised him. He said to David, "Am I a dog, that you come at me with sticks?" And the Philistine cursed David by his gods. "Come here," he said, "and I'll give your flesh to the birds and the wild animals!"

David said to the Philistine, "You come against me with sword and spear and javelin, but I come against you in the name of the Lord Almighty, the God of the armies of Israel, whom you have defied. This day the Lord will deliver you into my hands, and I'll strike you down and cut off your head. This very day I will give the carcasses of the Philistine army to the birds and the wild animals, and the whole world will know that there is a God in Israel. All those gathered here will know that it is not by sword or spear that the Lord saves; for the battle is the Lord's, and he will give all of you into our hands."

As the Philistine moved closer to attack him, David ran quickly toward the battle line to meet him. Reaching into his bag and taking out a stone, he slung it and struck the Philistine on the forehead. The stone sank into his forehead, and he fell face down on the ground.

So David triumphed over the Philistine with a sling and a stone; without a sword in his hand he struck down the Philistine and killed him.

David ran and stood over him. He took hold of the Philistine's sword and drew it from the sheath. After he killed him, he cut off his head with the sword.

David had confidence that the Lord would deliver him. David possessed this confidence because the Lord defended him in the past. David knew God would honor those who take their stand in defense of His good name. The accusation against the giant was: "He has defied the armies of the living God" (1 Samuel 17:36). Because the giant stood against the authority of God, he would fall. David chose to stand in the authority of the Lord and levy the Lord's will. David chose to walk in his purpose, defending the name of the Lord for the preservation of those who are of worth. Those of worth are God's people. But not only are they God's people, those of worth are all who will be given opportunity to hear the message of salvation because of the diligence of God's people to profess truth. David acted in preservation of the saints for the glory of God so His Word could be carried forth.

Upon confronting the giant, David proclaimed the folly of Goliath's tongue. David declared judgment against the giant. David declares that he will stand against the enemy of God because, "I come against you in the name of the Lord Almighty, the God of the armies of Israel, whom you have defied" (1 Samuel 17:45). Goliath defiled the purity of God's name. In response, David acted:

As the Philistine moved closer to attack him, David ran quickly toward the battle line to meet him. Reaching into his bag and taking out a stone, he slung it and struck the Philistine on the forehead. The stone sank into his forehead, and he fell face down on the ground. (1 Samuel 17:48–49)

The giant moved to attack and David ran. David ran straight at this giant. David ran to confront the enemy of God. David ran. He did not cower. He did not hide. He did not make excuses to avoid the conflict. He ran. He ran straight at the enemy, striking him down in defense of God's holy name. David ran, his face set like flint, bound and determined to represent the authority of God in the face of trial. David, by God's provision, has given all of us encouragement as to how we should respond.

We too shall run. We too shall bear His name *in valor*, defending those who come after. Our purpose is to bear His name with integrity. I remind you of the words from the prophet Jeremiah:

"Behold, I am going to send for many fishermen," declares the Lord, "and they will fish for them; and afterwards I will send for many hunters, and they will hunt them from every mountain and every hill and from the clefts of the rocks. For My eyes are on all their ways; they are not hidden from My face, nor is their iniquity concealed from My eyes. I will first doubly repay their iniquity and their sin, because they have polluted My land; they have filled My inheritance with the carcasses of their detestable idols and with their abominations." (Jeremiah 16:12–18)

God has sent out the fishermen. He continues to send them forth. They are to carry out the message of salvation, delivering from death those who choose to receive the message. But the Lord declares that "afterwards" He will send out hunters. We live in the "afterwards." We live in the age when God is revealing sin and calling for a people who will eradicate sin from the camp indiscriminately. No longer can we allow the people to comingle with death. No longer can we tolerate unrepentant sin in the camp. The enemy seeks to infiltrate the camp through deception, conformity, and contentment with the deception found in secular culture.

No longer can this be allowed to take place. The hunters are to seek out sin, reveal it for what it is, and pray that the Lord remove it from the camp and the heart of His people. The hunters run to meet the challenge of the day. The hunters do not cower in fear of what the enemy blasphemes about them or about the Lord. The hunters run to eradicate the enemy through the power of His Holy Spirit dwelling in us. The hunters find hope in the knowledge that God goes before them. God, Himself, is their banner. The battle is His, and the battle has already been won. Stand in the confidence of salvation. Stand in the hope of His name. God can work with those who are repentant for their mistakes. God cannot work with those who are unrepentant and refuse to soften their hearts toward healing. Allow the Lord to work in your heart to draw you closer to Him.

13

"NO GREATER VALOR"

Defend your faith. Defend the name of your Lord by standing firm on His Word. *For valor*, defend the faith for those of worth. That statement serves as the title for this work. It came to me as I was listening to a dear friend and fellow warrior in Christ speak at a conference I was attending. Bishop Edwin Felicie is a colleague whom I have had the pleasure of hearing speak at numerous events. He has proven to be a warrior for Christ and a compassionate brother in the Lord. I must give Bishop Edwin at least partial credit for inspiring the title of this writing to be developed. It was through a sermon presented by Edwin, titled "No Greater Valor," that the Lord gave me a title and a focus for this writing (the sermon is available to view by following the link provided in the endnote). At the time I heard this message from Edwin, I was congealing my thoughts for the work you are currently reading. The sermon given by Edwin as he was inspired by the Lord in turn gave me a title and a focus for the conclusion of this writing. I owe a debt of gratitude to Edwin for his willingness to hear from the Lord and share what God has given him. I now offer a brief introduction to Bishop Edwin and a summary of his sermon in order to collate the premises that were presented with this writing.

Bishop Edwin served in United States Army from 1977 to 1981. He was discharged honorably. During his service, Edwin attended Airborne School at Fort Benning, Georgia. He was also honored to serve in the

Second Infantry Division. I thank Edwin for his service to our country. Bishop Edwin began his sermon, "No Greater Valor," by sharing the "Soldier's Creed." The creed reads as follows:

I am an American soldier. I am a warrior and member of a team. I serve the people of the United States, and live the army values. I will always place the mission first. I will never accept defeat. I will never quit. I will never leave a fallen comrade. I am disciplined, physically and mentally tough, trained and proficient in my warrior tasks and drills. I will maintain my arms, my equipment and myself. I am an expert and I am a professional. I stand ready to deploy, engage, and destroy the enemies of the United States of America in close combat. I am a guardian of freedom and the American way of life. I am an American soldier.

These words, while written as a creed taken by those who enter military service, can be claimed, in part, by those who enter faith in our Messiah. Let me explain. When we claim Jesus as our Savior, we enter His service. We become His priesthood, as we discussed earlier. We become His representatives, bearing His name as we walk out the path of faith. We, similarly to this creed of a military warrior, become a soldier for Christ engaged in a spiritual war (Ephesians 6:12). We are a member of a team, the Body of Christ (1 Corinthians 12:27). The mission of the Lord in the proclamation of His gospel is the primary objective (Matthew 28:16–20). In this battle to proclaim truth in a world afflicted by chaos, we can never accept defeat. We must always strive to be a living testimony of truth (Galatians 6:9–10). We are to continually pray for those who are lost in an effort to open their eyes to receive grace, never leaving them to fall (Acts 26:16–18). We are to be disciplined by the Word of truth, champions of Christ finding victory in His deliverance (Proverbs 4:20–27). At all times we bear the armor of God, at the ready to stand firm in faith (Ephesians 6:10–18). We are guardians of His truth (Jude 1:3). We are a chosen people, a people of God's own possession, His royal priesthood (Exodus

19). We are His. Because we are His, we are to contend for our faith. *For valor*, for those of worth, we defend the truth in the face of our enemies.

The sermon continues by picking up this very point. Bishop Edwin points out the directive of Paul toward Timothy: "12 Fight the good fight of faith; take hold of the eternal life to which you were called, and you made the good confession in the presence of many witnesses" (1 Timothy 6:12). The term "fight" in this context is taken from the Greek ἀγωνίζομαι (G75- *agonizomai*). This word means "to contend, to endeavor with zeal, fight, to contend with adversaries." Edwin points out during his message that "it seems based on what the Apostle Paul wrote we must engage the wrong that is being done to the right."[153] As the people of God, we are called to contend for our faith. We are to fight for what is right, pushing back those who strike out against the truth of the Word. We have the authority, given to us through our Messiah, to stand our ground for the sake of His name, to contend for His truth.

The Church has been far too passive in light of the attacks from the enemy. We have willingly given up far too much ground in this spiritual battle. We have mistakenly adopted the phrase "turn the other cheek" (Matthew 5:39), applying it to mean that we, as the Church, must turn a blind eye toward deception. We are to keep quiet in our comfortable little gatherings and pray that the enemy pays us no attention. I admit that this is a noble prayer. We should never seek to confront the enemy head on. This is the task of Jesus, Himself. We should be praying for the freedom to continue to worship in peace. We must pray that the hand of the Lord protects us. In the effort to remain faithful, pray that He empowers us to endure trial. Stand behind your savior as He fights the battle for us. But in the spiritual battle, we cannot have a spirit of fear, but of confidence in His power, because we have been disciplined by His Word (2 Timothy 1:7). The phrase "turn the other cheek" serves as a reminder of the power of His sacrifice. Remember, Jesus set His face like flint. He was determined to carry out the purpose of His coming. Our Savior knew He would be struck. He knew the blows against Him would be the catalyst to ignite the fire of salvation in the hearts of mankind. He knew this, so He turned

His cheek. He turned His face of flint toward the enemy to be struck by the feeble blows of a defeated giant flailing to remain vibrant in the fight. Our efforts to remain faithful to Jesus will cause us to be struck; know this. The enemy will try to tear you down. He will try to bring chaos into your house and into your heart. Like Jesus, who set His face like flint, turning the other cheek to allow the blow of His enemy to cause glory to rain down from Heaven, endure trial, brothers and sisters, for His glory! **Set your face like flint, resolute to stand firmly in your faith for the exaltation of your Savior.** Pray that Jesus gives you the strength to know He is always with you; no one is able to take you from His mighty hand (John 10:25–30). Fight for what is right; fight for your faith. For your faith is not only yours. Your faith is the faith of all those whom you have the opportunity to influence. Your faith is for those who come after you. Your faith is a monument of God's mercy. **Be strong in faith, for those of worth, our children.**

Bishop Edwin continues in his sermon to recall the lives of many men and women who served during World War II. He talks about the hardships of this war and the extreme difficulty our soldiers had to endure to fight for freedom. Edwin goes into detail about a few service men and women who laid down their lives *for valor*. Many of the individuals Edwin spoke about served as chaplains dedicated to protecting the hope of God through their efforts to serve mankind. Edwin goes on to speak about the term "valor" and what it means be a man or woman of valor.

Bishop Edwin points out that the Hebrew word translated as "valor" is חַיִל (H2428- *khah'-yil*). This word means "strength, might, efficiency, ability, army." Those of valor possess strength to carry out the purpose of their lives with efficiency, ability, and might. The people of God are a people of valor through Jesus, who strengthens us. We are given and called to walk out the testimony of faith in our lives for the expression of grace to the world. Edwin points out the definition of "valor" in the English, which carries the connotation of worth or worthiness, courage, fearlessness. Edwin describes the sense *for valor* of those who fought for freedom during WWII. Many people laid down their lives *for valor*. They saw the worth of those they were protecting. The found the fight to be worthy because they protected the lives of others. Edwin explains that this is the attitude of those who serve in the military. They serve *for valor*. They serve because they see the worth of those whom they are protecting. They place themselves in harm's way to preserve the lives of those of worth. It is an honorable decision, and I thank our veterans and active military personnel for their dedication.

Jesus walked in valor. He saw the worth of His children. He loves us so much that He laid His life down to deliver us from sin and death. His sacrifice brought victory over the chaos that afflicts us. His death and resurrection grant us the gift of eternal life in His Kingdom. *For valor*, our Savior chose to endure unspeakable suffering because you are of worth. Do you stand in valor? Do you defend the faith to preserve those of worth? It is *for valor* that God calls us. He is calling for men and women to walk in valor this day and in this hour. He is calling for a people who are willing to fight for the faith of those who are yet to come. Fight for those of worth, our children. The faith we profess is the faith that we must pass down to our children. It is for this reason, and this reason alone, that I write. Our children are of worth. Our children are worth fighting for. I will not turn a blind eye to deception, pretending that if I do not admit deception is there, then it will have no effect. I will not cast my children to the wolves of this world without offering them tools of defense. I will not allow chaos to reign in my home. Our God is a God of order. He spoke order over chaos during the Creation (Genesis 1). God, through the impartation of His Holy Spirit dwelling in our hearts, gives us the authority to speak order over chaos as well. We do not have to allow the demands of a sinful culture gain influence over our children. We have His authority to stand and fight. We have His authority to shut the mouths of liars, thieves, and the vilest of predators who prey on the purity of our children. *For valor*, defend the faith for those of worth. The head of chaos has been crushed under the mighty power of our Savior, Jesus. To God be the glory, forever and ever!

Yet, even while this truth resounds in my heart, there are many people of faith who forget their purpose. So many choose to relinquish their authority in God. They give themselves over to complacency because they find it more comfortable to sinbathe under the shadow of chaos. Brothers and sisters, no longer can we regress to be content in this attitude. The days in which we live are dire. We must stand in our authority as children of God to express His light in a world that is racing toward darkness. This is the hope we can offer the lost. This is the hope we can provide the hopeless. This world offers no hope; it only offers increased confusion. I challenge you, therefore, to take your stand.

Stones of Remembrance

I remind you of an account found in the book of Joshua wherein the people of God were instructed to cross over the Jordan River to enter the land of promise. I want to take a moment to discuss this event, because it offers us insight into how we are to function as the people of God who offer hope in faith to others.

Then Joshua rose early in the morning; and he and all the sons of Israel set out from Shittim and came to the Jordan, and they lodged there before they crossed. At the end of three days the officers went through the midst of the camp; and they commanded the people, saying, "When you see the ark of the covenant of the Lord your God with the Levitical priests carrying it, then you shall set out from your place and go after it. However, there shall be between you and it a distance of about 2,000 cubits by measure. Do not come near it, that you may know the way by which you shall go, for you have not passed this way before."

Then Joshua said to the people, "Consecrate yourselves, for tomorrow the Lord will do wonders among you." And Joshua spoke to the priests, saying, "Take up the ark of the covenant and cross over ahead of the people." So they took up the ark of the covenant and went ahead of the people.

Now the Lord said to Joshua, "This day I will begin to exalt you in the sight of all Israel, that they may know that just as I have been with Moses, I will be with you. You shall, moreover, command the priests who are carrying the ark of the covenant, saying, 'When you come to the edge of the waters of the Jordan, you shall stand still in the Jordan.'" Then Joshua said to the sons of Israel, "Come here, and hear the words of the Lord your God." Joshua said, "By this you shall know that the living God is among you, and that He will assuredly dispossess from before you the Canaanite, the Hittite, the Hivite, the Perizzite, the Girgashite, the Amorite, and the Jebusite. Behold, the ark of the covenant of the Lord of all the earth is crossing over ahead of you into the Jordan. Now then, take for yourselves twelve men from the tribes of Israel, one man for each tribe. It shall come about when the soles of the feet of the priests who carry the ark of the Lord, the Lord of all the earth, rest in the waters of the Jordan, the waters of the Jordan will be cut off, and the waters which are flowing down from above will stand in one heap."

So when the people set out from their tents to cross the Jordan with the priests carrying the ark of the covenant before the people, and when those who carried the ark came into the Jordan, and the feet of the priests carrying the ark were dipped in the edge of the water (for the Jordan overflows all its banks all the days of harvest), the waters which were flowing down from above stood and rose up in one heap, a great distance away at Adam, the city that is beside Zarethan; and those which were flowing down toward the sea of the Arabah, the Salt Sea, were completely cut off. So the people crossed opposite Jericho. And the priests who carried the ark of the covenant of the Lord stood firm on dry ground in the middle of the Jordan while all Israel crossed on dry ground, until all the nation had finished crossing the Jordan. (Joshua 3:1–17)

The Lord instructed the people to cross the Jordan River leading into His promised land. The Levitical priests were to lead the march. As the priesthood, they set the example for others. They heard from the voice of God and responded in obedience to His call. The priests were charged with carrying the Ark of the Covenant before the people. The Ark of the Covenant represented God's eternal promises to His people. The covenant was given as an eternal reminder of God's mercy toward those who are His. The Word and the Lord went forth, leading those who were willing to follow. When the feet of the priests who carried the Ark entered into the waters of the Jordan, the waters stopped. The waters flowing from the north stood up in a heap. God parted the waters, again, so that His people could cross on dry ground. The priests took their stand in the middle of the Jordan as the rest of the camp passed through into the promise. What an amazing account of God's miraculous provision for His people.

The account of the Jordan crossing continues in the book of Joshua:

Now when all the nation had finished crossing the Jordan, the Lord spoke to Joshua, saying, "Take for yourselves twelve men from the people, one man from each tribe, and command them, saying, 'Take up for yourselves twelve stones from here out of the middle of the Jordan, from the place where the priests' feet are standing firm, and carry them over with you and lay them down in the lodging place where you will lodge tonight.'" So Joshua called the twelve men whom he had appointed from the sons of Israel, one man from each tribe; and Joshua said to them, "Cross again to the ark of the Lord your God into the middle of the Jordan, and each of you take up a stone on his shoulder, according to the number of the tribes of the sons of Israel. Let this be a sign among you, so that when your children ask later, saying, 'What do these stones mean to you?' then you shall say to them, 'Because the waters of the Jordan were cut off before the ark of the covenant of the Lord; when it crossed the Jordan, the waters of the Jordan were cut off.' So these stones shall become a memorial to the sons of Israel forever."

Thus the sons of Israel did as Joshua commanded, and took up twelve stones from the middle of the Jordan, just as the Lord spoke to Joshua, according to the number of the tribes of the sons of Israel; and they carried them over with them to the lodging place and put them down there. Then Joshua set up twelve stones in the middle of the Jordan at the place where the feet of the priests who carried the ark of the covenant were standing, and they are there to this day. (Joshua 4:1–9)

After the nation crossed into the land of promise, the Lord instructed Joshua to take up stones. These stones were to be set up in the camp. They were also to be set up in the middle of the Jordan, where the Ark of the Covenant had stood as the people crossed. These instructions given by God offer insight into how to actively defend our faith.

The stones God instructed the people to set up are referred to as a "sign among you" (Joshua 4:6). The word in the Hebrew translated as "sign" is אוֹת (H226-'ôt) meaning: "**sign**, mark, a non-verbal symbol or signal which has meaning, either as a crafted, or natural object, **banner**, standard, flag, **miracle**, wonder, sign, a mighty act of God which gives a message of wonder or terror, **example**."[154] The stones served as "a memorial to the sons of Israel forever" (Joshua 4:7). The people were to look upon the stones and remember what the Lord had done for them through this miraculous deliverance from the wilderness into the promise. The stones were a sign, mark, symbol, and banner declaring the wonder of an Almighty God as He pours out His grace upon those who are willing to follow. They were meant to remind the people of who they were in the midst of God's presence. The stones of remembrance served as stones to mark deliverance through faith. The stones marked the trust of the people in the provision of God. The Lord did not want them to forget their trust. They Lord instructed them to place these physical markers to serve as a reminder of His love for them. The Lord and only the Lord is the provider, sustainer, and banner of hope.

The Lord Our Banner

I am reminded of the account in the book of Exodus when Amalek came up against the people of Israel at Rephidim:

Then Amalek came and fought against Israel at Rephidim.

So Moses said to Joshua, "Choose men for us and go out, fight against Amalek. Tomorrow I will station myself on the top of the hill with the staff of God in my hand."

Joshua did as Moses told him, and fought against Amalek; and Moses, Aaron, and Hur went up to the top of the hill.

So it came about when Moses held his hand up, that Israel prevailed, and when he let his hand down, Amalek prevailed.

But Moses' hands were heavy. Then they took a stone and put it under him, and he sat on it; and Aaron and Hur supported his hands, one on one side and one on the other. Thus his hands were steady until the sun set.

So Joshua overwhelmed Amalek and his people with the edge of the sword.

Then the Lord said to Moses, "Write this in a book as a memorial and recite it to Joshua, that I will utterly blot out the memory of Amalek from under heaven."

Moses built an altar and named it The Lord is My Banner;

and he said, "The Lord has sworn; the Lord will have war against Amalek from generation to generation."[155]

Moses built an altar, naming it נִסִּי יְהוָה (H3071- *Jehovah Nissi*): "the Lord is my Banner." The Lord is to be lifted up as the sign or rallying point for the camp. The Lord is the identity, standard, or ensign of the soldiers under which they fight. The Lord goes before His people, a banner of truth declaring victory for those who follow. This is why this name of God was so significant to Moses. It was significant because of the grace of the Lord who delivered them from plight.

It is under this name that we fight. He is our banner, delivering us from the hands of our enemy. His name strikes terror in the hearts of those who position themselves as enemies of God. Our hope and refuge is in His great name. This is why it is vital that we, as God's people, remember what He has done for us. Like those stones of remembrance set up by the camp of Israel at the Jordan, we must set up stones of remembrance for ourselves and for our children. The Lord is our banner. He goes before us, fighting the battle, and brings victory to His people. It is our responsibility to lift our banner, exalting His name as the only source of consistency in an ever-changing world. He is our God. He is life and light and in Him is hope. We are His priesthood of believers carrying forth the Word of truth.

We must erect stones of remembrance to pass on the knowledge of God to those who follow after. The height of our calling as His people is to be witnesses of His glory to others. The task of believers is to demonstrate the power of God through the testimony of deliverance. We are set free of the bondage of the sin nature because of the sacrifice of our Great King, Jesus the Messiah! A great miracle is that of freedom from the slavery of the flesh. As His people, we must be living examples of this miracle. We are to set up stones or monuments in our lives so that we can talk about them with our children. Like Israel on the banks of the Jordan, or Moses on the hills at Rephidim, we must set up memorials to the great mercy of God; we too must remember. We are to remember His sacrifice leading to our deliverance. We must remember that He fought to win us back from captivity of the enemy. He is victorious; therefore, remember. Remember who you were before you were saved. Remember who you are now after coming to know salvation. Remember the Words that the Lord, Himself, speaks over you as a promise regarding who He sees you as, not as you see yourself. He sees you as His. In faith we are made complete, perfect, and restored through the blood of the Lamb. He does not see you in your failings; He sees you as His very own possession. Rejoice and remember that you are found chosen, set apart to be one of His own people. Therefore, exalt His name. Tell your children and those who come after you of the great provision of our King! Remember, lest you forget.

14

RESTORING THE MIRROR OF GOD ALMIGHTY!

Regarding remembering, A. W. Tozer, in his book *The Purpose of Man*, comments on the state of the Church in modernity. He writes:

> People do not know where they are, they do not know where they have been, they do not know why they are here, they do not know where they are going; and they do the whole thing on borrowed time, borrowed money, borrowed thinking, and the they die.[156]

The Church has lost its way. We have drifted far from the foundation of God's Word and allowed the culture to exert influence over what should be pure, holy, and distinct. As I have written earlier, there are so many avenues the enemy uses to attempt to deceive the people of God. As the writer of the book of Hebrews encourages, we must, as His people:

> ...lay aside every encumbrance and the sin which so easily entangles us, and let us run with endurance the race that is set before us, fixing our eyes on Jesus, the author and perfecter of faith, who for the joy set before Him endured the cross, despising the shame, and has sat down at the right hand of the throne of God. For consider Him who has endured such hostility by sinners

against Himself, so that you will not grow weary and lose heart. (Hebrews 12:1–3).[157]

This is the purpose of man: to run with endurance, enlivened by His Spirit, and to proclaim "good news to the afflicted; liberty to captives, freedom to prisoners and to comfort all who mourn."[158] We are to walk in the authority given us through our Savior, pushing back the evil spiritual influences that attempt to destroy hope. We do this by His strength, for His glory. We do this to preserve faith for those of worth, *for valor*. All of us who come to faith in salvation are given this purpose. Tozer offers these beautiful words as encouragement to take faith seriously. He wrote, "Man is the darling of the universe, the centerpiece of God's affection."[159] We are His joy, the joy set before Him as He looked down from the cross, blood stains on His face of flint—joy. He endured unspeakable ridicule, pain, and death for you. Rising again from the grave by His own power for you. For us, for His people, for joy He endured the cross. Our purpose is to be His, a testimony of mercy, each with a unique purpose in His Kingdom. Tozer continues: "You are a mirror of the Almighty, and this is the reason you were created in the first place. This is your purpose."[160] God imparted in all those of faith a special, essential, divine purpose, one founded on worship and reverence for our King. We carry this purpose into the world, establishing a fortification of holiness set apart from chaos. We exert the influence of His Kingdom over darkness. We are a people of God's own design, serving His purpose to be a light to this world (Matthew 5:14). Our purpose is to worship our Savior, to sing praises of hope, songs of true love. We must, as Tozer explains, "reflect back to God His own glory"[161] through the Holy Spirit. In obedience, because He first loved us, we must praise His name. It is in our reverence for a Holy God that we will begin to establish stones of remembrance to represent eternal markers of hope in the hearts of mankind. Tozer writes of a time when the Church was filled in jubilant splendor because they chose to remember God: "The church Militant conquered the world with their joyous religion because and only because they were worshippers."[162] They knew their purpose. They remembered the name of their Savior. They walked under the banner of His provision. They stood, as the priesthood of flint, called to defend faith for the preservation of the saints. They filled their hearts and their minds with things above (Colossians 3:2). Tozer comments on the condition of the human soul, suggesting: "The human soul is a vacuum, and we have filled it with trash."[163] I do not want to belabor this subject, but we all know we have fallen short of our purpose. We have allowed chaos to strike fear in the hearts of those who should walk in victory. We have filled our souls with things that are profane for far too long. It is time to take out the trash. It is time to clean house and repent , returning to the Lord in reverence. The Lord calls for revival. The Lord calls for purity in the hearts of humanity. We must respond. We must allow Him to restore our purpose as His mirrors of reflection. **For hope, for truth, and for our children we are to walk with determined integrity as mirrors of the Almighty. For valor, defend your faith for those of worth.**

The Zeal of Phineas

The Lord calls forth for a people of valor to walk in defense of holiness, to ascend the mountain and stand in faith alongside of the Lord, our hope. In the book of Numbers, we have an account of Phineas, a man of valor because he was zealous for the Lord. In chapter 25 of this book, Israel was camped in the region of Shittim. While the people camped there, Balak, king of Moab, enlisted the help of Balaam the seer in an attempt to curse the people of Israel. The curse, however, turned into a blessing as the Lord declared to deliver His people even through the mouth of this false prophet. Unfortunately, although the curse against Israel resulted in a blessing, the enemy of God's people continued to prey on the weakness of human flesh. The enemy of God was unrelenting in his pursuit to bring corruption to the camp. The text tells us that "the people began to play the harlot with the daughters of Moab. For they invited the people to the sacrifices of their gods, and the people ate and bowed down to their gods. So Israel joined themselves to Baal of Peor, and the Lord was angry against Israel" (Numbers 25:1–3).[164] Israel engaged in harlotry with the daughters of Moab. The sin of the flesh led them to be deceived further through participation in pagan sacrificial rituals. Because the people chose to fall victim to temptation, the Lord's anger burned against them. God was angry with the people because, through their participation in idolatry, they tied themselves to Baal of Peor (Numbers 25:2). Israel chose to ignore God's standard, seeking rather to neglect holiness in exchange for carnality.

Baal Peor is a Moabite deity. The Israelites were enticed to worship this false god when they had illicit sexual relations with Moabite women. "Baal" is a term meaning "owner, possessor, master, one who owns possessions, and controls the movement and/or activities of them, either inanimate or animate, including animals."[165] This is a term of Semitic origin applied to a number of varying pagan deities. The term connotes slavery to this god. The worship of Baal pervaded the region of Canaan. Iterations of Baal worship are found throughout the biblical text. When Israel succumbed to the worship of this god through lustful enticements, they rejected the purity of God for the slavery of sin. They fell victim to the false promises of this deity, shackling themselves to carnality. In their unfaithfulness to God, they chose subjugation to sinful desire. They turned their backs on deliverance, returning to enslavement. Baal is a god who deceives people into choosing slavery, willingly.

Baal (master/owner), god of Peor, is the designation identifying this iteration of Baal in the account found in Numbers. The term "Peor" signifies the region in which this god was worshipped. Peor is thought to signify a high mountain, possibly near Mount Nebo (Deuteronomy 4:3; Hosea 9:10+)[166] where this false god was venerated. The root of the term "Peor" is the Hebrew פָּעַר (H6473- pā· ʿăr), "meaning open wide."[167] Additionally, Gesenius' *Hebrew-Chaldee Lexicon* suggests the term also means to possess a wide gape as done by ravenous beasts.[168] Baal of Peor, a god possessing a gaping maw. A ravenous god that consumes its victims unreservedly. A god of lust and carnality. A god who salivates at the thought of bringing unto itself victims who have chosen to become slaves to what it falsely promises. Baal's adherents, slaves by choice, slaves of sin. This god, a master of lies and deceit, owning those who allow themselves to be enticed by deception. Baal of Peor, god of the open mouth, speaks violence and torment to deceive even those who have experienced freedom in deliverance by God, Almighty. How quickly the people turned from God to revel in the profanity offered by Baal. What power the flesh gives this false deity: to allow the lies spoken by the tongue of deceit to tempt one away from the only source of hope. Iniquity, unrepentant sin, taking root in the heart is the catalyst driving mankind to be given over to this vile demon. Baal is a god who brings chaos.

Chaos, disorder, and utter confusion are the antithesis of God. Chaos is the result of rebellion against the God of order. Chaos is a demon born out of the Fall from God's eternal Kingdom. In the Greek language, the term "chaos," ςοάχ (kʰá.os) means "gape, yawn, chasm or yawning space."[169] Chaos is used in Greek mythology to represent a place of emptiness, outer darkness, an abyss, or a place of gloom deep within the earth.[170] The term is also used to describe a primordial goddess preceding all of creation.[171] Myth surrounding the goddess suggests that she is the progenitor from which other gods of the Greek pantheon originate; gods such as Tartaros (the pit beneath the earth), Eros (love), Erebos (darkness) and Nyx (night) can be traced in origin to chaos.[172] The goddess Chaos is personified initially in the cosmology of Hesiod. Chaos is the personification of murky gloom and darkness.[173] Later authors suggest Chaos is connected with "the bad Demiurge,"[174] the Demiurge being "one of the forces of evil, who was responsible for the creation of the despised material world and was wholly alien to the supreme God of goodness."[175] In the biblical canon, chaos takes on numerous iterations.

> Throughout the Scriptures chaos is personified as the principal opponent of God. In ancient Semitic legends, a terrible chaos-monster was called Rahab (the proud one), or Leviathan (the twisting dragon-creature), or Yam (the roaring sea).[176]

Chaos, displaying its gaping maw of utter darkness, whispers deceit from the tree. Chaos is the lullaby we listen to on salvation's side of the glass divide. It is the lullaby that enthralls us to press our faces against the cold surface of the glass, yearning, in our fleshly selves, to fall into the abyss.

The voice of chaos lured even Solomon himself to depart from the knowledge of God:

> For when Solomon was old, his wives turned his heart away after other gods; and his heart was not wholly devoted to the LORD his God, as the heart of David his father had been.[177]

Solomon died a man of divided heart. He neglected to turn whole-heartedly toward God. Solomon clung to the promises of chaos found in lustful desire. Solomon erected idols to the desires of his flesh. He built an idol on the mountain east of Jerusalem to appease the voice of chaos ringing in his ears.

> Then Solomon built a high place for Chemosh the detestable idol of Moab, on the mountain which is east of Jerusalem, and for Molech the detestable idol of the sons of Ammon.[178]

Chemosh, a Moabite god is a god who conquers, demanding sub-mission. Chemosh is a god who dared to be venerated on the Mount of Olives, the mountain where Jesus spent His last hours in prayer, sweating blood under the thought of the cross (Luke 22:44). At Gethsemane once stood an idol dedicated to a god of calamity. Across from the Temple Mount, in the face of God Almighty, chaos.

How audacious can the enemies of God be? A prideful disrespect for purity is the language of their native tongue. Gods of unreserved pride, they are. Those who bow to these false gods of chaos, bound to pridefulness, become hopeless slaves to a god who possesses an insatiable appetite. Chaos will be unrelenting in its attempt to draw as many victims as possible to be lost to the abyss. What hope is there for deliverance if the voice of deception permeates our thoughts so readily?

Our hope is in He who divided the mountain under the weight of His foot:

> Then the LORD will go forth and fight against those nations, as when He fights on a day of battle.
>
> In that day His feet will stand on the Mount of Olives, which is in front of Jerusalem on the east; and the Mount of Olives will be split in its middle from east to west by a very large valley, so that half of the mountain will move toward the north and the other half toward the south. (Zechariah 14:3–4)[179]

Our hope is in our Lord Jesus, who goes before us fighting against our enemies. Our hope is in Messiah, who—by the mere fact of His presence—splits the profane asunder. Our hope is in He who will come on the clouds, in the midst of chaos, and establish an everlasting dominion. He is one that will have no end (Daniel 7). He will not be thwarted in His determination to stand as our Eternal King. Jesus is our strength, deliverer, and hope in all things (Isaiah 41:10; Psalm 62:7–8; John 16:33). He has overcome by His sacrifice. He is victorious through the power of the resurrection. He is King, awaiting His triumphal return. Fear not, though the world seems dark. We look forward to a day when the heavens will be peeled away; the sun, moon, and stars will be darkened because the light of His glory will be made known:

> But immediately after the tribulation of those days the sun will be darkened, and the moon will not give its light, and the stars will fall from the sky, and the powers of the heavens will be shaken.
>
> And then the sign of the Son of Man will appear in the sky, and then all the tribes of the earth will mourn, and they will see

the Son of Man coming on the clouds of the sky with power and great glory.

And He will send forth His angels with a great trumpet and they will gather together His elect from the four winds, from one end of the sky to the other. (Matthew 24:29–31)[180]

In the meantime, as we await the return of our King, hold the line. Stand firm in faith; be strong (1 Corinthians 16:13), for God Himself dwells in our hearts (John 14:26; 2 Timothy 1:14). Choose victory in Christ every day. The Lord goes before us, fighting against our enemy to save us (Deuteronomy 20:4). Identify deception. Turn a deaf ear to the whispers from the tree. Be alert for schemes to cause the brethren to stumble (Galatians 6). **Cast out sin, unrelentingly. Be unyielding in your determination to reject temptation.** No longer can we allow the profane to dwell among the holy. We are set apart as His precious possession (Exodus 19:5; 1 Peter 2:9). Be determined, you who are a priesthood of flint, to fix your eyes upon your King. **Take up your arms in the war of faith and stand in defense of truth.** *For valor,* **defend the faith for the sake of those of worth.**

In closing, I remind you of Phinehas. He was a man of valor, a man who sought out sin in the camp and eradicated its influence indiscriminately. Phinehas, a priest unto the Lord, was found among the camp as they fell victim to Baal Peor, the god of the open mouth, chaos yawning. I direct you back to the book of Numbers, where we left off just a moment ago:

While Israel remained at Shittim, the people began to play the harlot with the daughters of Moab.

For they invited the people to the sacrifices of their gods, and the people ate and bowed down to their gods.

So Israel joined themselves to Baal of Peor, and the LORD was angry against Israel.

The LORD said to Moses, "Take all the leaders of the people and execute them in broad daylight before the LORD, so that the fierce anger of the LORD may turn away from Israel."

So Moses said to the judges of Israel, "Each of you slay his men who have joined themselves to Baal of Peor."

Then behold, one of the sons of Israel came and brought to his relatives a Midianite woman, in the sight of Moses and in the sight of all the congregation of the sons of Israel, while they were weeping at the doorway of the tent of meeting.

When Phinehas the son of Eleazar, the son of Aaron the priest, saw it, he arose from the midst of the congregation and took a spear in his hand,

and he went after the man of Israel into the tent and pierced both of them through, the man of Israel and the woman, through the body. So the plague on the sons of Israel was checked.

Those who died by the plague were 24,000.

Then the LORD spoke to Moses, saying,

"Phinehas the son of Eleazar, the son of Aaron the priest, has turned away My wrath from the sons of Israel in that he was jealous with My jealousy among them, so that I did not destroy the sons of Israel in My jealousy.

"Therefore say, 'Behold, I give him My covenant of peace;

'and it shall be for him and his descendants after him, a covenant of a perpetual priesthood, because he was jealous for his God and made atonement for the sons of Israel.'" (Numbers 25:1–13)[181]

The people, enticed to sin, fell victim to Baal and the gaping maw speaking chaos. The Lord God calls for judgment because of this sin. He calls for the execution of the leaders who have allowed these vile acts to take place in the camp. The leaders of Israel are held responsible for the debacle with the Moabite women. They were responsible because they allowed it to happen on their watch. Those in positions of authority had the responsibility to warn the people of deception (Ezekiel 33). They chose, however, to turn a blind eye to the sin that crouched at the door (Genesis 4:7). Sin desired to ensnarl the people. Sin, unchecked, will whisper its song of false promise upon the ears of the negligent. Moses wept in the sight of the congregation. He wept at the doorway to the Tent of Meeting because of the heinous idolatry that was committed before the eyes of the Lord. Moses wept because unrepentant sin emboldened the sons of Israel to commit harlotry with the profane in the sight of all the people. Sin in the hearts of those who chose to listen to temptation was not hidden or done in the secret places of their inner being. Shameful acts of sin were being practiced without reservation for all to witness. Moses wept because he saw the seeds of revolt born in the hearts of those who embraced sin. The love for God grew cold.

> When Phinehas the son of Eleazar, the son of Aaron the priest, saw it, he arose from the midst of the congregation and took a spear in his hand. (Numbers 25:7)

Phinehas was a man zealous for God. He chose to remember holiness. Phinehas chose to remember that he was a chosen priest set apart for service to the Lord. He was determined to set his face like flint and hunt out the sin that was left to ravage the camp. He hunted sin, eradicating it with unreserved zeal in reverence for the Lord. Phinehas remembered what the Lord had done for Him. He remembered the love God poured out not only for him, but for all those who were willing to follow. Phinehas took up arms as a priesthood of flint, bound to fight for the preservation of faith. He saw the value in defending the truth. Phinehas saw the worth of those he could save. He refused to allow sin to continue to whisper enchantments amid the camp because he saw the hope of God for His people.

Because of the determination of Phinehas to preserve faith for those who come after, God blessed him. God's promise to Phinehas is one of eternality:

Phinehas, the son of Eleazar, the son of Aaron the priest, has turned away My wrath from the sons of Israel in that he was jealous with My jealousy among them, so that I did not destroy the sons of Israel in My jealousy.

Therefore say, "Behold, I give him My covenant of peace;

"and it shall be for him and his descendants after him, a covenant of a perpetual priesthood, because he was jealous for his God and made atonement for the sons of Israel." (Numbers 25:11–13)

Because Phinehas was jealous for the Lord, the wrath that was directed toward the sons of Israel was turned away. Phinehas was imparted from God a covenant of peace. The promise of the Lord's eternal peace was given to Phinehas as a sign of his perpetual priesthood. Phinehas was bestowed the honor of being called a priest unto the Lord because he defended the faith. Phinehas put an end to chaos.

Whatever Was Written Was Written for Our Instruction

While this account in the book of Numbers is wrought with violence, I again do not encourage violence to be committed against anyone in our walk of faith. I believe that often God uses a physical picture to teach a spiritual truth. The events surrounding the camp of Israel at the foot of the mountain of Baal Peor is a demonstration, in the physical, of a spiritual reality. Paul tells us in the book of Romans:

For whatever was written in earlier times was written for our instruction, so that through perseverance and the encouragement of the Scriptures we might have hope. (Romans 15:4)[182]

Let the Word of God give insight illuminating the path of faithfulness toward our Savior. God used these unfortunate events to bring about an understanding of the penalty of sin. If sin is allowed to take root in your heart, death follows. If we allow sin to run rampant in our churches, our homes, and our thoughts, chaos reigns. The gaping maw of the deceiver will inevitably swallow up the traces of faith. It is therefore imperative that we hunt out sin and call upon the Lord to destroy it. The Lord will "send for many hunters, and they will hunt them from every mountain and every hill and from the clefts of the rocks" (Jeremiah 16:16).[183] Ask the Lord to show you the sin that you harbor in your heart. Hunt out this sin and destroy any trace of it, indiscriminately. Search out the influence of sin in your home. Call upon the name of salvation to help you remove any sin, repenting and turning to your hope. Be watchful over your church family. Care for one another in love, restoring one another in gentleness as the Apostle Paul instructs us:

> Brethren, even if anyone is caught in any trespass, you who are spiritual, restore such a one in a spirit of gentleness; each one looking to yourself, so that you too will not be tempted. Bear one another's burdens, and thereby fulfill the law of Christ.
>
> For if anyone thinks he is something when he is nothing, he deceives himself.
>
> But each one must examine his own work, and then he will have *reason for* boasting in regard to himself alone, and not in regard to another.
>
> For each one will bear his own load.
>
> The one who is taught the word is to share all good things with the one who teaches him.
>
> Do not be deceived, God is not mocked; for whatever a man sows, this he will also reap.
>
> For the one who sows to his own flesh will from the flesh reap corruption, but the one who sows to the Spirit will from the Spirit reap eternal life.
>
> Let us not lose heart in doing good, for in due time we will reap if we do not grow weary. (Galatians 6:1–9)[184]

Encourage one another in faith so that we do not lose heart in the thrall of the battle. Sow into your faith and you will reap a harvest of blessing from God. Fight for the preservation of His Word for the sake of those who come after, for our children and others who follow. It is for them that we bear arms as the priesthood of flint. Set your face, then, fixing your eyes on salvation, determined to ignite the flame of faith in the heart of those who have ears to hear. *For valor*, for those of worth.

Therefore I, the prisoner of the Lord, implore you to walk in a manner worthy of the calling with which you have been called,

with all humility and gentleness, with patience, showing tolerance for one another in love,

being diligent to preserve the unity of the Spirit in the bond of peace.

There is one body and one Spirit, just as also you were called in one hope of your calling;

ne Lord, one faith, one baptism,

one God and Father of all who is over all and through all and in all.

But to each one of us grace was given according to the measure of Christ's gift. (Ephesians 4:1–7)[185]

Heed these words of Paul. Walk in a manner worthy of your calling bearing with integrity, zeal for God's Word.

Do Not Be Like Those in the Boat

Finally, I close with this reminder from the book of Matthew, in which we have an account of the disciples struck with fear at the sight of the storm. As Jesus was ministering in the region of Capernaum, large crowds of people followed. Jesus decided to cross over the sea of Galilee. Matthew wrote:

When He got into the boat, His disciples followed Him.

And behold, there arose a great storm on the sea, so that the boat was being covered with the waves; but Jesus Himself was asleep.

And they came to Him and woke Him, saying, "Save us, Lord; we are perishing!"

He said to them, "Why are you afraid, you men of little faith?" Then He got up and rebuked the winds and the sea, and it became perfectly calm.

The men were amazed, and said, "What kind of a man is this, that even the winds and the sea obey Him?" (Matthew 8:23–27[186]

As they crossed the sea in this boat, a great storm rose up. The disciples thought they would be swept into the waters due to the power of the storm. Jesus, sleeping in the boat, was not troubled by the torrent. The disciples cried out to Jesus to save them as they cowered in fear. Awakened by the cries for help, Jesus rebuked the storm and calmed the sea. Jesus put an end to chaos. The disciples were amazed that even nature itself obeyed the command of Jesus. While the storm raged, the only thing the disciples could focus on was the violence of the storm and the preservation of their own lives. They chose to forget the provision of their Savior. They forgot the authority of God. They, instead, chose to focus on the chaos of the storm. Rightly Jesus rebuked them for forgetting to trust Him. Rightly, He demonstrated His authority. For those who choose to not defend their faith in the shadow of the storm, chaos looms overhead, and they become like one of those of little faith. Those who cower in fear at the perceived power of chaos are like they who sit in the boat. While the storm rages, they whimper in awe of chaos, praising the storm in its fury. I charge you, do not fear, for God Himself is with us. Though chaos lashes out in rage because it knows that the day comes when the storm will be stilled forever, do not forget your hope. Do not be like those in the boat who forgot the power of salvation. You are a priesthood of the Most High God, a chosen possession of God Himself. Stand, *for valor*, defending the faith for those of worth. **To arms, brethren, as His priesthood of flint. For today is still called "today"** (Hebrews 3:12–19)! The Lord God goes before us in this fight. Stand firm and trust in His promises. The Lord gives us this promise in the book of Deuteronomy:

> When you go out to battle against your enemies and see horses and chariots *and* people more numerous than you, do not be afraid of them; for the LORD your God, who brought you up from the land of Egypt, is with you.
>
> When you are approaching the battle, the priest shall come near and speak to the people.
>
> He shall say to them, "Hear, O Israel, you are approaching the battle against your enemies today. Do not be fainthearted. Do not be afraid, or panic, or tremble before them, for the LORD your God is the one who goes with you, to fight for you against your enemies, to save you." (Deuteronomy 20:1–4)[187]

He fights for us! We are His! To God be the glory, forever!

CODA

¹ "For behold, the day is coming, burning like a furnace; and all the arrogant and every evildoer will be chaff; and the day that is coming will set them ablaze," says the LORD of hosts, "so that it will leave them neither root nor branch.

² "But for you who fear My name, the sun of righteousness will rise with healing in its wings; and you will go forth and skip about like calves from the stall.

³ "You will tread down the wicked, for they will be ashes under the soles of your feet on the day which I am preparing," says the LORD of hosts.

⁴ "Remember the law of Moses My servant, *even the* statutes and ordinances which I commanded him in Horeb for all Israel.

⁵ "Behold, I am going to send you Elijah the prophet before the coming of the great and terrible day of the LORD.

⁶ "He will restore the hearts of the fathers to *their* children and the hearts of the children to their fathers, so that I will not come and smite the land with a curse."

MALACHI 4:1–6 [188]

229

ABOUT THE AUTHOR

Corby Shuey serves as the senior pastor of a church located in Lebanon County, Pennsylvania. He is a graduate of Biblical Life College and Seminary where he earned a master of divinity degree. Corby seeks to encourage the church to stand in the hope of Jesus Christ, our King and Savior. It is only in this truth that we can find hope in a world given to disorder. Corby has written a number of books and Bible studies. He also publishes monthly blogs on his website, corbyshuey.com. The blog, books, and Bible studies are available on this site. There is also an archive of sermons on the church website. Be blessed knowing that you are the redeemed child of an eternal King! To God be the glory!

USE THE QR-CODE BELOW TO ACCESS MANY SPECIAL DEALS AND PROMOTIONS ON BOOKS AND FILMS FEATURING DISCOVERY, PROPHECY, AND THE SUPERNATURAL!

BIBLIOGRAPHY

Ancient Origins, 2019. "Quetzalcoatl: From Feathered Serpent to Creator God." https://www.
ancient-origins.net/myths-legends-americas/
rise-quetzalcoatl-plumed-serpent-creator-god-008959.

Anizor, Uche, PhD and Dr. Hank Voss. *Representing Christ: A Vision for
the Priesthood of all Believers*. (Downers Grove, IL: InterVarsity Press,
2016).

Arizona State University School of Mathematics and Statistical Sciences,
2021. "Theoretical Mathematics." https://math.asu.edu/research/
theoretical-mathematics.

Barclay, William, D. D. *Ethics in a Permissive Society*. (New York: Harper
and Row, 1971).

Barnett, Ronald A. "*The Books of Chilam Balam: Part One.*"
(MexConnect, 2021). https://www.mexconnect.com/
articles/538-the-books-of-chilam-balam-part-one/.

Beliefnet, Inc. "God Speaks to Each Person in Their Own Language."
beliefnet.com.

Berkeley Theatre, Dance, and Performance Studies, "Luis Valdez."
Accessed on July 29, 2021, https://tdps.berkeley.edu/luis-valdez.

Blue Letter Bible, 2021. Psalm 2 Commentary. https://www.blueletter-bible.org/Comm/spurgeon_charles/tod/ps002.cfm?a=480001.

Bohman, James. "Critical Theory" (Stanford Encyclopedia of Philosophy, Spring 2021 edition, Edward N. Zaltan, editor). https://plato.stanford.edu/entries/critical-theory/.

Bostrom, Nick. *Transhumanist Values* (Philosophical Documentation Center Press, 2003). https://www.nickbostrom.com/ethics/values.html.

Brainy Quote, 2021. "He alone, who owns the youth, gains the future." https://www.brainyquote.com/quotes/adolf_hitler_378177.

Bryan, Jenny and John Clare. "Frontline: Organ Farming Frequently Asked Questions." pbs.org, WGBH Educational Foundation, 2014. Accessed on July 20, 1017.

Cambridge University Press, 2021. "Identity." https://dictionary.cambridge.org/us/dictionary/english/identity.

Cherry, Kendra. "What Is Reciprocity." verywell-mind, 2020. https://www.verywellmind.com/what-is-the-rule-of-reciprocity-2795891.

Carl Jung Resources. "Concept of Collective Unconscious at Jung." carl-jung.net.

"Chaos Myths and Folklore." Wiki. https://mythus.fandom.com/wiki/Chaos.

Christian Discernment Publications Ministry, 1995. "The Teachings of Carl Jung: A Bizarre Blend of Blasphemy, Mythology, and Psychology." Christiandiscernment.com.

Chicago Tribune, 2017. "Scientists Take First Steps to Growing Human Organs in Pigs." https://www.chicagotribune.com/nation-world/ct-human-organs-pigs-science-20170126-story.html

Collins, A. O. (2003). Chaos. In C. Brand, C. Draper, A. England, S. Bond, E. R. Clendenen, & T. C. Butler (Eds.), *Holman Illustrated Bible Dictionary* (p. 278). Holman Bible Publishers.

Corradetti, Claudio. "The Frankfurt School and Critical Theory." (Internet Encyclopedia of Philosophy, 2021). https://iep.utm.edu/frankfur/ .

Crossman, Ashley. "Understanding Critical Theory" (ThoughtCo, 2019). https://www.thoughtco.com/critical-theory-3026623.

Denner, Joachim. "How Active Are Porcine Endogenous Retroviruses (PERVs)?" (National Center for Biotechnology Information, U.S. National Library of Medicine, 2016). https://www.ncbi.nlm.nih.gov/pmc/articles/PMC4997577/ .

Dictionary.com, LLC, 2017. "flint." dictionary.com.

Encyclopedia.com, 2021. "Aztec Mythology." https://www.encyclopedia.com/history/encyclopedias-almanacs-transcripts-and- maps/aztec-mythology.

Encyclopedia Britannica Inc, 2021. "Chimera." https://www.britannica.com/science/chimera-genetics.

Encyclopedia.com, 2019 "Chilam Balam" https://www.encyclopedia.com/humanities/encyclopedias-almanacs-transcripts-and-maps/chilam-balam.

Encyclopedia Britannica, 2021, "Covalent Bond." https://www.britannica.com/science/covalent-bond.

Encyclopedia Britannica. Demiurge. https://www.britannica.com/topic/Demiurge.

El Teatro Campesino, "Luis Valdez," https://elteatrocampesino.com/about-luis/ .

Fearon, James D. PhD. "What Is Identity (As We Now Use the Word?)" (Stanford, CA: Stanford University, 1999).

Felicie, Edwin. (2021, July 17). "No Greater Valor" [Video File]. Retrieved from https://www.youtube.com/watch?v=FzLU7Luu51A.

Garr, John, PhD. "Coequal and Counterbalanced: God's Blueprint for Men and Women." (Atlanta: Golden Key Press, 2012) 57.

Geology.com. 2005–2017. Flint. geology.com. Accessed on April 21, 2017.

Goodman, Brenda. "First Organ Grown from Stem Cells: Report." (WebMD, 2021) https://www.webmd.com/a-to-z-guides/news/20130703/first-organ-grown-from-stem-cells-alone-report.

Goudy, David J. "Without Virtue There Can Be No Liberty". (Mount Liberty College, 2018). https://mountlibertycollege.org/without-virtue-there-can-be-no-liberty/.

Griffiths A. J. F., Miller J. H., Suzuki D. T., "An Introduction to Genetic Analysis. 7th edition" (New York: W. H. Freeman). https://www.ncbi.nlm.nih.gov/books/NBK21881/.

Grossman, Ashley PhD. Virilization (Merck Manual: 2019) https://www.merckmanuals.com/home/hormonal-and-metabolic-disorders/adrenal-gland-disorders/virilization .

Gutierrez, Rochelle, PhD. "Living Mathematix: Towards a Vision for the Future." (Philosophy of Mathematics Journal, November 2017) https://files.eric.ed.gov/fulltext/ED581384.pdf.

Hanson, Molly. "What Is a Non-Human Person?" Bigthink.com, 2019. https://bigthink.com/culture-religion/non-human-person?rebelltitem=2#rebelltitem2.

History Stories, "How the Chicano Movement Championed Mexican-American Identity and Fought for Change." https://www.history.com/news/chicano-movement.

"History of Math." Historyworld, 2021. "History of Math." http://www.historyworld.net/wrldhis/plaintexthistories.asp?historyid=aa50.

Horkheimer, Max and Theodor Adorn.o "Dialectic of Enlightenment: Philosophical Fragments." (Stanford, CA: Stanford University Press, 2002).

Intersex Society of North America: 2008. Progestin Induced Virilization http://www.isna.org/faq/conditions/progestin).

Journal Psyche, copyright 1994– 2015. "Jung and His Individuation Process." journalpsyche.org.

Jung, C. G. "The Archetypes and the Collective Unconscious." (New York: Princeton University Press, 1969).

Knight, Jason. "Making Arrowheads: The Art of Flint Knapping." wildernesscollege.com. Alderleaf Wilderness College, 2006–2017.

Laurence, L.W. "The Lesser Key of Solomon Goetia: The Book of Evil Spirits." (Chicago, IL. De Laurence, Scott & Co. 1916).

Ligonier Ministries, 2020. "The State of Theology" https://thestateoftheology.com.

Lesbian, Gay, Bisexual, Transgender, Queer Plus (LGBTQ+) Resource Center, University of Wisconsin-Milwaukee, 2021. "Gender Pronouns." https://uwm.edu/lgbtrc/support/gender-pronouns/.

Lumenwaymaker, 2021. "The History of DNA." https://courses.lumenlearning.com/wm-biology1/chapter/reading-the-history-of-dna/.

Millar, Robert and Javier Tello. Gonadotrophin-releasing Hormone (Elsevier: Science Direct: 2019). https://www.sciencedirect.com/topics/neuroscience/gonadotropin-releasing-hormone.

Merriam-Webster, 2021. "Nonhomologous." https://www.merriam-webster.com/dictionary/nonhomologous.

Merriam-Webster, 2021. "Slavery." https://www.merriam-webster.com/dictionary/slavery.

National Center for Biotechnology Information, U.S. National Library of Medicine, 2021. "DNA Cloning with Plasmid Vectors." https://www.ncbi.nlm.nih.gov/books/NBK21498/.

National Cancer Institute. Gonadotropin-Releasing Hormone: https://www.cancer.gov/publications/dictionaries/cancer-terms/def/gonadotropin- releasing-hormone. accessed on 2/21/2019.

NHS. Treatment: Gender Dysphoria https://www.nhs.uk/conditions/gender-dysphoria/treatment.

Patton, Michael, ThM "Understanding the Postmodern Mind and the Emerging Church." (Bible.org, 2021). https://bible.org/article/understanding-postmodern-mind-and-emerging-church.

Peterson, Daniel, "Quetzalcoatl: Separating the Myths of Man from Those of Gods." *Deseret News*, 2020. https://www.deseret.com/faith/2020/3/26/21192451/daniel-peterson-quetzalcoatl-the-myths-of-the-man-and-god-mesoamerica-toltec-topiltzin.

Petty, Gary. "Secular Humanism: Between the Ideal and the Lie." (United Church of God, 2009). https://www.ucg.org/the-good-news/secular-humanism-between-the-ideal-and-the-lie.

Pray, Leslie PhD. "Recombinant DNA Technology and Transgenic Animals." (Scitable by Nature Education, 2008). https://www.nature.com/scitable/topicpage/recombinant-dna-technology-and-transgenic-animals-34513/.

Princeton, NJ. Princeton University Art Museum, 2021. "The Book of Chilam Balam of Chumayel." https://artmuseum.princeton.edu/transient-effects/eclipses-art/book-chilam-balam-chumayel.

Quirky Science. "Why Sparks from Flint and Steel." quirkyscience.com.

Roberts, Vaughan. "Transgender" (Good Book Company, 2016).

Roys, Ralph. "The Book of Chilam Balam of Chumayel" (Washington D.C., Carnegie Institution, 1933).

Scitable by Nature Education, 2021. "Plasmid/Plasmids." https://www.nature.com/scitable/definition/plasmid-plasmids-28/

Scobie, Linda. "Absence of Replication-Competent Human-Tropic Porcine Endogenous Retroviruses in Germ Line DNA of Inbred Miniature Swine." (American Society for Microbiology: *Journal of Virology*, 2020). https://journals.asm.org/doi/full/10.1128/JVI.78.5.2502-2509.2004

Scott, Charles, and Nancy Tuana. "Nepantla: Writing (from) the In-Between." *Journal of Speculative Philosophy* 31, no. 1 (2017): 1–15. https://www.jstor.org/stable/10.5325/jspecphil.31.1.0001?Search=yes&resultItemClick=t.

Slick, Matt. "What Is the Emerging Church." carm.org. Christian Apologetics and Research Ministry.

Snell, Marilyn Berlin. "The World of Religion According to Huston Smith." motherjones.com. Mother Jones, November/December 1997.

Spurgeon, C. H. "The Redeemer's Face Set Like a Flint." Sermon number 2738. spurgeongems.org. excerpt from Metropolitan Tabernacle Pulpit.

Stanford Encyclopedia of Philosophy, 2021. "Postmodernism." https://plato.stanford.edu/entries/postmodernism/#2 accessed on August 7, 2021.

The Stands4 Network, "Gabacho," https://www.definitions.net/definition/gabacho.

Swanson, J. (1997). In Dictionary of Biblical Languages with Semantic Domains : Hebrew (Old Testament) (electronic ed.). Logos Research Systems, Inc.

Synthego, 2021. "History of Genetic Engineering and the Rise of Gene Editing Tools." https://www.synthego.com/learn/genome-engineering-history.

The Intuition Network. "Beyond the Post Modern Mind with Huston Smith." intuition.org.

Lockman Foundation, 1995. New American Standard Bible: 1995 Update (La Habra, CA: 1995)

Tozer, A. W. *The Purpose of Man*. (Minneapolis, MN. Bethany House, 2009).

Unger, Cecile A. *Hormone Therapy for Transgender Patients*. (Translational Andrology and Urology: 2016 http://tau.amegroups.com/article/view/11807/13169).

VanDerwarker, Amber. Popul Vuh. Brittanica.com, 2021 https://www.britannica.com/topic/Maya-people.

Van Der Toorn, Karel, Bob Becking and Pieter W. Van Der Horst editors. *Dictionary of Deities and Demons in the Bible*. (Grand Rapids, MI: Eerdmans, 1999).

Valdez, Luis. "Early Works" (Houston: Arte Publico Press, 1994).

Voices in Urban Education: Annenburg Institute for School Reform at Brown University. "In Lak'ech: You Are My Other Me." http://vue.annenberginstitute.org/perspectives/lak'ech-you-are-my-other.

World Health Organization, 2021. "Covid-19 and Manda-
tory Vaccination: Ethical Considerations and Caveats.
Policy Brief 13, April 2021." WHO/2019-nCoV/Policy_brief/
Mandatory_vaccination/2021.1.

World Health Organization, 2021. "DNA Vaccines." https://
www.who.int/teams/health-product-policy-and-standards/
standards-and-specifications/vaccines-quality/dna.

Yang, Eun Suk. "Predicting the Legal Personhood of AI through the
Fate of Two Chimpanzees in the Matter of Nonhuman Rights Project, Inc. v. Lavery." Business School Digest: USC Gould School of
Law, 2021. https://lawforbusiness.usc.edu/predicting-the-legal-
personhood-of-ai-through-the-fate-of-two-chimpanzees-in-the-
matter-of-nonhuman-rights-project-inc-v-lavery/.

NOTES

1. New American Standard Bible: 1995 Update (La Habra, CA: Lockman Foundation, 1995), Is. 43:1–3.
2. "Luis Valdez," El Teatro Campesino. Accessed on July 29, 2021, https://elteatrocampesino.com/about-luis/.
3. "Luis Valdez," Berkeley Theatre, Dance, and Performance Studies. Accessed on July 29, 2021, https://tdps.berkeley.edu/luis-valdez.
4. "How the Chicano Movement Championed Mexican-American Identity and Fought for Change," History Stories, accessed on July 29, 2021, https://www.history.com/news/chicano-movement.
5. "Gabacho," The Stands4 Network, 2021, https://www.definitions.net/definition/gabacho. Accessed on July 30, 2021.
6. "Quetzalcoatl: From Feathered Serpent to Creator God." Ancient Origins, 2019. https://www.ancient-origins.net/myths-legends-americas/rise-quetzalcoatl-plumed-serpent-creator-god-008959. Accessed on July 30, 2021.
7. Peterson, Daniel, "Quetzalcoatl: Separating the Myths of Man from Those of Gods." Deseret News, 2020. https://www.deseret.com/faith/2020/3/26/21192451/daniel-peterson-quetzalcoatl-the-myths-of-the-man-and-god-mesoamerica-toltec-topiltzin accessed on July 30, 2021.
8. Ibid.
9. Valdez, Luis. "Early Works" (Houston: Arte Publico, 1994).

10. "In Lak'ech: You Are My Other Me." Voices in Urban Education: Annenburg Institute for School Reform at Brown University. http://vue.annenberginstitute.org/perspectives/lak'ech-you-are-my-other. Accessed on August 2, 2021.

11. VanDerwarker, Amber. Popul Vuh. Brittanica.com, 2021 https://www.britannica.com/topic/Maya-people. Accessed on August 3, 2021.

12. Roys, Ralph. "The Book of Chilam Balam of Chumayel" (Washington DC: Carnegie Institution, 1933).

13. "Chilam Balam" Encyclopedia.com, 2019 https://www.encyclopedia.com/humanities/encyclopedias-almanacs-transcripts-and-maps/chilam-balam. Accessed on August 4, 2021.

14 ."The Book of Chilam Balam of Chumayel." (Princeton, NJ: Princeton University Art Museum, 2021). https://artmuseum.princeton.edu/transient-effects/eclipses-art/book-chilam-balam-chumayel. Accessed on August 4, 2021.

15. Ibid.

16. Barnett, Ronald A. "The Books of Chilam Balam: Part One." (MexConnect, 2021). https://www.mexconnect.com/articles/538-the-books-of-chilam-balam-part-one/. Accessed on August 4, 2021.

17. Laurence, L. W. "The Lesser Key of Solomon Goetia: The Book of Evil Spirits." (Chicago: De Laurence, Scott & Co., 1916).

18. Ibid.

19. "Aztec Mythology." Encyclopedia.com, 2021. https://www.encyclopedia.com/history/encyclopedias-almanacs-transcripts-and-maps/aztec-mythology. Accessed on August 5, 2021.

20. Hanson, Molly. "What Is a Non-Human Person?" Bigthink.com, 2019. https://bigthink.com/culture-religion/non-human-person?rebelltitem=2#rebelltitem2. Accessed on August 7, 2021.

21. Yang, Eun Suk. "Predicting the Legal Personhood of AI through the Fate of Two Chimpanzees in the Matter of Nonhuman Rights Project, Inc. v. Lavery." Business School Digest: USC Gould School of Law, 2021. https://lawforbusiness.usc.edu/predicting-the-legal-personhood-of-ai-through-the-fate-of-two-chimpanzees-in-the-matter-of-nonhuman-rights-project-inc-v-lavery/. Accessed on August 7, 2021.

22. "Theoretical Mathematics." Arizona State University School of Mathematics and Statistical Sciences, 2021. https://math.asu.edu/research/theoretical-mathematics. Accessed on August 7, 2021.

23. "Postmodernism." Stanford Encyclopedia of Philosophy, 2021. https://plato.stanford.edu/entries/postmodernism/#2. Accessed on August 7, 2021.

24. Gutierrez, Rochelle, PhD. "Living Mathematix: Towards a Vision for the Future." (Philosophy of Mathematics Journal, November 2017): 2. https://files.eric.ed.gov/fulltext/ED581384.pdf. Accessed on August 7, 2021.

25. Ibid.

26. Cherry, Kendra. "What Is Reciprocity." verywellmind, 2020. https://www.verywellmind.com/what-is-the-rule-of-reciprocity-2795891. Accessed on August 7, 2021.

27. Gutierrez. "Living Mathematix" 6.

28. Scott, Charles, and Nancy Tuana. "Nepantla: Writing (from) the In-Between." Journal of Speculative Philosophy 31, no. 1 (2017): 1–15. https://www.jstor.org/stable/10.5325/jspecphil.31.1.0001?Search=yes&resultItemClick=true&searchText=Nepantla%20Writing%20(from)%20the%20In-Between&searchUri=%2Faction%2FdoBasicSearch-%3FQuery%3DNepantla%253A%2BWriting%2B%2528from%2529%2Bthe%2BIn-Between%26acc%3Don%26wc%3Don%26fc%3Doff%26group%3Dnone%26refreqid%3Dsearch%253Ab1b3f4b00906bf89cef838cb3a369174&ab_segments=0%2Fbasic_search_gsv2%2Fcontrol&refreqid=fastly-default%3Afe8223b70bb24c47288eac38e3632c05. Accessed August 7, 2021.

29. Gutierrez. "Living Mathematix" 11.

30. Gutierrez. "Living Mathematix" 16.

31. Gutierrez. "Living Mathematix" 5.

32. Gutierrez. "Living Mathematix" 11.

33. Ibid.

34. "History of Math." Historyworld, 2021. http://www.historyworld.net/wrldhis/plaintexthistories.asp?historyid=aa50. Accessed on August 9, 2021.

35. Gutierrez. "Living Mathematix" 18.

36. Gutierrez. "Living Mathematix" 3.

37. "Identity." Cambridge University Press, 2021. https://dictionary.cambridge.org/us/dictionary/english/identity. Accessed on August 11, 2021.

38. Roberts, Vaughan. "Transgender" (Good Book Company, 2016) 26.

39. Ibid.

40. Roberts. "Transgender" 30.

41. Fearon, James D. PhD. "What Is Identity (As We Now Use The Word?)" (Stanford, CA: Stanford University, 1999). Accessed on August 12, 2021.

42. Roberts. "Transgender" 31.

43. Garr, John PhD. "Coequal and Counterbalanced: God's Blueprint for Men and Women." (Atlanta: Golden Ket, 2012) 57.

44. Ibid.

45. Garr, Coequal: 58.

46. Garr, Coequal: 61.

47. Unger, Cecile A. Hormone Therapy for Transgender Patients. (Translational Andrology and Urology: 2016. http://tau.amegroups.com/article/view/11807/13169). Accessed on 2/20/2019.

48 Progestin Induced Virilization (Intersex Society of North America: 2008 http://www.isna.org/faq/conditions/progestin). Accessed on 2/20/2019.

49 Grossman, Ashley PhD. Virilization (Merck Manual: 2019 https://www.merckmanuals.com/home/hormonal-and-metabolic-disorders/adrenal-gland-disorders/virilization). Accessed on 2/20/2019.

50. Ibid.

51. Unger, Cecile A. Hormone Therapy for Transgender patients. (Translational Andrology and Urology: 2016 http://tau.amegroups.com/article/view/11807/13169). Accessed on 2/20/2019.

52. Treatment: Gender Dysphoria (NHS, https://www.nhs.uk/conditions/gender-dysphoria/treatment). Accessed on 2/20/2019.

53. Millar, Robert and Javier Tello. Gonadotrophin-releasing Hormone (Elsevier: Science Direct, 2019). https://www.sciencedirect.com/topics/neuroscience/gonadotropin-releasing-hormone accessed on 2/21/2019.

54. Ibid.

55. gonadotropin-releasing hormone: (National Cancer Institute). https://www.cancer.gov/publications/dictionaries/cancer-terms/def/gonadotropin-releasing-hormone. Accessed on 2/21/2019.

56. Treatment: Gender Dysphoria. (NHS, https://www.nhs.uk/conditions/gender-dysphoria/treatment). Accessed on 2/20/2019.

57. "Slavery." Merriam-Webster, 2021. https://www.merriam-webster.com/dictionary/slavery. Accessed on August 14, 2021.

58. "Gender Pronouns" (Lesbian, Gay, Bisexual, Transgender, Queer Plus (LGBTQ+) Resource Center, University of Wisconsin-Milwaukee, 2021). https://uwm.edu/lgbtrc/support/gender-pronouns/. Accessed on August 27, 2021.

59. Bostrom, Nick. Transhumanist Values (Philosophical Documentation Center Press, 2003). https://www.nickbostrom.com/ethics/values.html. Accessed on August 27, 2021.

60 "The History of DNA." (lumenwaymaker, 2021). https://courses.lumenlearning.com/wm-biology1/chapter/reading-the-history-of-dna/. Accessed on September 4, 2021.

61. "History of Genetic Engineering and the Rise of Gene Editing Tools." (Synthego, 2021) https://www.synthego.com/learn/genome-engineering-history. Accessed on September 4,2021.

62. Ibid.

63. "DNA Cloning with Plasmid Vectors." (Bethesda, MD. National Center for Biotechnology Information, U.S. National Library of Medicine, 2021). https://www.ncbi.nlm.nih.gov/books/NBK21498/. Accessed on September 5, 2021.

64. "Plasmid/Plasmids." (Scitable by Nature Education, 2021) https://www.nature.com/scitable/definition/plasmid-plasmids-28/. Accessed on September 6, 2021.

65. Griffiths A. J. F., Miller J. H., Suzuki D. T, "An Introduction to Genetic Analysis. 7th edition" (New York: W. H. Freeman). https://www.ncbi.nlm.nih.gov/books/NBK21881/. Accessed on September 9, 2021.

66. Ibid.

67. Ibid.

68. Griffiths A. J. F., Miller J. H., Suzuki D. T., "An Introduction to Genetic Analysis. 7th edition" (New York: W. H. Freeman). https://www.ncbi.nlm.nih.gov/books/NBK21881/. Accessed on September 9, 2021.

69. Pray, Leslie PhD. "Recombinant DNA Technology and Transgenic Animals." (Scitable by Nature Education, 2008). https://www.nature.

com/scitable/topicpage/recombinant-dna-technology-and-transgenic-animals-34513/. Accessed on September 6, 2021.

70. Griffiths A. J. F., Miller J. H., Suzuki D. T., "An Introduction to Genetic Analysis. 7th edition" (New Uprl" W. H. Freeman). https://www.ncbi.nlm.nih.gov/books/NBK21881/. Accessed on September 9, 2021.

71. "Nonhomologous." (Merriam-Webster, 2021) https://www.merriam-webster.com/dictionary/nonhomologous. Accessed on September 9, 2021.

72. "Covalent Bond." (Encyclopedia Britannica, 2021). https://www.britannica.com/science/covalent-bond. Accessed on September 6, 2021.

73. Pray. "Recombinant DNA." (Scitable By Nature Education, 2008). https://www.nature.com/scitable/topicpage/recombinant-dna-technology-and-transgenic-animals-34513/. Accessed on September 6, 2021.

74. "DNA Vaccines." (World Health Organization, 2021). https://www.who.int/teams/health-product-policy-and-standards/standards-and-specifications/vaccines-quality/dna. Accessed on September 6, 2021.

75. "Covid-19 and Mandatory Vaccination: Ethical Considerations and Caveats. Policy Brief 13, April 2021." (World Health Organization, 2021). WHO/2019-nCoV/Policy_brief/Mandatory_vaccination/2021.1. Accessed on September 8, 2021. The notation I have made reference to is from a document offered by the WHO as a consideration in the development of policy pushing mandated vaccinations. The document is a PDF download available through the WHO web address.

76. Ibid.

77. Lowercased intentionally throughout the book as a visual reminder that the devil is defeated.

78. Goodman, Brenda. "First Organ Grown From Stem Cells: Report." (WebMD, 2021) https://www.webmd.com/a-to-z-guides/news/20130703/first-organ-grown-from-stem-cells-alone-report. Accessed on September 9, 2021.

79. Bryan, Jenny and John Clare. Frontline: Organ Farming Frequently Asked Questions. pbs.org, (WGBH Educational Foundation, 2014). Accessed on July 20, 1017.

80. Ibid.

81. Ibid.

82. "Chimera." (Encyclopedia Britannica Inc, 2021). https://www.britannica.com/science/chimera-genetics. Accessed on September 13, 2021.

83. "Scientists Take First Steps to Growing Human Organs in Pigs." chicagotribune.com, Chicago Tribune, 2017. Accessed on July 20, 2017.

84. Scobie, Linda. "Absence of Replication-Competent Human-Tropic Porcine Endogenous Retroviruses in Germ Line DNA of Inbred Miniature Swine." (American Society for Microbiology: Journal of Virology, 2020). https://journals.asm.org/doi/full/10.1128/JVI.78.5.2502-2509.2004. Accessed on September 14, 2021.

85. Denner, Joachim. "How Active Are Porcine Endogenous Retroviruses (PERVs)?" (National Center for Biotechnology Information, U.S. National Library of Medicine, 2016). https://www.ncbi.nlm.nih.gov/pmc/articles/PMC4997577/. Accessed on September 14, 2021.

86. Ibid.

87. Goudy, David J. "Without Virtue There Can Be No Liberty". (Mount Liberty College, 2018). https://mountlibertycollege.org/without-virtue-there-can-be-no-liberty/. Accessed on September 9, 2021.

88. Slick, Matt. "What Is the Emerging Church." carm.org. Christian Apologetics and Research Ministry. Accessed on October 3, 2016.

89. Ibid.

90. Patton, Michael, ThM. "Understanding the Postmodern Mind and the Emerging Church." (Bible.org, 2021). https://bible.org/article/understanding-postmodern-mind-and-emerging-church. Accessed on September 17, 2021.

91. "Concept of Collective Unconscious at Jung" carl-jung.net Carl Jung Resources, 2016. Accessed on October 4, 2016.

92 .Jung, C. G. "The Archetypes and the Collective Unconscious." (New York: Princeton University Press, 1969), 287.

93. "Jung and His Individuation Process." journalpsyche.org. Journal Psyche, 1994–2015. Accessed on October 4, 2016.

94. Ibid.

95. "The Teachings of Carl Jung: A Bizarre Blend of Blasphemy, Mythology, and Psychology." Christiandiscernment.com. Christian

Discernment Publications Ministry, 1995. Accessed on October 4, 2016.

96. "God Speaks to Each Person in Their Own Language." beliefnet.com. Beliefnet, Inc. Accessed on October 4, 2016.

97. "Beyond the Post Modern Mind with Huston Smith." intuition.org. The Intuition Network. Accessed on October 4, 2016.

98.. Snell, Marilyn Berlin. "The World of Religion According to Huston Smith." motherjones.com. Mother Jones, November/December 1997. Accessed on October 4, 2016.

99. Ibid.

100. "Beyond the Post Modern Mind with Huston Smith." intuition.org. The Intuition Network. Accessed on October 4, 2016.

101 Petty, Gary. "Secular Humanism: Between the Ideal and the Lie." (United Church of God, 2009). https://www.ucg.org/the-good-news/secular-humanism-between-the-ideal-and-the-lie. Accessed on September 18, 2021.

102. Ibid.

103. "The State of Theology" (Ligonier Ministries, 2020). https://thestateoftheology.com. Accessed on September 18, 2021.

104. Ibid.

105. Ibid.

106. Bohman, James. "Critical Theory" (The Stanford Encyclopedia of Philosophy, Spring 2021 edition, Edward N. Zaltan, editor). https://plato.stanford.edu/entries/critical-theory/. Accessed on October 1, 2021.

107. Corradetti, Claudio. "The Frankfurt School and Critical Theory." (Internet Encyclopedia of Philosophy, 2021) https://iep.utm.edu/frankfur/. Accessed on October 1, 2021.

108. Crossman, Ashley. "Understanding Critical Theory" (ThoughtCo, 2019). https://www.thoughtco.com/critical-theory-3026623. Accessed on October 1, 2021.

109. Corradetti, Claudio. "The Frankfurt School and Critical Theory." (Internet Encyclopedia of Philosophy, 2021). https://iep.utm.edu/frankfur/. Accessed on October 1, 2021.

110. Ibid.

111. Horkheimer, Max and Theodor Adorno. "Dialectic of Enlightenment:

Philosophical Fragments." (Stanford, California, Stanford University Press, 2002): 1.

112. Ibid.

113. Ibid., 5

114. Ibid.

115. Ibid., 6.

116. Ibid., 15.

117. Ibid., 11.

118. Ibid, 9.

119. Ibid., 125.

120. Ibid., 9.

121. Ibid., 11.

122. Ibid., 72.

123. "He alone, who owns the youth, gains the future." (Brainy Quote, 2021) https://www.brainyquote.com/quotes/adolf_hitler_378177. Accessed on September 18, 2021.

124. New American Standard Bible: 1995 Update (La Habra, CA: Lockman Foundation, 1995), Romans 1:28–32.

125. Psalm 2 Commentary (Blue Letter Bible, 2021). https://www.blueletterbible.org/Comm/spurgeon_charles/tod/ps002.cfm?a=480001. Accessed on 11/8/2021.

126. Anizor, Uche, PhD. and Dr. Hank Voss. Representing Christ: A Vision for the Priesthood of All Believers. (Downers Grove, IL: InterVarsity Press, 2016) 14.

127. Ibid., 15.

128. Ibid.

129. Ibid., 27.

130. Ibid., 30.

131. Ibid., 31.

132. Barclay, William, D. D. Ethics in a Permissive Society. (New York: Harper and Row, 1971) 182.

133. Ibid.

134. Ibid., 184.

135. Anizor and Voss, Representing Christ, 34.

136. "flint." Dictionary.com, 2017. Accessed on April 21, 2017.

137. Flint. Geology.com. 2005–2017. Accessed on April 21, 2017.

138. Ibid.

139. Knight, Jason. "Making Arrowheads: The Art of Flint Knapping." wildernesscollege.com. Alderleaf Wilderness College, 2006–2017. Accessed on April 21, 2017.

140. "Why Sparks from Flint and Steel." quirkyscience.com. Quirky Science. Accessed on April 21, 2017.

141. Spurgeon, C. H. "The Redeemer's Face Set Like a Flint." Sermon number 2738. spurgeongems.org. excerpt from Metropolitan Tabernacle Pulpit. Accessed on April 22, 2017.

142. Ibid.

143. Ibid.

144. Ibid.

145. Ibid.

146. Ibid.

147. Ibid.

148. Ibid.

149. Ibid.

150. Ibid.

151. "flintDictionary.com, LLC, 2017. Accessed on April 21, 2017.

152. Spurgeon, C. H. "The Redeemer's Face Set Like a Flint." Sermon number 2738. spurgeongems.org. excerpt from Metropolitan Tabernacle Pulpit. Accessed on April 22, 2017.

153. Felicie, Edwin, (2021, July 17). No Greater Valor [Video File]. Retrieved from https://www.youtube.com/watch?v=FzLU7Luu51A.

154 Swanson, J. (1997). In Dictionary of Biblical Languages with Semantic Domains : Hebrew (Old Testament) (electronic ed.). Logos Research Systems.

155. New American Standard Bible: 1995 update (Ex 17:8–16). (1995). Lockman Foundation.

156. Tozer, A. W. The Purpose of Man. (Minneapolis, MN: Bethany House, 2009) 30.

157. New American Standard Bible: 1995 update (Heb 12:1–3). (1995). Lockman Foundation.

158. New American Standard Bible: 1995 update (Is 61:1–2). (1995). Lockman Foundation.

159. Tozer, Purpose of Man. 42.

160. Ibid., 43.

161. Ibid., 58

162. Ibid.

163. Ibid., 144.

164. New American Standard Bible: 1995 update (Nu 25:1–3). (1995). Lockman Foundation.

165. Swanson, J. (1997). In Dictionary of Biblical Languages with Semantic Domains : Hebrew (Old Testament) (electronic ed.). Logos Research Systems.

166. Ibid.

167. Ibid.,

168. פָּעַר. https://www.blueletterbible.org/lexicon/h6473/kjv/wlc/0-1/. Accessed on 1/21/2022.

169. Van Der Toorn, Karel, Bob Becking and Pieter W. Van Der Horst, editors. Dictionary of Deities and Demons in the Bible. (Grand Rapids, MI: Eerdmans, 1999) 185.

170. Ibid.

171. "Chaos Myths and Folklore." Wiki. https://mythus.fandom.com/wiki/Chaos. Accessed on 1/24/2022.

172. Ibid.

173. Van Deer Toorn, Karel. Dictionary of Deities and Demons, 185.

174. Ibid., 186.

175. Demiurge. The Encyclopedia Britannica. https://www.britannica.com/topic/Demiurge Accessed on 1/25/2022

176. Collins, A. O. (2003). Chaos. In C. Brand, C. Draper, A. England, S. Bond, E. R. Clendenen, & T. C. Butler (Eds.), Holman Illustrated Bible Dictionary (p. 278). Holman Bible Publishers.

177. New American Standard Bible: 1995 update (1 Ki 11:4). (1995). Lockman Foundation.

178. New American Standard Bible: 1995 update (1 Ki 11:7). (1995). Lockman Foundation.

179. New American Standard Bible: 1995 update (Zec 14:3–4). (1995). Lockman Foundation.

180. New American Standard Bible: 1995 update (Mt 24:29–31). (1995). Lockman Foundation.

181. New American Standard Bible: 1995 update (Nu 25:1–13). (1995). Lockman Foundation.

182 New American Standard Bible: 1995 update (Ro 15:4). (1995). Lockman Foundation.

183. New American Standard Bible: 1995 update (Je 16:16). (1995). Lockman Foundation.

184. New American Standard Bible: 1995 update (Ga 6:1–9). (1995). Lockman Foundation.

185. New American Standard Bible: 1995 update (Eph 4:1–7). (1995). Lockman Foundation.

186. New American Standard Bible: 1995 update (Mt 8:18–27). (1995). Lockman Foundation.

187. New American Standard Bible: 1995 Update (La Habra, CA: Lockman Foundation, 1995), Dt 20:1–4.

188. New American Standard Bible: 1995 update (Mal 4:1–6). (1995). Lockman Foundation.